GENDER AND INSECURITY

For Stuart, Olivia and Juliette

Critical Security Series

Gender and Insecurity

Migrant Women in Europe

Edited by
JANE FREEDMAN

Routledge
Taylor & Francis Group

LONDON AND NEW YORK

First published 2003 by Ashgate Publishing

Reissued 2018 by Routledge
2 Park Square, Milton Park, Abingdon, Oxon OX14 4RN
711 Third Avenue, New York, NY 10017, USA

Routledge is an imprint of the Taylor & Francis Group, an informa business

A Library of Congress record exists under LC control number: 2003056288

ISBN 13: 978-1-138-70845-7 (hbk)
ISBN 13: 978-1-138-70843-3 (pbk)
ISBN 13: 978-1-315-19849-1 (ebk)

Contents

PART III: NEGOTIATING SOCIAL AND POLITICAL IDENTITIES

List of Contributors

Jane Anderson is senior lecturer in HIV Medicine at Barts and the London School of Medicine. Her current research focuses on the lives and experiences of African HIV-positive women in London.

Sabah Chaib is a researcher working on issues concerning immigration and economic activity. She has recently completed a report for a French Trade Union on immigrant women's labour market insertion.

Emma Clarence is a research assistant in the department of politics and international relations at the University of Aberdeen. Her research interests include nationalism, multiculturalism and public policy making.

Colectivo Ioé is a sociological research team based in Madrid, specialised in migration and the labour market. It is made up of the sociologists Carlos Pereda, Walter Actis and Miguel Ángel de Prada.

Umut Erel was born in Turkey and has studied in both Germany and the UK. Her research has focused on women in migration. She is currently working on a European research project on Racism, Anti-Racism and the Trades Unions at London Metropolitan University. Her recent publications include *Gender on the Move: Crossing Borders – Shifting Boundaries* (edited with M. Morokvasic and K. Shinozaki), 2003, Opladen: Leske and Budrich.

Jane Freedman is a lecturer in politics at the University of Southampton. Her research focuses on issues of gender, citizenship and migration. Recent publications include *Women, Immigration and Identities in France*, 2001, Oxford: Berg, and *Citizenship and Immigration in France*, forthcoming, Aldershot: Ashgate.

Gabriella Lazaridis lectures in sociology at the University of Leicester. She has published extensively in the field of migration in Europe and is currently involved in one research project on migration dynamics and social exclusion of Albanians in Italy and Greece, and another on immigrants and ethnic minorities in European cities.

Claudie Lesselier is a researcher and founder member of RAJFIRE, a French women's organisation which campaigns for the rights of migrant and refugee women in France.

Laura Oso Casas is currently lecturing and researching in the Faculty of Sociology at the University of La Coruña (Spain). She has acted as an advisor for a number of international organisations. To date her research has focused mainly on the issue of female immigration in Spain. She has published two monographic studies, as well as around fifteen chapters in books and articles for specialised journals. One of her most important publications was the monographic study entitled *La migración hacia España de mujeres jefas de hogar*, 1998, Madrid: Instituto de la Mujer.

Francesca Scrinzi is currently a research fellow working on a joint project between the University of Genoa, Italy, and the University of Nice – Sophia Antipolis, France. Her research centres on the position of migrant workers in domestic services in Italy and France. She has published several articles on this subject.

Chapter 1

Introduction: A Gendered Analysis of Migration in Europe

Jane Freedman

Since the 1960s a number of major developments in global migration patterns have placed the phenomenon at the heart of global politics. First, the scale of movements has increased exponentially. In the 1960s only a handful of countries, mainly the traditional immigration nations of North America and Oceania, were significantly affected by international migration, but by 2000 the International Organisation for Migration reported that over 2.5 per cent of the world's population was living outside of their country of birth (IOM, 2000),[1] and virtually every nation was influenced in some way by immigration or emigration of various kinds. Secondly, there has been an enormous increase in the diversity of international population movement. Whereas in the past the bulk of such movement involved permanent, or at least long term, settlement at the destination, world migration is now characterised by not only increased levels of permanent settlement in foreign countries but also by a myriad of temporary, circular migrations of varying duration with a range of purposes. Thirdly, and perhaps inevitably, there has been a dramatic increase in the number of global institutions in shaping the level and patterning of international migration. On the one hand government involvement is increasing not only in destination countries where attempts to limit the number and characteristics of immigrants have escalated, but also in origin countries where nations have realised the benefits of remittances to national development and actively encouraged emigration of various kinds.

These factors have reinforced each other to change the racial mix of many countries and cities beyond all recognition. Simultaneously, the increase in global migration has also given rise to paranoia and xenophobia. Migrants everywhere live a tenuous existence – rarely gaining the same rights as non-migrants, their hosts always aloof. Blamed for a range of ills – from unemployment to crime, strained social services to lack of national unity – migrants are aware of just how easily their rights can be swept away. Focusing on the European Union, this project emerges out of a serious concern for the plight of women without states and those who fall victim to the states that are supposed to offer them some basic protection.

---

[1] This figure is seen as a conservative estimate by many as it does not include the many undocumented migrants. Others have suggested that if all undocumented migrants were accounted for the figure would rise to about 7 per cent.

Across the EU, immigrant women often find themselves in particularly insecure positions because of their lack of independent legal status, the difficulty of access to adequate health and social security provision, and because of their particular vulnerability to both domestic and institutional forms of violence. They are often in economically weak positions, either unemployed or in badly paid part-time or domestic jobs with no forms of social protection. The book will address these various forms of insecurity and attempt to detail ways in which they might be addressed. Further, it will look at the ways in which immigrant women have themselves tried to fight against these insecurities through their own political mobilisation.

The Context of Immigration in Europe

Over the past decades, immigration has become an increasingly central and contentious political issue for the states of the European Union. There has been both a conceptual and a geo-political widening of the migration issue (Geddes, 2003) with new types of migration emerging alongside new forms of state and regional response, and with the impact of international migration spreading beyond the more traditional countries of immigration (e.g., France, Germany, the UK), to include the countries of Southern Europe. These developments have helped to bring the control of immigration to the centre of the political agenda.

It is usual to make a distinction between three (or sometimes four) different historical phases of migration into Western Europe since 1945. In the immediate post-War period, immigration was generally encouraged by many West European countries in order to combat labour shortages experienced as a result of the war and the need for post-war reconstruction. The models of immigration adopted by each country varied, from the German 'guest-worker' model to the British 'post-colonial' model (with France adopting some elements of each). State policies and strategies in relation to migration clearly had an important effect on the experiences and status of immigrants in each country, framing the general conditions of entry, work and residence, and determining the citizenship status of migrants. The continuing effects of these different migratory regimes can be seen even today, as the European Union attempts to create a unified immigration and asylum policy. However, the effects of state control of migration were somewhat limited in this first post-war period by the urgency of the need for labour which meant that in many cases industry led the recruitment of migrants, and any 'illegal' migration was overlooked by government officials. Following the oil crisis and the economic slowdown of 1973-1974 many countries imposed restrictions or a complete stop on labour migration. After the suspension of labour migration, other forms of migration became relatively more important such as migration for family reunification. As the first generation of labour migrants settled and had families, the political debates around migration centred on the implications of permanent settlement (Geddes, 2003). A further change in migratory patterns emerged in Europe after the end of the Cold War, when there was a massive movement of migrants from Eastern Europe to the West. The period following the end of the

Cold War has been characterised by an increase in the number of asylum seeking migrants entering Europe, as this is now one of the only legal channels open to immigrants. This is because most EU countries have now stopped or severely limited labour migration (although there has been, especially recently, a renewed interest in the migration of some categories of highly skilled labour), and have placed greater restrictions and conditions on migration for family reunification. Governments have increasingly attempted to control migration both through external and internal measures. The last decade has also seen an increasing Europeanisation of immigration and asylum policy, as the European Union attempts to find a unified stance on the issue, which has become increasingly important since the creation of a single market in Europe has led to the opening up of internal borders.

The division of migratory histories into various periods like this, has also had gendered implications for the understanding of migration into Europe. Many of the earlier analyses of migration assumed that the first period of post-war labour migration consisted almost entirely of young, single men who had come to work, and that any women who did migrate at this time, did so only as dependents of these male labour migrants. Within this type of analysis, women's migration began seriously only after the end of labour migration, when women came mainly through family reunification. This analysis has been challenged, however, for the way in which it marginalises the role of women in migration, and assumes that their migratory experiences are secondary, dependent as they are on following a male family member. More recent studies and analyses have pointed out that women's independent migratory projects and experiences must not be ignored in any understanding of the recent history of immigration in Europe. Women, it is argued have been a constant factor in migratory flows, even though this might have been in smaller numbers during some periods. Migrant women have always participated to some extent in the labour market, and although many women have migrated through family reunification after the suspension of labour migration in many countries, this means of entering Europe has not precluded active economic, social and political roles for these women.

Moreover, the current period of migration, a period where governments both at a national and a supra-national European level are increasingly striving to restrict migration, and particularly to limit the number of asylum seekers and 'illegal' migrants, also has clearly gendered effects, which must be analysed in any complete examination of current migration patterns and processes. As will be discussed below, the increasing restrictions on migration, which have often been justified in terms of guaranteeing the security of European citizens, have in fact led to increasing insecurities for immigrants within Europe. And the developing policies and strategies for restricting migration have had differing impacts on male and female migrants. In any history or analysis of migration and immigration policies in Europe, it is necessary, therefore, to take into account the different positions of men and women migrants, and their differing migratory trajectories. In the following section, we will discuss the efforts to achieve a common European immigration and asylum policy, before going on to examine the particular insecurities faced by women migrants in contemporary Europe.

An Evolving European Union Immigration Policy

The difficulties involved both in agreeing common immigration and asylum policies for all the member states of the EU, and then in implementing such policies if they were agreed, have been well-documented (Geddes, 2000). The general direction of these attempts to agree a common policy, however, demonstrate a growing tendency amongst European countries to commit to ever-more restrictive targets on immigration and asylum, leading to the creation of what some have termed 'Fortress Europe'. One of the contributory elements to the maintenance of restrictive immigration targets has been their perceived electoral appeal, with governments thus wanting to appear 'tough' on immigration issues in order to win the support of voters. And on the opposite side of the coin, there have been few politicians willing to take the electoral risk of highlighting the benefits of migration. As Geddes remarks: 'It is a sad fact that there are few votes in being nice to immigrants' (Geddes, 2000: 26). Further, immigration has been seen more and more in terms of security, and this rationale has encouraged tighter and tighter controls being put in place. Immigration and asylum are seen as threats to the 'societal security' of states (Waever et al., 1993), hampering governments in their quest to control their populations. Increasingly also, immigration and asylum have been linked with the security threat posed by terrorism (Koser, 2001). This perceived relationship between immigration and security was highlighted by the effects of the terrorist attacks of September 2001 in the USA, and their aftermath on the treatment of immigrants (particularly Muslim immigrants) in the EU. Indeed, recent anti-terrorist legislation introduced in several EU countries and designed to increase the security of European citizens has been criticised for infringing the rights of non-EU citizens resident in Europe, laying them open to arbitrary arrest and detention.

These types of security concerns have been heightened particularly as a result of the process of European integration, and the opening up of internal borders within Europe. In many ways, this process has had consequences which have increased the differences in status and rights between European citizens and others living in Europe. The putting into place of a system of free movement of goods and of people in the EU has had clear legal and political implications for the movement of third country nationals both into and within the EU, but it may be argued that these third country nationals are largely overlooked by the provisions of the various EU Treaties which enshrine free movement, and that in fact, their existence somehow disturbs the basic philosophy of the European Union. As Brochmann remarks: 'The legal status of third country nationals living in an EU memberstate (resident aliens) was not contained in the Single European Act, even though this group now constitutes the majority of the immigrant population in Western Europe' (Brochmann, 1999: 18).

As remarked above, attempts to agree on a common European immigration and asylum policy are closely linked to the moves towards creating European citizenship and guaranteeing free movement of European citizens within the EU. In order to open up internal borders within Europe, member states have felt the need to impose stricter controls on the external borders of the EU. One of the most significant steps towards opening internal frontiers was the Schengen Agreement of 1985, of which France was one of the initial signatories (along with Belgium, Germany, Luxembourg and the Netherlands). The Agreement was implemented in 1995 and the Schengen system included within the full EU structure in the Amsterdam Treaty of 1997 (with provision for the UK and Ireland to continue to opt out of the Schengen area). Although there have been many difficulties in implementing the Schengen acquis, the agreement and its implementation remain important as a key to understanding the direction in which European border control is moving. The Agreement of 1985 stated that:

> In regard to the free movement of persons, the Parties shall endeavour to abolish the controls at the common frontiers and transfer them to their external frontiers. To that end they shall first endeavour to harmonise, where necessary, the laws and administrative provisions concerning prohibitions and restrictions which form the basis for the controls and to take complementary measures to safeguard security and combat illegal immigration by nationals of States that are not members of the European Communities.[2]

The emphasis here is clearly on the need to install further safeguards on external borders in order to realise the opening of internal borders. Immigration is thus placed firmly in the realms of security. The implementation of Schengen should have had some benefits for non-European citizens – principally the right to free movement for third country nationals who have entered the Schengen area legally. However, this right to free movement within the Schengen area has not been fully realised because of the difficulties they have encountered in receiving and using their Schengen visas. And even in this supposed right of free movement, a clear distinction is made between EU and third country nationals with the latter being subject to myriad conditions on their movement, including, for example, the obligation to report to the appropriate authorities within three days of their arrival in another country. Further, the granting of such a right to free movement for third country nationals within the Schengen area has been balanced by the imposition of more restrictive conditions on entry into the Schengen area and an increasing internal controls through the Schengen information system (a vast computerised database) and greater police powers to stop and control identity. These types of controls have, as argued above, made it harder for third country nationals residing legally within the EU to exercise their rights of free movement, but have also made Europe an increasingly insecure destination for illegal migrants. These increasing border controls, coupled with the more restrictive immigration policies of European states have, it is argued, contributed to the growth of people smuggling and trafficking, as some try and profit from the increasing difficulties migrants have in crossing the borders into Europe. This type of smuggling and trafficking has been brought to public attention in some of the tragic cases where large numbers of migrants have died whilst they were being smuggled across borders in lorries or boats, but beyond this organised and large-scale smuggling, there is, as

---

[2] Article 17, Schengen Agreement.

Oso Casas argues (Oso Casas, this volume), a whole array of small-scale profiteering at the expense of those desperate to enter Europe.

The use of the Schengen area as a way of attempting to increase border controls and limit immigration more strictly can be seen as part of a general trend whereby European states have used the EU and the supranationalisation of immigration policy as a way of reasserting control over 'unwanted' migration (Geddes, 2001). And this use of the EU to reduce 'unwanted' migration can be seen to be extending to the areas of refugee and asylum policy as well. As Lavenex argues with regard to refugee and asylum policy in Europe: 'European integration does have an important impact by providing a forum for the pursuit of predominantly restrictive policies' (Lavenex, 2000: 179). Thus the 'communitarisation' of immigration and asylum policy through its move to the first pillar of the EU under the Amsterdam Treaty of 1997, should not be seen merely as a loss of control for European states as immigration moves from the intergovernmental to the supranational policy-making arena. In fact, rather than penalising the individual member states through a loss of control over immigration and asylum policy, this change might be seen as useful in advancing the 'selfish' interests of these member states in limiting immigration (Van Selm, 2002).

As mentioned above, a key area on which European countries have tried to gain agreement and cooperation is that of asylum and refugee policy. Under the terms of the Schengen agreement, member countries could and should refuse to grant asylum to any asylum seeker having passed through a safe third country, whilst the Dublin Convention of 1990 signalled that an asylum claim could only be made in one country of the EU – the country that the asylum seeker had arrived in, unless they had relatives in another EU country – and that once a decision was made on this claim that decision should stand for all of the EU countries. The aim of the Dublin Convention was to avoid one person making multiple asylum claims in different countries and asylum seekers being sent, or trying to move from one country to another to find one which would grant them refugee status. The discourse amongst the member states of the EU has talked of a communitarisation of asylum issues, which together with other immigration issues have been moved from the Third to the First Pillar of the Maastricht Treaty and are thus liable to a more supra-national and less intergovernmental approach. In reality, however, there has been little agreement on reaching a common asylum policy with all states attempting to minimise their commitment to sharing the burden of receiving refugees. A significant example of the failure to reach any agreement over the treatment of asylum seekers was the continuing dispute between France and the UK over the Sangatte refugee camp. The problem of Sangatte was clearly linked to the absence of a real unified European policy on asylum which has meant that: 'hypocrisy and lack of cooperation prevail with each country trying to get rid of asylum seekers judged undesirable by moving them on to a neighbouring country or by shifting the burden of protection outside of the EU thanks to readmission agreements' (Wihtol de Wenden, 2002: 9). Further there has been an increasing tendency amongst both politicians and the media to focus on the issue of so-called 'bogus' asylum seekers and to condemn them as 'economic migrants' rather than true political refugees. This may be seen as one of the damaging effects that has arisen as immigration and asylum have been treated as one and the same issue (Joppke, 1997). As European states have closed their borders to labour migration and have at the same time reduced or stopped completely resettlement programmes for political refugees, asylum seeking has become one of the major routes of legal migration into Europe, and consequently politicians have begun to treat immigration and asylum as one single issue. However, the perception of many that most asylum seekers are in fact economic migrants ignores both data on the outcome of asylum claims, and also the fact that for many asylum seekers there are both political motivations for leaving their own country and also economic and social reasons for choosing a particular country in which to claim asylum. As Koser argues, the perception that most asylum seekers are 'bogus', 'fails to take account of data showing that consistently across the European Union over the last decade up to fifty per cent of asylum applicants are granted either refugee status or some kind of temporary protection. It also confuses motivations for leaving with motivations for selecting a country of asylum. It is reasonable to expect that someone fleeing persecution will at the same time try to apply for asylum in a country where he or she has an existing social network, understands the language and has a chance to work' (Koser, 2001: 88).

This emphasis on the need to reduce the number of asylum seekers granted refugee status, and to crack down on the so-called 'bogus' asylum seekers, together with a determination to stop all 'illegal' immigration, have led to increasingly insecure conditions for those migrants who do enter Europe, even for those who may have been resident in Europe for a long period or who may in fact have gained EU citizenship. Whilst some would argue that the development of a form of post-national citizenship within Europe means that migrants often enjoy the same citizenship rights as EU nationals (Soysal, 1994), it might be stated on the contrary that in recent years many of the rights of migrants have been eroded by governments attempts to limit immigration. In fact, rather than the development of post-national citizenship rights enjoyed by all whether migrants or nationals, it might be more accurate to describe a continuing stratification of rights (Morris, 2002), with increasing differences between the rights and entitlements of different groups (EU citizens and non-EU citizens, legal and illegal migrants, asylum seekers and refugees etc.). This stratification of rights has led to increasing insecurity for various groups of immigrants. Many European countries have, for example, restricted or attempted to restrict the health and social security benefits to which certain categories of migrants are entitled. In addition, the general climate of xenophobia which has been created by the public discourses on immigration (particularly surrounding illegal immigration and 'bogus' asylum seekers) has impacted on many immigrants, even those who may have acquired European citizenship. In this way, even where an immigrant's security is not threatened by the withdrawal or limitation of formal rights, they may experience insecurity as a result of the particular societal conditions within which these rights are exercised. Contemporary discourses and policies on immigration in Europe may thus be seen to be contributing to an increasing insecurity and vulnerability amongst many migrants. These insecurities and vulnerabilities relate to legal status, social rights and physical and mental well-being amongst others. The effects of insecurity are of course experienced differently by various groups and individuals. As argued above, it is important to consider gender as a variable when assessing the impact of immigration policies in Europe, and this book will attempt to look specifically at the insecurities faced by migrant women in Europe. The next section deals with the issue of 'feminisation' of migration, and examines the ways in which migrant women have been particularly exposed to vulnerability and insecurity.

The 'Feminisation' of Migration in Europe

One of the tendencies noted in contemporary studies of global migration patterns, is the feminisation of migratory flows (Castles and Miller, 1993; Phizacklea, 1998). As argued above, it would be wrong to see women's migration as merely 'secondary' migration in relation to primarily male labour migration. Women may have been overlooked or ignored in many classic studies of migration (Barison and Catarino, 1997; Golub et al., 1997), but women have always had their own independent migratory projects. Independent female migration may have escaped accurate documentation in ostensibly gender neutral studies because women were seen as less threatening than men to the receiving country (Skrobanek et al., 1997). However, recently more studies have taken account of the particular role played by female migrants, and researchers have made reference to the 'feminisation' of migration. This reference to the feminisation of migration indicates a growing number of women who are involved in the migratory process. Although accurate figures are difficult to produce because of the lack of gender disaggregated statistics on migration, it is estimated that women now make up at least half of the world's migrant population, and in some cases, particular migratory flows are almost entirely female (e.g., figures for Italy show that migrant populations from the Philippines and Somalia are largely composed of women, Andall, 2000; Scrinzi, this volume).

The reasons for this feminisation of migration are complex and varied. Clearly the conditions of globalization have played a major role in the acceleration of all types of migration, not just that of women, but the particular impacts of globalization on women must be seen as playing a role in their migratory trajectories. In particular, the feminisation of poverty has been highlighted as a major cause of women's migration, as they seek to obtain economic security through finding employment in different countries. The impact of poverty is clear in the growing numbers of women becoming involved in the transnational domestic work and sex work industries for example (see chapters 5 and 8, this volume). However, it is necessary to avoid casting migrant women merely as the victims of globalizing forces (Phizacklea, 2003). Clearly the forces of globalization have an impact on migrant women's daily lives, but their decisions regarding migration are influenced by other factors such as achieving greater personal freedom. As Phizacklea points out in relation to her research on migrant domestic workers in London: 'Relieving poverty at home, building a better future for their children and escaping from unsatisfactory marriages are just some of the motivational factors for migrating' (Phizacklea, 2003: 34).

Together with increasing pressures and reasons for migrating, women are also faced with increasingly restrictive immigration and asylum regimes in many European countries, as outlined above. The causes of insecurity for migrants are reinforced in many cases for women, by an underlying public/private divide which assumes that their role will be a domestic one, and thus ignores their very real presence in the labour market and all that this entails. One of the major sources of insecurity for migrant women in Europe lies in their legal status. Although, contrary to some models, women have always been involved in labour migration, there has often been a reluctance to accept their status as labour migrants, and since the official suspension of labour migration many women have had to enter Europe on the basis of family reunification as this was the only legal means of entry. This means that often they may find themselves dependent on a male relative for their legal residence status, and may be prevented from working legally. The underlying assumption in many immigration policies and in the application of these policies by immigration officials, has been that women would be economically dependent on a man whom they had come to join, thus the issue of migrant women's economic integration into the labour market has not been considered. In France, for example, women *sans-papières* (literally 'without papers' i.e. illegal residents), who had won their fight to gain residence papers, found that police prefectures tended to give them a visitor's card which did not give them the right to work (Cissé, 2000). The assumption was that they would be dependent on a male relative (husband or father). This type of assumption and the legal implications that it has mean that immigrant women may be forced into positions of dependency and vulnerability. Not only have they been dependent on male relatives economically, but their relationship with these men has also been the legal foundation for their residence in Europe. Thus some women have been forced to stay in violent or abusive relationships in order to maintain their legal residence status. Cissé recounts the experiences of some women migrants in France whose attempts to leave their violent husbands were blocked by these husbands threats to take their wives' residence cards to the police prefecture and ensure that their right to stay in France was withdrawn (Cissé, 2000). This lack of an independent legal status is clearly a cause of insecurity and has been the focus of several campaigns for migrant women (Lesselier, this volume).

Further, there have been criticisms of the way in which the asylum system in Europe operates in ways which have particular negative impacts on women. Statistics regarding the proportion of asylum seekers who are female are often unavailable or inaccurate (Crawley, 2001), which may seek to disguise the inherent gender blindness of research on refugees and asylum seekers. In fact, one of the major problems for women refugees is the lack of recognition of many gendered forms of persecution in assessing claims for asylum, due to the continuing operation of a public-private division (Crawley, 2000). Issues such as the threat of forced marriage, or of female genital mutilation, for example, are often not considered seriously as grounds for granting of asylum, or may be assigned to 'cultural differences' which are part of the order of things. To address these types of problems, the European Parliament adopted a resolution in 1984 which called upon states to consider women who had been the victims of persecution because of their sex, as a particular social group, under the terms of the Geneva Convention. The issue of whether or not it would be beneficial for women asylum seekers to be classified as a social group in this way have been debated, with some arguing that this would be inappropriately comprehensive (Crawley, 2001; Kofman et al., 2000). However, campaigners have pointed to the limitations that the non-recognition of women as a social group in this context poses for female asylum seekers (Lesselier, this volume). Further, even beyond the legal process of assessment of asylum claims, women asylum seekers have been particularly affected by social policies introduced by many European governments in order to reduce the entitlements of asylum seekers and thus discourage further claimants. In the UK, for example, the introduction of a voucher system for asylum seekers had particular negative impacts on women, as did the policy of dispersal (Clarence, this volume).

Migrant women are also faced with growing economic insecurities. These are in part related to assumptions about women's role (or non-role) in the labour market as outlined above, and the policies which have built on these assumptions. Migrant women's labour market participation is often invisible, but it is clear that they play a growing role in particular sectors in many European countries. Notably, it has been pointed out the growing role that migrant women play in both the domestic work and sex work industries in Europe (see chapters 5 to 8, this volume). The types of jobs which migrant women occupy are often unskilled and low-paid jobs which are temporary or part-time. The growing demand for flexible labour and working patterns in Western European labour markets has been well-documented, and within this changing pattern of employment there is a clear demand for migrant women's labour. Although official statistics still reveal that more men than women migrate for the purposes of finding work (Zlotnik, 1995), estimates as to the number of undocumented migrant workers reveal that there are as many women as men. As Lim and Oishi argue, in relation to the migration of women from Asia, official statistics take no account of women who migrate on a tourist or student visa and who end up working (usually illegally) in the country of destination, or of those women who migrate illegally and are therefore not documented (Lim and Oishi, 1996). The structure of migrant women's employment in Western Europe is conditioned both by transformations in the global economy and by particular factor in European societies, such as the demand for services of care for the young and elderly. This demand has been fuelled both by a restriction or withdrawal of state services of care, or a basic inadequacy in these services which has not been addressed (Truong, 1996), and by the changing nature of European women's work. Whilst European women have moved in greater and greater numbers into the paid labour market, the traditional divisions of labour within the family have not been modified at the same rate, and so European women are increasingly buying the services of immigrant women to do the tasks for which they are still held responsible, but for which they have little time. The types of jobs into which migrant women are recruited are as argued above, largely unskilled, low-paid and insecure in terms of having little social or legal protection. The fact that many of these women are working illegally because they do not have the requisite work permits makes their conditions of work even more insecure.

Anderson lists some of the problems faced by migrant domestic workers in Europe: 'excessive working hours, working with animals, working for no extra money in the homes of employers' families, having to provide free "trial" labour (and often not employed at the end of it), sexual harassment and false accusations of stealing' (Anderson, 2000: 76). And being without legal residence papers as many of these women are merely intensifies their problems and their dependence on their employers:

> If their rights are abused they have no recourse to authority, since they are likely to end up in prison. As women they face particular problems with pregnancy, often losing their job in consequence, and with no rights to state health care during their pregnancy and birth. When born their children often have no rights to health or education. Being undocumented does not mean that workers are independent of their employers; indeed it gives the employers a direct hold over the workers: if they are dissatisfied with them they may simply report and deport them, or may even do so to avoid paying their wages. (Anderson, 2000: 179)

Whilst the picture of migrant women's work must obviously be nuanced by examining differences in employment patterns in women from different origins and of different generations, it can be argued that the opportunities for migrant women to enter the labour market in contemporary Europe are limited both by stringent immigration controls and by racial discrimination operating within these labour markets (Kofman et al., 2000). Thus, although there remains a 'demand' for migrant women's work, employment may often be a source of various insecurities.

Closely related to migrant women's position in the labour market is their role as providers of welfare. As argued above, the restructuring of European labour markets and welfare states has led to an increased demand for migrant women's work as care givers. In addition, governments' attempts to discourage migration through internal restrictions, such as the limitation of health and welfare services and benefits available to migrants has impacted heavily on women, who are generally expected to remain the main providers of welfare both within and outside of the family. The insecurities caused to female asylum seekers in the UK by the government's attempts to limit their access to welfare have already been mentioned (Clarence, this volume). A similar pattern can be seen to be emerging in other European countries whereby attempts to limit access to health and welfare benefits has caused a stratification of migrants' rights, with a gap between needs and provision emerging, particular for those who have arrived most recently. This gap has specific gendered effects because of the gendered divisions of labour that exist. When women are expected to provide for their family's welfare, the burden of cuts and restrictions in access to education, medical care and welfare benefits may have a specifically negative impact on them. For example, Anderson (this volume) explores the experiences of migrant women in London living with HIV/AIDS, and relates how the difficulties of living with this illness are compounded by the problems they encounter stemming from their situations as women and as migrants. Moreover, the impacts of lack of access to adequate housing, health care etc. may compound the insecurity of migrant women due to their vulnerability to different forms of gender-based violence. The Refugee Women's Resource Project, for example, has pointed to the issue of housing for female asylum seekers in the UK, and has highlighted the ways in which inadequate or shared housing may increase the risks of these women experiencing violence or sexual attack (Refugee Women's Resource Project, 2001).

All of these sources of insecurity may be reinforced by 'culturalist' understandings of migrant women's position, which attributes inequalities in their position to differences between European culture and their 'culture of origin'. This results in essentialised and stereotyped perceptions of migrant women as bearers of 'traditional' cultures. Such essentialised and essentialising representations lead to preoccupations such as that with Islamic women wearing the veil. As Ahmed has argued, both the narrative of the Islamic veil as an oppression, and the counternarrative of the veil as a resistance are misperceptions which are based in and reinforce colonial discourse (Ahmed, 1992). Such racialized representations and discourses which represent a continuation of colonialist perceptions, are also present in the debates over issues such as sexual trafficking (chapter 8, this volume). It is within the context of such discourses that migrant women seek to establish their own social and political identities (Erel, Lazaridis, this volume), and it might be argued that unless such discourses are challenged, the realities of the insecurities facing migrant women in Europe cannot be fully understood.

Organization of the Book

This book seeks to address some of the multiple insecurities facing migrant women living in Europe. The book will examine the impact of globalization and of contemporary immigration and asylum policies on these women's lives, but will attempt to avoid the portrayal of migrant women as mere 'victims' of such processes, examining their role as active agents in the migratory process.

Part One looks at political and legal insecurities facing migrant women as a result of contemporary immigration and asylum policies and examines the strategies that migrant women adopt to overcome the obstacles posed by these policies. In chapter 2 Emma Clarence examines the challenges posed to women asylum seekers in the UK by the new legislation introduced by the government, whilst in chapter 3, Claudie Lesselier examines the problems of dependency faced by migrant women in France as a result of the gender differentiated effects of immigration and asylum policies. Following this in chapter 4, Laura Oso Casas looks at the migratory strategies adopted by Colombian and Ecuadorian women trying to enter Spain, and the ways in which they seek to avoid the hurdles of the Spanish immigration authorities on the one hand, and the dangers of the trafficking networks which seek to exploit them on the other.

In Part Two, chapters deal with the position of migrant women in the labour market in Europe, highlighting economic insecurities and strategies for overcoming these. Chapter 5, by Francesca Scrinzi analyses the phenomenon of the globalization of neo-domesticity, taking the example of migrant domestic workers in Italy. Whilst in chapter 6, the Colectivo Ioé address the issue of the socio-economic insertion of migrant women into the Spanish labour market, and in chapter 7 Sabah Chaib highlights the labour market position of migrant women in France. In chapter 8, Jane Freedman addresses a particular aspect of migrant women's work, looking at the growing involvement of migrant women in the prostitution and sex work industries in Western Europe, and arguing for an end to the simplistic division between 'forced' and 'voluntary' prostitution.

Finally, Part Three will examine social insecurities faced by migrant women, and the ways in which they seek to negotiate their identities within their particular situations. In chapter 9, Jane Anderson examines the lives of African women in the UK who are living with HIV/AIDS, highlighting the particular problems these women face because of their gender, their situation as migrants and their illness. And in chapters 10 and 11, Umut Erel and Gabriella Lazaridis both use biographical narratives to analyse the experiences of Turkish women in Germany, and African women in Greece, and the ways in which these are negotiated in the face of racism and discrimination. These different chapters seek to highlight the multiplicity of migrant women's experiences in Europe, drawing out the challenges posed by contemporary immigration and asylum policies, by the economic conditions shaped by processes of globalisation, and by the various forms of xenophobia, racism and discrimination which these women face. They also aim to point to these women's multiple strategies for facing these challenges, and to portray them not only as passive victims but as active agents negotiating the challenges of the various insecurities which they face.

References

Ahmed, L. (1992), *Women and Gender in Islam*. New Haven: Yale University Press.
Andall, J. (2000), Organizing Domestic Workers in Italy: The Challenge of Gender, Class and Ethnicity, in F. Anthias and G. Lazaridis (eds), *Gender and Migration in Southern Europe*. Oxford: Berg.
Anderson, B. (2000), *Doing the Dirty Work? The Global Politics of Domestic Labour*. London: Zed Books.
Barison, N. and Catarino, C. (1997), 'Les femmes immigrées en France et en Europe', *Migrations Société*, 9, 52, pp. 17-19.
Bommes, M. and Geddes, A. (eds) (2000), *Immigration and Welfare: Challenging the Borders of the Welfare State*. London: Routledge.
Brochmann, G. (1999), 'Controlling Immigration in Europe', in G. Brochmann and T. Hammar (eds) *Mechanisms of Immigration Control*. Oxford: Berg.
Castles, S. and Davidson, A. (2000), *Citizenship and Migration*. Basingstoke: Macmillan.
Castles, S. and Miller, M. (1993), *The Age of Migration*. Basingstoke: Macmillan.
Cissé, M. (2000), The sans-papières, in J. Freedman and C. Tarr (eds), *Women, Immigration and Identities in France*. Oxford: Berg.
Crawley, H. (2000), 'Gender, persecution and the concept of politics in the asylum process', *Forced Migration Review*, 9, pp. 17-21.
Crawley, H. (2001), *Refugees and Gender: Law and Process*. Bristol: Jordan.
Fassin, D. (1996), *L'Espace politique de la santé*. Paris: Presses universitaires de France.
Freedman, J. and Tarr, C. (eds) (2000), *Women, immigration and identities in France*. Oxford: Berg.

Geddes, A. (2000), *Immigration and European Integration: Towards Fortress Europe?* Manchester: Manchester University Press.

Geddes, A. (2001), 'International Migration and State Sovereignty in an Integrating Europe', *International Migration*, 39, 6, pp. 22-42.

Geddes, A. (2003), *The Politics of Migration and Immigration in Europe*. London: Sage.

Golub, A., Morokvasic, M. and Quiminal, C. (1997), 'Evolution de la production des connaissances sur les femmes immigrées en France et en Europe', *Migrations Société*, 9, 52, pp. 17-36.

IOM (2000), *World Migration Report 2000*. Geneva: IOM.

Joppke, C. (1997), 'Asylum and state sovereignty: a comparison of the United States, Germany and Britain', *Comparative Political Studies*, 30, 3, pp. 259-98.

Joppke, C. (ed) (1998), *Challenge to the Nation State: Immigration in Western Europe and the United States*. Oxford: Oxford University Press.

Kofman, E., Phizacklea, A., Raghuram, P. and Sales, R. (eds) (2000), *Gender and International Migration in Europe*. London: Routledge.

Koser, K. (2001), 'New approaches to asylum?', *International Migration*, 39, 6, pp. 85-100.

Kostakopoulou, T. (2001), *Citizenship, Identity and Immigration in the European Union*. Manchester: Manchester University Press.

Lavenex, S. (2000), 'France: international norms, European integration and state discretion', in J. van Selm (ed) *Kosovo's Refugees in the European Union*. London: Pinter.

Lim, L. and Oishi, N. (1996), International Labour Migration of Asian Women: Distinctive Characteristics and Policy Concerns, *Asian and Pacific Migration Journal*, 5, 1, pp. 85 – 116.

Lutz, H. (1997), 'The limits of European-ness: immigrant women in Fortress Europe', *Feminist Review* 57, pp. 93-111.

Morris, L. (2002), 'Britain's asylum and immigration regime: the shifting contours of rights', *Journal of Ethnic and Migration Studies*, 28, 3: 409-425.

Phizacklea, A. (1998), Migration and Globalization: A Feminist Perspective, in K. Koser and H. Lutz (eds), *The New Migration in Europe: Social Constructions and Social Realities*. Basingstoke: Macmillan.

Phizacklea, A. (2003), Gendered Actors in Migration, in J. Andall (ed), *Gender and Ethnicity in Contemporary Europe*. Oxford: Berg.

Quiminal, C. (2000), 'The associative movement of African women and new forms of citizenship', in J. Freedman and C. Tarr (eds) *Women, immigration and identities in France*. Oxford: Berg.

Refugee Women's Resources Projet (2001), *Women's Asylum News*, 7, February 2001. London: Asylum Aid.

Skrobanek, S., Boonpakdi, N. and Janthakeero, C. (1997), *The Traffic in Women*. London: Zed.

Soysal, Y. (1994), *Limits of Citizenship. Migrants and Postnational Membership in Europe*. Chicago: Chicago University Press.

Truong, T. (1996), Gender, international migration and social reproduction, *Asian and Pacific Migration Journal*, 5, 1, pp. 27 – 52.

Van Selm, J. (2002), 'Comprehensive immigration policy as foreign policy?', in S. Lavenex and E. Ucarer (eds), *Externalities of Integration: The Wider Impact of the EU's Migration Regime*. Lexington MA: Lexington Books.

Waever, O., Buzan, B., Kelstrup, M. and Lemaitre, P. (1993), *Identity, Migration and the New Security Agenda in Europe*. London: Pinter.

Wihtol de Wenden, C. (1988), *Les immigrés et la politique*. Paris: Presses de la fondation nationale des sciences politiques.

Wihtol de Wenden, C. (2002), 'La crise de l'asile', *Hommes et Migrations*, 1238, pp.6-12.

Yuval-Davis, N. and Anthias, F. (1989), *Woman-Nation-State*. London: Macmillan.
Zlotnik, H. (1995), The South to North Migration of Women, *International Migration Review*, 29, 1, pp. 229 – 254.

PART I
POLITICAL INSECURITIES: THE GENDERED EFFECTS OF IMMIGRATION AND ASYLUM POLICIES

Chapter 2

Ignored and Isolated: Women and Asylum Policy in the United Kingdom

Emma Clarence

Introduction

As governments across the world seek to limit and control the number of people entering their states, it is unsurprising to find that those who do enter are subject to formal and informal restrictions and control. Social policies directed at refugees, and the way in which services are delivered, have an impact beyond simply determining access to resources. The language of 'bogus asylum seekers', accompanied by the introduction of policies aimed at making Britain 'unattractive' to those seeking refuge, provides an indication of the way in which the British government has sought to diminish the experiences and needs of refugees. Whilst it is clear that the majority of asylum claimants in Britain face hostility and even incredulity from government officials, the specific experiences of women need to be drawn out from the experiences of refugees in general if we are to understand the differential impact asylum policies can have on one specific group.

Drawing on the British experience this chapter examines the impact of contemporary social policies upon women asylum claimants. Since the election of the Labour government there have been two pieces of legislation focussing upon asylum processes, one in 1999 and the next in 2002. These pieces of legislation have, amongst their many initiatives, introduced a new government agency, the National Asylum Support Service, whose function it is to oversee the assistance asylum claimants receive. Accompanying this has been the introduction and ultimately the replacement of a voucher system, the formalised dispersal of asylum claimants across Britain, the withdrawal of services to asylum claimants who did not register for asylum on their arrival and proposed greater use of asylum accommodation and detention centres. All of these have had a profound impact on the lives of those people claiming asylum in the United Kingdom. By considering the impact of such policies on the lives of women asylum claimants in Britain, the plight of women, and the insecurity of their position, can be analysed in detail. Before doing so it is necessary to understand the current political approach to asylum in the United Kingdom.

Asylum in the United Kingdom

Governments and the media are often found referring to Britain's 'proud history' of welcoming those who seek asylum and refuge (Audit Commission, 2000: 3; Home Office 1998: 8.1) before going on to highlight the increase in the number of people claiming asylum, the 'burden' that such a rise places on the asylum system and suggesting that the increase can be attributed to 'bogus' asylum claimants. It is important to contextualise such claims and the figures that invariably accompany them. Whilst it is not disputed that the number of people claiming asylum has increased in the United Kingdom (from 26,260 in 1990 to 71,100 in 1999 and 110,700 in 2002) other European countries have had not dissimilar experiences. Indeed the United Kingdom ranks only ninth amongst European Union states for the number of asylum claimants per head of population (Home Office, 2001: 4.12). In such a context the claim of a 'burden' of asylum claimants, with the implication that the United Kingdom is doing (significantly) more than other (European) states, fails to withstand scrutiny. In an international context the UK's claim of being 'burdened' is weaker still; the UK actually receives only approximately two per cent of the world's refugees (Refugee Action, 2002: 2). The majority of refugees are in the developing world, crossing borders to flee persecution or civil strife, and remaining within their region rather than entering the West.

        The perception that economic refugees rather than 'genuine' claimants have targeted the UK is one that has been propounded both by the media and some sections of the government. Use of words such as 'swamping' (in reference to asylum claimants and public services) by the Home Secretary, David Blunkett, in 2002, has only further served to reinforce negative images of asylum claimants. Rather than attempting to tackle the growing public unrest and hostility towards refugees by focusing on the reality of both the numbers applying and the fact that 'the overwhelming factor affecting asylum claims...is what goes on in terms of political stability in other countries in the world' (Jack Straw to the Special Standing Committee in respect of the Immigration and Asylum Bill Col 470 22, March 1999) the government has instead effectively reinforced such perceptions with its policies directed towards asylum claimants. Thus, the harsh measures that have been introduced since 1998 are based on the idea of deterring 'bogus' asylum seekers from entering the UK in order to take advantage of the welfare system.

The Asylum System in Practice

The asylum system in the United Kingdom, as it currently operates, suffers from significant problems. Report after report from non-governmental agencies involved in the care and representation of asylum claimants highlight the problems of the asylum system, particularly at the initial decision making stage (see, for example Asylum Aid, 1999; National Association of Citizens' Advice Bureaux, 2002; Refugee Action, 2002). Such criticisms include the apparent lack of understanding of changing international political situations, the failure of immigration officers to accept evidence of torture, unrealistic demands of asylum claimants (such as producing evidence of their own arrest warrants) and general inconsistencies in decision making (Asylum Aid, 1999). Furthermore, the process of claiming asylum can be exceptionally long and time consuming, taking years in some cases. The length of time that the process takes is something which the government has sought to address through its reforms although the emphasis on speed has, arguably, compromised fairness and justice.

In this context, both male and female asylum claimants confront a system whose adequacy is questioned. Women, however, face a system which compounds such problems with its failure to recognise sex as a factor which must be considered not only in the asylum decision making process but in the policies to support claimants whilst that decision is being made. As it stands, despite the drafting of gender guidelines by the Refugee Women's Legal Group in 1998 there remain no official gender guidelines for use by immigration officers in their decisions on asylum cases. The Immigration Appellate Authority has issued gender guidelines (2000), but these are for use in the appeals process. The failure to produce similar guidance for the initial decision stage has important consequences for the way in which women experience the asylum process. From the very moment they are interviewed women are subjected to treatment which ignores their experiences and the need for sensitivity. Women interviewers and translators are provided only 'where possible' rather than as a matter of course, and thus women claimants may be interviewed by male immigration officers, in front of their children or even male family members, clearly limiting the likelihood of sexual violence being reported.

It is important to recognise that the way in which women experience the persecution which leads them to seek asylum may be different from men. In the Immigration Appellate Authority's Asylum Gender Guidelines (2000) it is acknowledged that whilst women have the same experiences as men, they also suffer persecution and have unique experiences because they are women. This is not simply because of the use of sexual violence against women but also because of the way in which women engage in political activities may be different, and harder to document. Women may be persecuted because they are associated with the activities of male family members and they are also seen as being more vulnerable and less able to move or relocate quickly because of children. The failure of women to meet social expectations can also result in ill-treatment. It is for all these reasons that the Asylum Gender Guidelines argues that 'Even where gender is not a central issue in an asylum claim, giving consideration to gender-related aspects of a case will assist in fully understanding and determining the whole of an asylum claim' (2000: 2).

However it is clear that such guidance is not being used. Despite the United Kingdom's 1995 commitment to meeting the United Nation's call for all legislation to be assessed for its gender impact, it is clear that such a commitment does not extend as far as asylum policy (Refugee Action, 2002: 2). Women have been marginalised, if not ignored, and their special needs as asylum claimants consistently overlooked (Crawley, 2001). The government's own data collection service fails to record how many women enter the United Kingdom seeking refuge. In 2001, 22 per cent of applications for asylum were from women. However the

government only notes the 'head of the household' and thus many women will not
be counted or acknowledged (Refugee Action, 2002: 4). This is a consequence of
the way in which women register for asylum: when a woman arrives with her
husband, her claim for asylum is not considered separately but is linked to that of
her husband. The implicit presumption in this is that a woman's claim for asylum
is for the same reasons as that of her husband. Not only does this marginalise
women at the very beginning of the asylum claim process, it also fails to recognise
that there may be specifically gender-based reasons for seeking asylum.

Research by the Refugee Women's Resource Project in 2003 noted that
asylum decisions in the United Kingdom are made on a 'gender blind' basis – that
is, gender plays no role in the decision making process – and that there is a clear
lack of understanding of specific gender issues. Home Office refusal letters have,
for example, repeatedly referred to 'low level' political activities as a reason for
rejecting applications, rather than recognising that there are different ways of
engaging in political activity (Refugee Women's Resource Project, 2003: 68). This
is in stark contrast to the Asylum Gender Guidelines which specifically highlight
such issues (Refugee Women's Resource Project, 2003: 71; Immigration Appellate
Authority, 2000). Given the lack of gender awareness in the asylum decision
making process it is perhaps unsurprising that the support programmes for women
claiming asylum have also proven to be insensitive to their needs.

Immigration and Asylum Act (1999)

The Immigration and Asylum Act (1999) radically altered the way in which
asylum claimants were treated upon entering the United Kingdom. The White
Paper, *Fairer, Faster and Firmer* (1998), which preceded the Act, highlighted the
government's new approach. Those claiming asylum were to have their cases
decided speedily and then, if necessary, be deported quickly following any appeal
process. This in turn would 'help to promote race equality' (1998: 2.13). Broadly, a
key part of the 1999 Act was the government's desire to minimise the claimed
'economic incentives' for people to enter the United Kingdom and claim asylum or
to claim asylum having been located in the UK on other visas (such as student
visas) which had expired (Oxfam, 2000). Many of its key reforms were designed to
control the way in which asylum claimants received support and thus make the
United Kingdom 'less attractive' to 'bogus' claimants.

The changes initiated by the Act were radical. Whereas previously
assistance had been provided to asylum claimants by local authorities and Benefits
Agencies, a single central government body, the National Asylum Support Service
(NASS) was to be established. This began operating in April 2000, charged with
the responsibility for overseeing the support which was to be made available to
asylum claimants whilst they waited for their claim to be heard. Accompanying the
establishment of NASS was a new way of providing support. A system was
introduced in which claimants received a weekly allowance paid in vouchers that
could only be used at participating stores (Shaw, 2002: 12). Vouchers were worth
70 per cent of Income Support for adults and 100 per cent for children. What that

meant in 2002 was that an adult received £59.26 and each child £33.50 (Oxfam, 2002: 8). Claimants also received £10 per week paid in cash which was to be used for all travel, telephone and incidental expenses. To enable claimants to purchase clothes and other such items a grant of £50 per person was made available every six months. The grant was not automatically paid by NASS and had to be applied for, in writing, in English, before it would be issued. It is important to note that the level at which Income Support is set is at the minimum considered for an 'acceptable standard of living' (Oxfam, 2002: 4) and acts as a gateway for a series of other welfare benefits all of which were therefore denied to claimants.

The justification for the low levels of financial support was given by the then Home Secretary, Jack Straw, when he told the House of Commons that the 'asylum support system is intended to be on a short-term basis, a safety net arrangement, and it should be possible to live on these amounts for short periods only' (cited in Oxfam/Refugee Council, 2002: 19). Furnished accommodation would be provided and utility bills paid under a dispersal programme, detailed below, allowing the government to argue that the level of support from vouchers was acceptable as the shelter needs of claimants would be met (Audit Commission, 2000:12). The Audit Commission reported an average wait of 12 months for an initial decision, against the government's target that a decision on an asylum application would be reached in, on average, two months and any subsequent appeals would be heard within four months (2000: 8, 14). These delays challenge the idea of vouchers being only a 'short-term' safety net, and therefore also challenge the claim that the amount of support provided was adequate. In research conducted amongst forty organisations for a joint Oxfam/Refugee Council Report (2002) it was found that 85 per cent of organisations reported that the asylum claimants they worked with had experienced hunger as a result of the inadequacy of the vouchers (2002: 4). This was further supported by a Maternity Alliance/Bail for Immigration Detainees (2002) Report which detailed mothers going hungry in order to ensure that their children had adequate food and clothing.

Not only were the vouchers providing inadequate support but actually using them was an often demeaning experience as they very clearly and publicly labelled people as 'asylum seekers'. For women there was also an added dimension to the problems associated with vouchers. Women who seek refuge in the UK with their husbands usually have their application linked to that of their husbands who are deemed to be the 'principal applicant'. Vouchers were printed with the name of the principal applicant on them, although other applicants connected to the principal applicant were also intended to use them. However, reports highlighted the difficulties women had when trying to use vouchers that did not have their name on them (Medical Foundation for the Care of Victims of Torture, 2000a: 28). Home Office research accepted that women had been prevented from using the vouchers because they had the name of the principal (male) applicant and shops had refused to accept them (Eagle, 2002: 20). Public refusal, in what was already considered to be a difficult and potentially demeaning situation, contributed to women feeling isolated and marginalised. It also lessened the control and influence women could have over the way in which vouchers were spent.

Although this refusal was not a policy of the government, it was a failure of the design of the scheme. In effect the voucher policy was being implemented by supermarket staff who were responsible for both checking the eligibility of the individual using the vouchers and ensuring that their shopping did not contain 'prohibited items' such as cigarettes or alcohol (Sales, 2002: 464). The role of supermarket staff in implementing a policy as sensitive as asylum support is highly questionable. However, this was not the only problem which claimants confronted. Other failings of the voucher system quickly became evident with the repeated and well documented problems individuals and organisations had in trying to contact NASS. The long delays in receiving vouchers experienced by some claimants and the fact that NASS helpline was available in English (although the private company who ran the vouchers offered a multi-lingual phone service, it was not well publicised) further highlight the administrative inefficiencies of NASS and the lack of awareness of the needs of asylum claimants.

The decision of the government to exclude travel from NASS's definition of essential living needs also had a detrimental impact upon women. Any travel costs were to come from the £10 cash element of their assistance. This created significant hardship for all asylum claimants in that it made it difficult (if not impossible) for people to travel to medical appointments, to see friends and relatives or to make use of local facilities such as libraries, colleges, etc. For women taking children to school the lack of travel payment meant that they were required to walk children to school, sometimes over long distances. The dispersal programme (discussed below) separated women from friends and relatives and the small cash allowance left them with little financial ability to maintain contact either by telephone or visiting. Thus, women found themselves isolated from potential support networks in geographic areas which were often hostile to the very presence of asylum claimants.

The voucher system was, on the whole, insensitive to the needs of women who were pregnant or had young children. Even the maternity grant of £300 (payable in vouchers) was implemented in such a way that women had difficulties in accessing it. The grant was available, on application, within four weeks of the birth or two weeks after it. No extra support was available earlier in the pregnancy to buy maternity clothing or any other items which pregnant women may require; those extra needs had to be met out of the standard voucher and cash payments. In an Oxfam/Refugee Council survey 65 per cent of organisations reported that the maternity grant was an inadequate amount to meet the needs of women in the period immediately before and after birth (Oxfam/Refugee Council, 2002: 12-13). Organisations reported that women had entered hospital for the birth of their child without such basics as nappies because vouchers had not arrived in time. The six-week application 'window' ignored the potential difficulties which impacted upon the ability of women to meet the deadlines. Women who had not applied before the birth and remained in hospital for more than two weeks found themselves without the grant because they had missed the deadline (Oxfam/Refugee Council, 2002: 12-13). Compounding all of these difficulties was the requirement to spend maternity grant vouchers only in specific stores – the option of buying (cheaper) second-hand baby goods was not one therefore available to women claimants.

Such insensitivity and lack of awareness of the needs of women claimants is more than an inconvenience. The stress of applying for asylum, coupled with other potential problems such as language difficulties and a lack of understanding of how British administrative systems and institutions work, at the same time as being pregnant, have the potential to harm both the development of the unborn child and the health of the mother. However, more threatening to the welfare of women claimants was the failure of the government to consider the needs of women who were HIV positive. The low weekly allowance precluded the purchase of infant formula – crucial for those women who were HIV positive and therefore unable to breastfeed – and they were ineligible to receive the milk tokens available to UK residents on low incomes through the 'benefits gateway' aspect of Income Support. The government claimed in a joint Department of Health/Home Office statement that 'Selective provision of formula milk (through milk tokens) to HIV-infected asylum seeking mothers could result in deductive disclosure of the women's HIV status' (Community Care, 2002). It went on to claim that if all asylum claimants were given milk tokens it would have a negative impact on breast-feeding promotions, although this ignored another government campaign to reduce mother to baby transmissions of HIV of which the provision of milk formula is a key component. The statement pointed to the vouchers provided by NASS and the additional maternity allowance as evidence of the government's financial assistance to asylum claimants and stated that 'Asylum seekers may be able to access formula milk free or at reduced prices through local schemes operated by community clinics or hospital services' (Community Care, 2002). This failed to acknowledge that the National Health Service did not accept vouchers and thus women were unable to purchase the reduced cost milk formula on sale within hospitals unless they used their small cash allowance, which was also required to fund their travel and communication needs.

Dispersal and Accommodation and Detention Centres

Accompanying the introduction of vouchers was a formalised dispersal programme. Apparent political and social discontent at the concentration of asylum claimants in London and Kent was addressed by central government with the introduction of a 'no-choice' dispersal scheme, whereby people would be sent to accommodation centres or private accommodation across the United Kingdom (Home Office, 1998: 8.22). If asylum claimants rejected the location they were to be sent to, they became eligible for subsistence support only (Shaw, 2002: 12-13). It was intended that 'placements would take account of the value of linking to existing communities and the support of voluntary and community groups' (Home Office, 1998: 8.22). A concession was granted to the Medical Foundation for the Care of Victims whereby people under their care would be accommodated in London to enable them to access the services of the Foundation. However, there is evidence of the government's failure to actually heed its own guidance. The plan of NASS to 'cluster' people together after dispersal has not been successful. Dispersal has been on 'ad hoc' basis with little meaningful attempt to group asylum claimants together (Medical Foundation for the Care of Victims of Torture, 2000b) leaving people isolated from their own communities and potential support networks. Highly vulnerable individuals are actually made more vulnerable by the uncertainty and insecurity which accompanies the dispersal process.

The system of dispersal and accommodation centres pursued by the government, from the evidence of asylum claimants, lacks cultural sensitivity. Women, including those who are pregnant, are housed in mixed private accommodation (Refugee Action, 2002: 11) with little concern as to social customs which may require the exclusion of male non-family members. Many women in such circumstances effectively found themselves confined to their bedrooms (Refugee Action, 2002: 11). Whilst NASS claimed that it was not opposed to considering single sex accommodation it identified difficulties in finding adequate accommodation as an explanation of why it had not yet done so. Even those dispersal policies which would appear to be supportive of women in vulnerable situations – such as the development of nationality and/or language clusters – may in fact be detrimental to some women who come from communities with only small number of claimants because they may find themselves more isolated (Refugee Action, 2002: 12).

Women who are dispersed to accommodation centres may also find themselves victims of harassment from other asylum claimants. Such victimisation within accommodation centres has been repeatedly highlighted by voluntary and non-governmental organisations as an area that the government has failed to meaningfully address (Community Care, 2001; Maternity Alliance, 2000). There is no segregation of single women and women with children within accommodation centres, and groups caring for, and representing asylum claimants highlight the unsatisfactory nature of this (Medical Foundation for the Victims of Torture, 2000a). A lack of (female) interpreters for women asylum claimants is also an issue which remains to be resolved. Women, often traumatised by the experiences which have contributed to their decision to seek asylum, are required to discuss intimate medical or psychological problems with male interpreters, or even male family members (Refugee Action, 2002: 15). In one reported case the decision to perform a caesarean birth on a woman who did not speak English was taken without an interpreter being present (McLeish, 2002).

The Audit Commission (2000) in its report into the dispersal system has highlighted the lack of support for asylum claimants. It found that outside of London there were inadequate support structures. Interpreting services are 'ad hoc' and limited. This only increases the vulnerability of some of the most vulnerable people within society as the example above illustrates. Nor is it only the area of interpreting that services are inadequate. For those women who have been raped or sexually assaulted the way in they been dispersed has left them, at best, without continuity of medical care or counselling and at worst uninformed of the services and assistance that are available to them. Refugee Action's research highlighted that two thirds of asylum claimants were from countries where women were highly unlikely to report rape because of the shame. Accompanying this fear was the fact that 49 per cent did not know that counselling and other forms of assistance was available to them (Refugee Action, 2002: 13). Continuity of care and the provision of services which understand the complex problems women asylum claimants who have experienced sexual violence present with, are crucial if the physical and mental health needs of such women are to be addressed. Dispersal clearly does not consider such needs.

For pregnant women dispersal has compounded the problems they confront. Research for the Maternity Alliance/Bail for Immigration Detainees (2002) further highlighted the insensitivity which the government's policies, and the way in which they have been implemented. It was not uncommon for women to be dispersed even when they are close to giving birth, including those whose birthing arrangements had already been made (Medical Foundation for the Care of Victims of Torture, 2000a). Women have also been dispersed after the birth, separating women from friends and family who could offer support. Nor is it uncommon for women with young babies to be 'repeatedly moved' around accommodation centres (Maternity Alliance/Bail for Immigration Detainees, 2002). For those women who were placed in full board accommodation other problems emerged. Medical appointments were missed if transport was not available and the provision of meals also created difficulties. There was often a lack of flexibility surrounding meal times and thus women missed meals completely if they were attending hospital appointments. Pregnant women often prefer (and are advised) to eat little and often, but this was not available for women in full board accommodation. Having given birth accommodation centres continued to prove unresponsive to the needs of mothers and babies. 'Solid' baby food was not provided and HIV positive women did not have access to baby milk formula in the accommodation and were required to purchase it themselves (Maternity Alliance/Bail for Immigration Detainees, 2002).

Compounding the sense of isolation women experience in the dispersal process have been problems in the way in which claimants have been dispersed. Usually, dispersal has been to areas of high deprivation and social exclusion where 'public services are not meeting the needs of [the] population' (Medical Foundation for the Care Victims of Torture, 2000a: 13). In such a situation hostility to claimants is easily generated. Dispersal has also taken place into areas where there is no visible ethnic minority community making asylum claimants highly visible and potentially vulnerable to racially motivated attacks. This failure to be aware of underlying socio-economic issues in dispersal areas has only served to heighten tensions between local residents and asylum claimants rather than alleviate them as was the government's reasoning in its 'firm but fair' asylum policy. Asylum claimants have reported racial victimisation, and there have been a number of racially motivated murders of claimants. In such an environment of hostility it is unsurprising that women have found themselves effectively confined to indoors, leaving as little as practicable, so as to avoid racial harassment. Myths abound as to the level of support claimants receive which invariably suggest that claimants receive far more assistance then they actually do. The government has done little to tackle such misconceptions preferring to rely upon the image of itself as a 'strong' government tackling the difficult issue of asylum. This has done little to address the negative experiences of asylum claimants and has instead left them

Gender and Insecurity

isolated in communities often convinced of the correctness of the rhetoric of 'bogus asylum seekers'.

Although the 1998 *Fairer, Faster and Firmer* White Paper argued that families should only be detained for a few days prior to removal after an unsuccessful asylum application (Home Office, 1998: 12.5) there has been a clear shift away from that approach. In 2001 the Director of Immigration Services signalled a change of policy when an increase in family detention accommodation was announced. What had been 'particularly regrettable' in 1998 had become an acceptable part of having 'effective immigration control'. Nor is it unknown for families to be divided – with the 'head of the family' (usually male) detained and the remaining family dispersed with no regard to where the detained family member is being held. This places a significant strain on the entire family, and pays no heed to the cultural and social issues which may emerge when a woman is placed in that position. Conversely, the importance of keeping families together has now been used to justify the detention of children signalled (Bail for Immigration Detainees, 2002: 38).

After a long campaign by voluntary and non-governmental organisations, trade unions and some parliamentarians a review into the voucher system was announced. In October 2001 Blunkett confirmed that the system would be phased out, but it was not until February 2002 that the White Paper formally announced the phasing out of vouchers and an increase in the cash benefit to £14. The success of the campaign to end vouchers for asylum claimants was not met however with a significant shift in the direction of government resources and policy. The level of financial support remained stable (only a 1.6 per cent rise was announced) and the opportunity to access other benefits open to those claiming Income Support was denied to those seeking asylum. The White Paper did not address the issue of payments for milk formula but following a campaign and a High Court ruling in July 2002 which ruled that the Home Secretary should reconsider the policy, the government finally altered its position, albeit only slightly, on its provision. From 3 March 2003 all women were granted an extra £3 per week if they were pregnant, £5 for a child under 1 and £3 for a child aged between 1 and 3.

The Nationality, Immigration and Asylum Act (2002)

Having already passed legislation in 1999, only two years later the government was again eager to reform the asylum process. In February 2002 the White Paper *Secure Border, Safe Havens: Integration with Diversity in Modern Britain* was published by the Home Office. The 2002 Act made no attempt to address the failures of the previous asylum legislation to consider the needs of women. Indeed the announcement that a list of 'safe countries' had been drawn up and incorporated into the Act (with the Home Secretary retaining the power to add countries as and when considered necessary) highlights the way in which the government actually chose to ignore the experiences of women and the well-documented instances of gender based persecution in some states. The list of safe countries in 2003 included the European Union states, the ten EU accession countries and a further seven countries including Albania, Macedonia and Serbia/Montenegro (*The Guardian*, 7 February 2003). People from such countries will be deported without appeal on the basis that 'It is frankly absurd that people can routinely claim they are in fear of their lives...These are democratic countries which live under the rule of the law' according to David Blunkett (quoted in *The Guardian*, 24 October 2002).

The attempt to identify 'safe' countries is telling in that it highlights the continuing lack of gender awareness in the government's policies. Women may confront forms of persecution because of their sex which a blanket idea of a 'safe country' overlooks. A case in point is the treatment of Roma, and specifically Roma women, across Europe. A United Nations Development Programme Report in 2003 highlighted that the living conditions of Roma in Central and Eastern Europe were in fact closer to those experienced by populations in sub-Saharan Africa than to those of the majority of European citizens. Roma women, in particular, have become a target. A Report by the Center for Civil and Human Rights, a Slovak human rights group, released in January 2003 presented evidence of the forced sterilisation of Roma women in Slovakian public hospitals (Center for Reproductive Rights, 2003). For the UK government to claim that such a country is 'safe' ignores both the reality of the plight of all Roma, who confront racism and discrimination, and the specifically gendered experiences of women. It is worth noting that between 1990 and 1999 over seven thousand Roma were granted asylum within the European Union.

Within Britain, the White Paper, and the National Immigration and Asylum Act (2002) which accompanied it, saw the proposed introduction of induction centres and the expansion of accommodation centres for asylum claimants. It was intended that induction centres would house between 200 and 400 asylum claimants and would serve as a reception centre. Asylum claimants would stay at the centres for approximately seven days whilst the National Asylum Support Service decided if they were eligible for support and informed them of the asylum process. Following this claimants would then be dispersed or placed in accommodation centres whose use was to be expanded. It was intended that they would ultimately house approximately 3000 to 4000 claimants throughout their application periods, with the remaining applicants continuing to be dispersed. Accommodation centres would effectively be 'closed', with meals, health and legal services, as well as education provided within the centre, with claimants receiving only a small cash allowance.

Although the government claimed that asylum claimants would not be 'detained' in such accommodation centres, there would be a residence requirement in operation, and non-residence 'may affect the outcome of their asylum claim where the non-compliance damages their credibility' (Shaw, 2002: 16). Part of this plan was the controversial decision to no longer allow the children of asylum claimants to access mainstream education services. There has been significant concern at the potential for this policy to institutionalise claimants and hamper the integration of successful refugees into wider society. Furthermore, the government had failed to meaningfully address the well-documented problems experienced by women claimants within such centres.

The Nationality, Immigration and Asylum Act (2002) introduced assistance measures which have had a profound impact upon the support available to asylum seekers. Those claimants who did not claim asylum at their first port of entry into the United Kingdom had their right to claim assistance removed unless good cause could be shown why there had been a delay and they had independent, verifiable evidence of the date and method of their arrival in the United Kingdom. The reasons why individuals do not immediately claim asylum have been well documented. They include language difficulties, fear of the state and a general lack of knowledge as to how the asylum process operates. However the government's policy ignores such issues and instead introduces punitive measures which could only lead to increased poverty and destitution amongst refugees. This policy has echoes of an earlier failed one. The Conservative government had, in 1996, passed the Asylum and Immigration Act which had denied welfare benefits to those who claimed asylum 'in-country' (Fiddick, 1999; Sales, 2002: 462). Following a legal challenge the policy was effectively overruled when a court ruling decided that it was the duty of local authorities to provide assistance to those people deemed to be 'destitute', and that this included asylum claimants. Despite opposing the 1996 Conservative government policy when it was announced, and given the nature of the 1996 court ruling, the Labour government went ahead with its own version of the policy.

It should be made clear that there is no significant difference between the number of 'in-country' asylum claimants being granted refugee status as those who claim asylum 'at port' (Asylum Aid, 1999; *The Guardian*, 17 January 2003). Indeed the Home Office's own figures highlight that around 65 per cent of 'in-country' applications are successful (Refugee Council, 2002b: 16). Despite this it is still perceived by the government that a 'genuine refugee' would claim asylum upon arrival (Crawley, 1999: 25). Thus, assistance was only to be granted to those claimants who could prove they had claimed for asylum, met the (new) criteria for destitution, and applied for asylum 'as soon as reasonably practicable'. It quickly became apparent that this was being strictly interpreted as the Refugee Council reported benefits being refused to someone who registered for asylum within one day of arriving (*The Guardian*, 17 January 2003). Even before the eligibility criteria were instituted on 8 January 2003, asylum organisations were expressing their concern at the impact of the legislation (Refugee Council, 2002b). By 19 February 2003 six test cases in the High Court had seen the court rule that the new eligibility criteria were in breach of the European Convention on Human Rights. The government appealed and the High Court ruled on 18 March 2003 that in the test cases brought to court, assistance had been wrongly denied. However, the ruling left the way open for the system to be implemented if changes were made. It remains unclear how the policy will be altered and what the implications of such changes shall be for asylum claimants. What is clear is that the government will not fundamentally alter its policy direction based on its continuing use of the rhetoric of 'bogus asylum seekers'.

Conclusion

Asylum claimants who enter Britain are vulnerable. The very act of leaving one country, usually with very little and often leaving family behind, to seek refuge in another country is a period of insecurity. In the midst of that insecurity they are confronted by a state whose rhetoric has emphasised the likelihood of the 'bogus' nature of their claims. Women claimants in particular encounter a state that not only doubts their claim for asylum but ignores their specific needs and perpetuates their insecurity. In every aspect of the asylum process women are marginalised and isolated. At the initial decision making stage the specifically gendered nature of some forms of persecution are ignored by immigration officers, despite detailed guidance from the Immigration Appellate Authority. The very policies and programmes that are meant to offer support and act as a safety-net for women claimants have served to disadvantage them. The voucher system, with its emphasis on the (male) principal applicant stigmatised women who were refused goods because they were not explicitly named on them. Furthermore, vouchers proved inadequate in meeting the most basic needs of women and children, including providing adequate food. Pregnant women have lacked the necessary resources to purchase items required in the periods before and after birth. Prior to 2003 the government went so far as to refuse extra financial support for women who were HIV positive in order to allow them to purchase milk formula, in direct contravention of a stated government policy to reduce the transmission of HIV from mother to baby. Women were faced with difficult choices as to how best to meet the needs of their child without endangering it, frequently to the detriment of their own health. Whilst much is made by central government of its commitment to a fair and just asylum policy, it is clear that fairness and justice do not extend to ensuring that the needs of some of the most vulnerable people are addressed or even recognised.

References

Asylum Aid (1999), *Still No Reason At All: Home Office Decisions on Asylum Claims*, London: Asylum Aid.

Audit Commission (2000), *Another Country: Implementing Dispersal under the Immigration and Asylum Act 1999*, London: Audit Commission.

Bail for Immigration Detainees (2002), *Immigration Detention in the United Kingdom*: Submission to the United Nations Working Group on Arbitrary Detention.

Bloch, A. and L. Schuster (2002), Asylum and Welfare: Contemporary Debates, *Critical Social Policy*, 22, 3, pp. 393-414.

Center for Reproductive Rights (2003), *Freedom News*, Vol. XII, No. 3, March.

Child Poverty Action Group (2003), Asylum seekers milk tokens success http://www.cpag.org.uk/

Cohen, S. (2002), The local state of immigration controls, *Critical Social Policy*, 22/3, pp. 518-543.

Community Care (2001), Isolated by Gender, *Community Care*, November 22.

Community Care (2002), Denial of Milk Tokens Exposes Babies to HIV Risk, Claim Campaigners, *Community Care*, February 14.

Crawley, H. (1999), *Breaking Down the Barriers: A Report on the Conduct of Asylum Interviews at Port*, London: Immigration Law Practitioners' Association.

Crawley, H. (2001), *Refugees and Gender: Law and Process*, London: Jordan.

Eagle, A. et. al. (2002), *Asylum Seekers' Experiences of the Voucher Scheme in the United Kingdom – Fieldwork Report*, London: Home Office Research, Development and Statistics Directorate.

Fiddick, J. (1999), *Immigration and Asylum*, Research Paper 99/16, London: House of Commons Library.

Gibney, M. (2001), *The State of Asylum: Democratisation, Judicilisation and Evolution of Refugee Policy in Europe*, Working Paper No. 50, New Issues in Refugee Research, Oxford: Refugee Studies Centre.

Home Office (1998), *Fairer, Faster and Firmer*, London: Home Office.

Home Office (2001), *Report of the Operational Reviews of the Voucher and Dispersal Schemes of the National Asylum Support Service*, London: Home Office.

Home Office (2001), *Secure Border, Safe Havens: Integration with Diversity in Modern Britain*, London: Home Office.

Home Office (2002), *Understanding the Decision-Making of Asylum Seekers*, Home Office Research Study, London: Home Office.

Immigration Appellate Authority (2000), *Asylum Gender Guidelines*, London: Immigration Appellate Authority.

Maternity Alliance/Bail for Immigration Detainees (2002), *A Crying Shame: Pregnant Asylum Seekers and Their Babies in Detention*, London: Maternity Alliance.

McLeish, J. (2002), *Mothers in Exile: Maternity Experiences of Asylum Seekers in England*, London: Maternity Alliance.

Medical Foundation for the Care of Victims of Torture (2000a), *Response of the Medical Foundation for the Care of Victims of Torture to the National Asylum Support Service Vouchers Review*, London: Medical Foundation for the Care of Victims of Torture.

Medical Foundation for the Care of Victims of Torture (2000b), *Asylum Detention is Not Fair (Policy Statement)*, London: Medical Foundation for the Care of Victims of Torture.

National Association of Citizens' Advice Bureaux (2002), *Distant Voices: CAB Clients' Experience of Continuing Problems with the National Asylum Support Service*, London: National Association of Citizens' Advice Bureaux.

Oxfam (2000), *Token Gestures – The Effects of the Voucher Scheme on Asylum Seekers and Organisations in the UK*, Oxford: Oxfam.

Oxfam and the Refugee Council (2002), *Poverty and Asylum in the UK*, London: Refugee Council.

Refugee Action (2002), *Is it Safe Here? Refugee Women's Experiences in the United Kingdom*, London: Refugee Action.

Refugee Council (2002a), *The Nationality, Immigration and Asylum Act 2002: changes to the asylum system in the UK*, London: Refugee Council.

Refugee Council (2002b), *Withdrawal of In-Country Asylum Support*, Refugee Council Briefing 2 December, London: Refugee Council.

Refugee Women's Resource Project (Asylum Aid) (2003), *Women Asylum Seekers in the UK: A Gender Perspective*, London: Refugee Women's Resource Project.

Refugee Women's Resource Project, *Women's Asylum News* available at http://www.asylumaid.org.uk/RWRP/RWRP.htm

Sales, R. (2002), The deserving and the undeserving? Refugees, asylum seekers and welfare in Britain, *Critical Social Policy*, 22/3, pp.456-478.

Schuster, L. and J. Solomos (2001), Asylum, Refuge and Public Policy: Current Trends and Future Dilemmas, *Sociological Research Online*, Vol. 6, No. 1.

Shaw, M. (2002), *The Nationality, Immigration and Asylum Bill: Immigration and Asylum*, Research Paper 02/26, London: House of Common Library.

Standing Committee in Respect of the Asylum and Immigration Bill (1999).

Chapter 3

Women Migrants and Asylum Seekers in France: Inequality and Dependence

Claudie Lesselier

Women migrants and asylum seekers in France find themselves confronted with a range of policies, legislation and administrative practices which impose highly restrictive conditions on the entry and residence of foreigners. As a consequence of these policies, laws and practices, migrant women suffer from arbitrary and often violent treatment, and many of them are forced into a situation of illegality and great insecurity, that of the *sans-papiers*.[1]

The law which regulates the entry and residence of foreigners in France is that of 2 November 1945, which has been modified several times as a result of changes in immigration policy. The most recent modification dates from May 1998 following the arrival of the 'plural Left' government in 1997.[2] The law of 11 May 1998 allows for the regularization of certain *sans-papiers* thanks to an article which permits the granting of a one year residence permit to those who have been living in France for ten years, who have medical needs which can only be met in France, or who have family members in France.[3] This law is complemented by numerous decrees and circulars emanating mainly from the Ministry of the Interior. The right of asylum and the procedures for claiming asylum are regulated by the

---

[1] *Sans-papiers* meaning literally those 'without papers', is the term generally used to refer to those residing in France 'illegally', without the necessary residence permits. Although some of these 'illegal' residents may have entered France outside of the legal channels, others may have been residing legally in France for varying lengths of time, and have seen their status 'illegalised' through changes in laws and policies which have led to non-renewal of their residence papers. There have recently been large scale mobilisations of *sans-papiers*, including hunger strikes and occupations of buildings, in support of their claims to gain legal residence status in France.
[2] The Right-Wing government of Jean-Pierre Raffarin, elected in 2002, is currently in the process of introducing new legislation on immigration, which will in particular affect the asylum determination process.
[3] This law of 11 May 1998 is often called the 'Chèvenment law' after the Minister of the Interior in the government of the time (that of Lionel Jospin). It is useful to specify that in France, it is the Ministry of the Interior and its representatives in each department, the prefects, who are responsible for affairs concerning the entry and residence of foreigners. However, it is possible to appeal against the decisions of the Ministry or the Prefect in an administrative tribunal.

OFPRA (Office français pour les réfugiés et apatrides) which examines all 'conventional' or 'political' asylum claims and decides on whether or not to attribute the status of refugee. In 1998 a second type of procedure for claiming asylum was introduced. This 'territorial' asylum is a manner of granting 'subsidiary protection' for those whose claims are considered as not falling within the framework set out by the Geneva Convention. The status conferred by this 'territorial' asylum gives rise to only temporary rights of residence in France.

International treaties (bilateral agreements) define the particular conditions of entry and residence for nationals of certain countries. Notably, the Franco-Algerian bilateral agreements do not permit Algerian nationals to benefit from new dispositions introduced in the law of 1998.[4] Other bilateral agreements fix the conditions within which laws regulating personal status will be applied (all that concerns marriage, divorce, guardianship of children etc.). The Foreign Ministry, embassies and consulates, also have power over the entry and residence of foreigners in France through their decisions on whether or not to grant visas, and the establishment of a list of so-called 'safe' countries whose nationals' claims for asylum will not be admitted, or will be the subject of accelerated procedures.

It must be stated that these laws and regulations concerning the entry and residence of foreigners in France are in no way gendered, and establish no distinction between men and women. Male and female immigrants are often confronted with very similar situations. However, it may be seen as important to analyse these laws in a way which takes into account the gender relations in society and which highlights the particular situations of insecurity in which women may find themselves. For, if the laws themselves are not gendered, it is clear that the social, economic and familial realities with which women are faced are gendered. The interactions between the legislation and the material and ideological realities affecting migrant women, must thus be examined.

This chapter will argue that French policies and laws on immigration and asylum support and even aggravate situations of inequality and dependence for migrant women. They do this partly by defining the place of migrant women solely in terms of the framework of the family, a family conceived in a highly traditional and normative fashion, marked by the continuing pre-eminence of men over women. Concerning asylum, these policies and laws hardly recognise the persecutions experienced by women. Female migrants and asylum seekers who have already suffered from multiple oppressions, and who are attempting to free themselves from such oppressions in leaving their countries of origin, thus encounter in France complex situations within which they face interlocking oppressions as a woman and as a foreigner.

---

[4] These Franco-Algerian bilateral agreements date from 1968. Amongst the major differences from the laws applicable to those of other nationalities, Algerians must have resided in France for at least 15 years (rather than 10) in order to be able to claim regularisation. An addition to the agreements designed to iron out some such discrepancies was signed on 11 July 2001 by the French and Algerian governments. However, the new agreement was ratified by the Algerian national assembly but not by the French national assembly, and despite campaigns this ratification has still not taken place.

As an activist in a feminist collective which supports and helps migrant women confronted with such situations, I have been able to support them in their actions and their struggles, and have collected numerous accounts of their experiences. This analysis is based upon my experiences of working with migrant women, together with the experiences of other similar associations with whom we are linked.

Law and Family

With the closure of the borders to labour migration in 1974, familial and conjugal links became determining factors in obtaining the right to entry and residence in France, either through marriage to a French man or woman, through family reunification, or finally through the recognition of a migrant's private and familial life in France (an addition due to the law of 1998 which enforces the application of the European Convention of Human Rights concerning the respect of private life). In all of these cases, a woman who wishes to enforce the respect of her right to a family life will come up against restrictive and very often arbitrary conditions.

Family Reunification

The laws concerning family reunification permit a foreigner residing in France in a regular situation to bring his or her close relations (spouse and minor children, plus in some cases parents) to France. Those being brought into the country under these conditions will obtain the same rights of residence as those who they are coming to join (a residence card for either one year or ten years). Currently, three quarters of those coming to join a spouse in France are women. To claim the right to family reunification, the family member living in France must prove that they have a certain level of resources, a job, and housing. In cases of polygamous marriage, family reunification can only be claimed for a first wife and her children. And finally, and most importantly, family reunification must be claimed whilst the family members who wish to come to France are still living abroad.[5]

In reality, many women and children arrive in France with a tourist visa, and ask to be regularised once this visa has run out. Foreign women who are in an irregular situation and then marry in France find themselves facing the same difficulties when they attempt to regularise their situation following this marriage. In effect, family reunification 'sur place' (once the family members have already arrived in France) is allowed only in very exceptional circumstances at the discretion of the prefecture.[6] Laura V., for example, is a Romanian, married to a compatriot resident in France, with two children, one of them born in France. Her husband attempted to regularise her situation by applying for family reunification

---

[5] Family reunification is regulated by articles 29, 30 and 31 of the 1945 law. Statistics concerning family reunification are published by the Ministry of Social Affairs' Migration and Population Division.

[6] Circular of 1 March 2000 relative to the family reunification of foreigners.

'sur place'. This request was refused and Laura was informed that she would have to go back to Romania in order that her husband could then ask for her to rejoin him in a family reunification. Her appeal against this judgement, based on the fact that she had been resident in France since her oldest child had started school, remained without any response.

Marriage to a French National

Marriage to a French national, whether this marriage occurred in France or abroad, gives a person the right to a French residence permit.[7] Such marriages, however, are often the object of great suspicion, and certain mayors refuse to authorise marriages between a foreign man or woman in an irregular situation, and a French person, fearing that this is purely a marriage of convenience. The foreign partner in such a marriage will first receive a one year residence permit, and then following this a ten year permit. The renewal of a one year permit and the delivery of the ten year permit, are both subject to the fact that the spouses have been living together continuously. This is a cause of great difficulty for women in cases of separation or domestic violence. In some cases women feel unable to leave a violent partner because of the fear that they will not be able to renew their residence permit, or will have it withdrawn from them.

Recognition of Private Life: the Arbitrary Reigns

The law of 1945, modified in 1998 by the Chevènement law, now stipulates that the granting of a residence card is a right for a foreigner living in France who does not qualify under the conditions for family reunification but for whom 'personal and family ties in France are such that a refusal to authorise residence would bring a disproportionate harm to their private and family life' (article 12b, line 7). An analysis of the application of this article, the ways in which applications are treated and the arguments of the representatives of the prefecture both in written responses and evidence given to tribunals, indicates that their interpretation of the term 'private and family life' falls within very strict social and moral norms and models. The 'private and family life' of the applicant must conform to these strict norms if they are to be granted the right to residence in France. Further, the prefectures always have the right to respond that a person can go and lead their private and family life elsewhere than in France.

For the application of this right, a person must have been living in France for longer than five years, and must have close family in the country. If they are living with a partner this relationship must be a stable and long-term one, preferably with children. A relationship between a woman and a man who is

---

[7] Marriage to an EU national living in France gives the same rights and the delivery or renewal of a residence permit is subject to the same conditions.

married to someone else is not recognised,[8] and neither is a relationship between two people who are not actually living together. Non-conjugal relationships, with brothers, sisters, cousins, for example, even if they are very important on a human, social scale, count for very little in the judgements of the prefecture. The fact of being the mother of a child born in France is not taken into consideration.[9] Mina B., a Moroccan woman, has been in France for over ten years, she lives with her Tunisian partner (who has been married in Tunisia) and with a child born in France and recognised by his father. The prefecture has refused her claims for a residence permit, arguing that she lacks proof of her length of residence in France and that her relationship is not sufficiently stable. They added that her parents are still living in Morocco, and that she could go and rejoin them there.

In effect, the existence of parents still living in an immigrant's country of origin does provide an obstacle to the granting of a residence permit on the basis of the right to private and family life. It is not rare to read in the negative responses of the prefectures that 'you have family ties in your country of origin'. This type of response has been found in letters addressed to forty year old women, whose elderly parents of over 70, live on the money sent home to them by their daughter. This point is particularly frustrating for the *sans-papiers* who feel that they are considered as eternal minors. Elisa G., a woman from Senegal, who has no close family in Senegal, came to France to rejoin her daughter and her brother. She made and application to regularise her residence papers in 1997, but this application was rejected because she could not provide her parents' death certificates. She was later able to obtain these certificates and has made a new application which may have a chance of success.

The PaCS (Pacte civil de solidarité) is an official recognition of a relationship which can be obtained either by same-sex or different-sex couples. This new status which was introduced by a law of 15 November 1999, is one element which should be taken into consideration when considering a person's right to residence in terms of their private and family life. A PaCS can be contracted between a French national and a foreigner, or between two foreigners living in France (even in an irregular situation). If one of the partners is French or a foreigner with a regular residence permit (except if he/she is a student), then the other partner should also be able to obtain a residence permit. A circular from the Interior Ministry stipulated that a couple should have been living together in a PaCS for three years before the foreign partner could obtain residence status, but this was shortened to one year in a telegram to the prefects from the Ministry in April 2002. However, couples who are in a PaCS have had great difficulty in getting this measure applied, showing the level of discrimination which exists towards gay and lesbian couples (because it is gay and lesbian couples who are primarily concerned with the PaCS, not being legally allowed to marry). A statement by the ARDHIS (Association pour le droit au séjour des personnes

---

[8] There are many cases where foreign women are living with men who have immigrated to France, often a long time ago, and left their wives and children in their country of origin.

[9] Except if this child has French nationality, in other words, if his/her father is French and has recognised him/her.

homosexuelles et transexuelles) of 2 July 2002, explains that numerous prefectures are refusing to implement this new law. And when immigration tribunals cancel deportation orders against a person in a PaCS, the prefects systematically appeal against these judicial decisions. Whilst this procedure is going on the immigrant still has no residence papers. Thus an Algerian woman who waited for two years to obtain a visa to join her French female partner, and then entered into a PaCs with her as soon as she arrived in France, was refused a residence permit, and also lost her appeal. The women are continuing to fight for their right to live together in France.

Dependence and Vulnerability within the Family

From what has already been discussed, it is clear that the law both supports and promotes situations of conjugal dependence to the extent that for many women, marriage is the only way to ensure that they have the right to enter or to remain in France.

Marriage and Migration

One of the effects of this legislation is that strategies to marry in order to receive residence papers have developed. Women who marry for these reasons can find themselves in very difficult situations, open to all types of deceptions, blackmail, denunciations, and violence. The system of such arranged marriages functions more and more to the benefit of men. Families organise the wedding of their daughters, who have French nationality or residence status, to a compatriot, often in the cases of North Africa and Turkey, a cousin, who will then also gain the rights to residence in France. Samira, a young French woman of Moroccan origin, was married in Morocco to a young man who turned out to be violent towards her. 'I was his visa for France', she explains. Depressed and guilty, it was only with a lot of help from friends that she succeeded in starting divorce proceedings. This type of marriage is systematic for young people of Turkish origin in France. Gaye Petek-Salom estimates that 98 per cent of young women and 94 per cent of young men in the Turkish community in France will marry another Turk (Petek-Salom, 2001). These marriages are arranged by the family and often involve a large dowry to be paid by the future wife, a practice which is diminishing in Turkey itself. The women who are brought from Turkey to marry, come to live in the house of their husband's family where they are subject to the authority of their mother-in-law and often to norms and constraints more limiting than those in their country of origin. As for young women of Turkish origin in France who marry a man brought over from Turkey, they are in a situation of lesser dependency (if they are bringing over a husband under the laws on family reunification they will have to have a job and sufficient economic resources), and usually hope to construct and egalitarian relationship within their couple. However, frequently the influence of the community and of the family means that they are forced to resort to more traditional models of married life.

Under a Husband's Control

French law concerning residence permits obtained through marriage leaves women without any defence in the face of their husband's power over them, at least during the first few years of marriage or of residence in France. In effect, when a person obtains a residence permit because of their marriage, as in the case of family reunification, or marriage to a French national, their temporary residence permit will not be renewed, or a ten-year residence card granted, if they cease to live with their partner. When a wife presents her application for a residence permit, her dossier must contain her husband's identity card or his residence permit and receipts for rent or utility bills proving that they live together. Thus a husband's agreement is necessary for a wife to make an application. In certain cases, the civil servants processing the application will demand a husband's physical presence in order to agree to process the dossier. If a husband refuses to provide her with his identity papers, a woman cannot lodge a claim for residence papers. Certain men (both French nationals and foreign nationals with French residence status) profit from this situation in order to keep their wife in a position of dependence, or bring a young woman to France promising to marry her and then separate from her, leaving her without hope of obtaining residence status. This situation is also clearly propitious to domestic violence. Our organisation has lost count of the number of calls for help it has received from battered women who have no legal residence papers. Battered women's hostels have few free places for these women, and if they leave their husband they will have no right to residence in France.

Numerous women recount experiences of insecurity and vulnerability resulting from their legal dependence on their husbands (Grosjean and Rotman, 2003). M., a Cuban woman, got married in France to a French man whom she had met in Cuba. However, soon after her arrival in France and her marriage, her husband decided to start divorce proceedings. Her residence permit was not renewed. In an even worse situation is F., a Moroccan woman married to a compatriot who was resident in France. She sold her business in Morocco to come to France to live with him. She entered France on a tourist visa as he had informed her that this was the easiest way to arrange things. She has spent two years virtually imprisoned by her husband who beats her, and has refused to allow her to apply for a residence permit, leaving her without papers, an illegal resident. She cannot return to Morocco because she no longer has anything there, and her family who disapproved of her marriage have disowned her. She would like to divorce and to continue living in France. But if she does so she will remain an illegal immigrant without papers for at least another eight years.

These measures concerning married life concern both husbands and wives, but women are far more often in situations where they are forced to stay in an unhappy or violent relationship. These situations of violence and illegality are contributed to by patriarchal traditions which maintain the authority of a husband over his wife, and by the ease with which a husband may repudiate or divorce his wife under certain laws on personal status (see below for a discussion of the impact of foreign laws on personal status). Added to this is the isolation which many immigrant women suffer in France, and the impossibility for many of them of returning to a country of origin where a divorced woman will be stigmatised.

Polygamous Marriages

The situation of wives in polygamous marriages is particularly dramatic. Since 1993, French law has stipulated that those living in polygamous situations are not entitled to acquire or to renew a residence permit.[10] Wives of polygamous men are thus doubly penalised by a situation for which they are not responsible. A polygamous man can divorce or throw out those wives he no longer wishes to keep, and thus regularise his situation by having only one wife left. This course of action is even encouraged by a circular of the Ministry of the Interior published in April 2000 which applies to families that arrived in France before 1993. In the case of these families, the circular informs, the husband's residence permit will be renewed if he ceases to live polygamously. What will become of the rejected wives? They will be unlikely to be able to claim residence status in France on the grounds of the length of time that they have been in the country or by the fact that they have close family ties in the country. These women are for the most part Africans from the countries of the Sahel. They come from rural backgrounds and will often speak little or no French, and will be unable to read or write. They usually have no job and have children to support. In the Paris region, where these rejected wives are the most numerous, many of them have been forced to live in squats with their children (Bissuel, 2002). In other situations polygamous men bring their wives over to France to live with them in turn, using false papers to get them into the country, and thus maintaining them in a situation of illegality and dependence.

Young People without Rights

Berthe N., is a young woman born in 1980 in Côte d'Ivoire, who came to rejoin members of her family in France in 1995 at the age of fifteen. Her mother sent her to Paris so that she could benefit from the best living conditions possible. When she reached the age of eighteen she found herself without residence papers, living in France illegally. It was impossible for her to continue her studies, and in order for her residence status to be regularised she would have had to have been living in France since before she was twelve. The situation of foreign minors is becoming more and more worrying. If boys tend to come to France alone, girls are generally sent by their parents to live with relatives. Often they also end up becoming servants for these relatives. Before the age of eighteen these minors do not need a residence permit. If they are alone they are taken care of by the Social Services. But as soon as they reach the age of eighteen they enter a situation where they are living in France illegally and their requests for residence permits are often refused. Recently both teachers and students have mobilised to protests against this

---

[10] These measures were inscribed in the 1993 law by a Right-Wing government (the law was named the Pasqua law after the Minister of the Interior at the time).

situation and to stop deportations of young foreign nationals. But their situation remains uncertain.

Forced Departures

Sometimes young girls find themselves constrained by their families into a forced return to their country of origin (or that of their parents), notably in view of marriage (Jama, 2001). On other occasions a new wife will be forced to leave France with her husband. If, after several years, these women manage to come back to France, they will find themselves without any rights of residence because even ten year residence permits will become invalid after three years of absence. Nawel, who was born in Lyon, was forced by her parents to return to Algeria in 1982, at the age of twenty. Unaccustomed to the restrictions imposed on women in Algerian society she found life there impossible:

> Here in France I felt free. In Algeria I had to be accompanied even to go to the cinema. I waited eight years to get a visa to come back to France. The idea of life on the other side of the ocean was the only thing that kept me going. But when I returned to France I was completely disillusioned ... At the prefecture they told me that I had no chance of obtaining residence papers. And yet I was born here in France and did all of my education here. (Collectif de soutien aux démocrates et aux victimes de la violence politique en Algérie, 2001)

Malika D., lived in France with her parents, brothers and sisters, and had French residence papers. But family pressure obliged her to go and get married in Algeria. She was badly treated by her husband, and returned to France thirteen years later with her son, coming to live with her parents. Her husband sent two of his brothers from Algeria to take away her son, and he then started divorce proceedings against her under Algerian law. Despite the fact that the French judicial system granted Malika a separation from her husband which gave her custody of her son, she was refused residence papers by the Ministry of the Interior, and was sent a deportation order. She remains without papers, unable to bring her son back to France.

French law does not protect women when they return to 'their country' even when they have French nationality. For many countries, particularly Islamic countries, nationality is passed down only through birth and is never lost. A young French woman whose parents are Moroccan, Algerian or Tunisian, for example, will always keep the nationality of these countries. Of course, this dual nationality may be an advantage, but it can also have negative effects in that the French authorities will not intervene to protect a woman in the other country of which she holds the nationality. A young French Malian woman, who got married to a Malian man during her holidays there, found herself locked up in a small village, beaten and raped. Although she had French nationality, having been born and brought up in France, the French consulate in Bamako refused to help her because she also had

Malian nationality through her parents. It was only thanks to friends and the intervention of an international women's association that she was able to flee.[11]

A Double Judicial System

French law considers that all residents of foreign nationality are subject, in so far as their personal status is concerned, to the laws of their country of origin. In many cases these laws are more or less identical to French laws, but with regard to Muslim countries, in particular, there can be important contradictions between the application of their laws on personal status and the respect of fundamental principles of French law. The Algerian Family Code, the Moroccan Mudwana or the Egyptian code of personal law, for example, are all deeply inegalitarian in terms of gender relations, notably with respect to divorce, custody of children, and inheritance. A man of Algerian, Moroccan or Egyptian nationality living in France who wishes to divorce would thus have a much easier time if he undertook divorce proceedings in one of these countries and then had the decision recognised in France. International private law, does however, allow a factor of public order to intervene when foreign laws are manifestly contrary to French law. To defend her rights, therefore, a woman in this situation can call on the French judicial system to support her. The problem is that any such procedures, involving as they do two legal systems, are long and costly, and few women are informed as to the possibility of invoking French legal support[12] (Rochart, 2001). Associations of Algerian women in France are fighting for the modification of the bilateral agreements between the two countries in order to end French recognition of the Algerian Family Code. They also support Algerian women's associations who are fighting for the total abolition of this Family Code. The effects of the recognition of this Code in France are evident in the case of Madame S., an elderly woman, married and living in France in an apartment which she shared with her husband. Her husband returned to Algeria and obtained a divorce without Madame S. being informed or asked for her consent. Two years later he asked his wife to leave their apartment, and she discovered for the first time that she had been divorced. She turned to the French legal system to contest the Algerian ruling and the Appeal Court ruled that the Algerian divorce was in fact not valid. However, her husband has pursued the case to the Court of Cassation, where the case is still being decided.

Even more serious are the consequences of the intervention of foreign law on children. Sérénade Chafik, a woman of Egyptian origin who has obtained French nationality and is living in France, turned to the French judicial system to

---

[11] This association, the Groupe pour l'abolition des mutilations sexuelles (GAMS) is comprised of French and African women who wish to fight against genital mutilation and forced marriages.

[12] To try and inform more women of their rights under French law, a group called Femmes contre les intégrismes (Women against fundamentalism) has published a practical guide for women of North African origin living in France, entitled *Madame vous avez des droits* (You do have rights, Madam).

obtain protection for her daughter Laila. Laila's father, who was still living in Egypt wished his daughter to undergo a process of genital mutilation and Sérénade wanted the French courts to protect her from this practice. However, the French legal system ruled eventually in favour of the father, arguing that French law could not prohibit the father from carrying out the genital mutilation which was permitted (and even encouraged) under the customary laws of Egypt. Sérénade is still protesting against this decision.

Nationality

The dispositions in the Civil Code which relate to obtaining French nationality seem at first examination very favourable in comparison to those other countries. To be naturalised, for example, it is required that a person has lived continuously in France for the past five years and that they can demonstrate a 'sufficient assimilation to the French community', notably by a sufficient command of the French language. However, the decisions on requests for naturalisation are completely discretionary. Experience has shown that a married person's request for naturalisation will not be accepted unless their spouse has requested naturalisation as well. And if a woman is divorced or separated, she will need to provide proof of this which can be difficult to obtain in the case of certain countries. Malika N. has been resident in France since 1970 and her children have French nationality. She has been divorced for many years and the divorce was recognised in France. Her husband has since returned to Morocco. She has requested naturalisation but the French authorities will not agree to her request unless she provides a transcript of the divorce from the Moroccan Civil Register. This is proving impossible because of the opposition of her ex-husband.

Rights of Asylum

The policy of restricting those able to claim the right to asylum in France is having a significant effect on women.[13] Statistics from the OFPRA (Office français pour la protection des réfugiés et apatrides), the body responsible for regulating the asylum process in France, show that for the years 1991 to 1998, between 30 and 35 per cent of those claiming asylum were women. Women accounted for between 46 and 49 per cent of those accorded refugee status over the same period, indicating that women are not disadvantaged compared to men in the process of claiming asylum. However, women do experience particular difficulties relating to failures to take into account persecutions feared or experienced because of their sex. It is also interesting to note that the majority of these female asylum seekers are either single, widowed or divorced (about 60 per cent). And in a more general picture it must be remembered that the majority of the world's refugees are women, but women are in a minority amongst those seeking asylum in France and elsewhere in

---

[13] Figures from the OFPRA show that only 17.3 per cent of those claiming political asylum in 2001 received positive responses.

Europe. This leads to the conclusion that very few women refugees actually manage to reach Europe in order to lodge a claim for asylum.

Asylum Procedures

To claim asylum in France it is necessary to reach French territory and to do that both money and travel documents are vital. Transport companies are careful to check passengers' visas for fear of sanctions if they are caught transporting people without the necessary documents. And those who undertake such a voyage take the risk of ending up in a 'waiting zone' in an airport and being sent back on the next aeroplane. In August 2001 a young woman from Sierra Leone was placed in a 'waiting zone' at Roissy airport (near Paris) where the police refused to register her claim for asylum. She was beaten when she refused to get into the aeroplane to take her back to Sierra Leone. It was only with the intervention of Amnesty International that she was finally able to make an asylum claim in France. This case is typical of what may happen to asylum seekers arriving in France, and especially in the case of women from Africa who are often suspected of being not genuine asylum seekers, but prostitutes coming to seek work in France.

The procedure for claiming political or conventional asylum (under the terms of the Geneva Convention) consists of submitting a dossier to the OFPRA in which the persecution a person has suffered is detailed, together with proof of this persecution. OFPRA will not grant refugee status unless the person has been a victim of actual persecution (and is not just in valid fear of persecution), which is very serious and individualised (the person must have been directly and personally a victim of this persecution), and which is carried out by state agents (unless the victim can prove that they asked for the help of public authorities with no response). In case of a refusal from the OFPRA the asylum seeker can have his/her claim re-examined by an appeals committee. Whilst his/her case is being examined (it takes several months to obtain the necessary papers and interview and between one and two years for the case to be processed and a decision reached), an asylum seeker does not have the right to work, but receives an allowance of 280 euros a month for one year (a sum which is clearly insufficient to live on and pay rent), and is affiliated to the social security. Centres for housing refugees have an extremely limited number of places and a woman will have no chance of receiving a place unless she has children with her.

A second type of procedure for claiming asylum is that of territorial asylum which is a new status introduced under a law of 1998 to deal in particular with the situation of asylum seekers fleeing from Algeria (Freedman, 2003). This asylum procedure is regulated by the Ministry of the Interior. It is a simplified procedure which guarantees only temporary rights of asylum (a residence card of one year and not a ten-year residence permit). In fact, the rate of rejection for those claiming territorial asylum is huge. More than 98 per cent of those who claimed territorial asylum between the creation of this status in 1998 and the end of 2000, were refused.

Female asylum seekers have lived through dramatic events in their countries of origin and often speak of their bad reception in France. This is the experience of Louisa B., an Algerian woman who applied for territorial asylum in France, after having resisted the Islamic militants in Algeria and in fear for her life and that of her children:

> I brought my children with me from Algeria to save us all from a certain and violent death. It was extremely sad and painful to leave behind us our bloodstained country. And having arrived in France we were confronted with a very harsh reality. We discovered the indifference or incredulity of those who heard our story, and above all the intolerance and severity of those who refused us the chance of survival and of putting our nightmare behind us. I am mute and my struggle is in vain, faced with the draconian laws with which we are faced, despite all that is happening in Algeria ... Put yourself in our place and imagine the ordeal we are living through in your 'country of asylum' and of 'human rights'. (RAJFIRE, 2001)

Recognition of Gendered Persecution

For several years, feminists have been undertaking a political and legal fight to obtain greater recognition for the forms of persecution suffered by women because they are women, and in some cases to have women recognised as a 'social group' under the terms of the Geneva Convention. The type of persecutions experienced specifically by women because of their sex are persecutions relating to the transgression of discriminatory laws, practices and customs; acts of sexual violence such as rape and genital mutilation; forced marriages; and also indirect persecutions which are suffered because of the activities or opinions of another member of the family (ProAsile, 2000).

However, these types of violence and persecution against women are often considered as 'private' or incidental, or if the violence is widespread it is regarded as part of the normal order of things, of the 'culture' of a certain country. Such persecutions are not regarded as political or as violations of human rights, especially if they are not committed by public authorities but by families or community groups.

Certain women have obtained refugee status because of violence that they suffered as women (several Algerian women for example), but these individual decisions have not lead to the recognition of women as a social group under the terms of the Geneva Convention. On the contrary, it has been clearly specified in the judgements of the Asylum Appeals Committee that the granting of refugee status should not be interpreted as the recognition of women as a persecuted social group. In July 1994, for example, the Appeals Committee overturned the decision by OFPRA to reject the asylum claim of Miss Nadia E., an Algerian woman. This decision took into consideration the fact that she had been a victim of 'repeated threats and violence by Islamic groups because of her continuing professional activity, and she because refused to submit to their demands to modify her lifestyle', and also the fact that the local authorities had tolerated this persecution. But one of the judges responsible for this decision took care to close the door to any recognition that Algerian women who resisted Islamic laws were being persecuted as a group:

> Considering that the dispositions of Algerian law that regulate the lives of women in Algeria apply to all women without distinction; and that the fact that certain women choose to contest these laws does not allow us to regard these women as belonging for this reason to a particular social group as stipulated in the Geneva Convention.[14]

In some kind of paradoxical way, it seems here that the fact that a discrimination is generalised (the fact that these discriminatory laws apply to all women in Algeria) means that it cannot be the basis for a claim for asylum.

Thanks in large part to the struggles of associations and some lawyers, several women have been granted refugee status on the grounds that they or their daughters were in danger of genital mutilation. It must be noted however, that it is always the Appeals Committee which takes such decisions, and not OFPRA itself. A Malian woman, Suzanne K., obtained refugee status from the Appeals Committee in March 2001, because she was at risk of suffering genital mutilation, because she had denounced such practices on the radio, and because she had been threatened and had not received any support from the authorities in her country.[15] Such decisions, however, remain very individualised. In this case, the applicant was helped in her claim for asylum by the fact that her daughters had suffered genital mutilation, by the fact that her husband's family had an large influence in the country, and that she herself was a Catholic. In another case a Somalian woman who had suffered genital mutilation herself and had seen her older daughter being infibulated against her wish, and dying as a result of this, had fled with her younger daughter whom her husband's family wished to undergo the same fate. The OFPRA refused her claim for asylum, but the Appeals Committee recognised her refugee status on the grounds that:

> In the prevailing situation in Somalia, women who refuse to allow their daughters to be subject to such practices are exposed to forced mutilation and to persecutions practiced with the assent of the population, without being able to claim the protection of public authorities.[16]

There has thus been some progress towards the recognition of gender based forms of persecution, but there is still no global recognition of persecutions suffered by women because of their sex.

Sexual Orientation

A similar problem arises in connection with those persecuted because of their sexual orientation. Beyond the restrictive interpretation of the notion of 'social group', the French authorities are highly reluctant to take into account any violence exercised by non-state authorities (family, community, religious groups etc.) The

---

[14] CRR decision 24 July 1994.

[15] CRR decision 19 March 2001.

[16] CRR decision 7 December 2001.

authorities consistently underestimate the levels of violence to which people are subjected because of their sexual orientation. Most of those having claimed asylum on this basis have been rejected. However, there have recently been two favourable decisions thanks to the mobilisation of homosexual groups and of Amnesty International. These decisions in favour of an Algerian transsexual and an Algerian homosexual, were both based on the recognition that the current situation in Algeria placed these people in danger of violence because of their 'belonging to a particular social group'.[17] There is little information about lesbians who have fled their country because of persecution based on their sexual orientation, but it seems that few claim asylum on these grounds, preferring to find other ways to remain in France.

An Impossible Return

Those whose claims for asylum are rejected find themselves 'invited to leave the territory'. If they do not leave they receive a deportation order, which will generally be enforced during an identity check in a public place. They will then be placed in a detention centre before being put on a boat or an aeroplane under heavy guard. If they resist they may be found guilty by a tribunal and placed in detention.[18] It seems that less women than men are the objects of the implementation of these deportation orders. This may be because women are less 'targeted' by the police, and also because they are less present in public places where they are likely to undergo identity checks. However, there are women who are found guilty and imprisoned for breaking the laws on the residence of foreigners in France, and there are women in detention centres.

And it is not only failed asylum seekers who must fear a forced return to their country of origin. All the immigrants that we have met are clear that they cannot and will not return to their countries of origin. What would be their place in society if they did return? How would they find employment? The women *sans-papiers* who drew up a manifesto in November 1999 underlined to what extent they would risk stigmatisation and exclusion if they were forced to return:

> Forced return destroys the lives and the relationships which we have built up here in France. We come from countries where the majority of the population lives in poverty and where there are not enough jobs; it is with our salaries that we support our families still living in those countries. If we go back without work, without income, what will we do? We will have to start again from nothing. Here we are accustomed to a certain lifestyle, there we risk becoming dependent on others. Here we can live alone if we wish, we can take responsibility for our own lives. There that would be very badly seen. Women who have lived alone in Europe are often considered as too free, and rejected as too emancipated because they will not do as they are told. Men say that a woman who has 'hung around' here for fifteen

---

[17] CRR decision 16 April 1999.

[18] There is the possibility of trying to use judicial means to resist these deportations, the details of which are too complex to explain here.

years will not make a good wife, and women who have lived alone in France are often considered as prostitutes. (Femmes Sans-Papiers, 1999)

Trafficking and Modern Slavery

The fate of foreign women who are the victims of international trafficking has also become a preoccupation. The illegal situation of these women prevents them from freeing themselves from this exploitation. They do not enter into the criteria for regularisation. Several associations have campaigned for these women to be given residence papers for humanitarian reasons or on the basis of asylum. H.S., who comes from a country in Sub-Saharan Africa, was brought to Belgium by pimps, unaware of what fate awaited her. Having been raped and forced into prostitution, she fled to Paris. All of her identity papers had been taken away from her. By chance she came into contact with our association. As she is a minor she was taken under the protection of the Social Aid to children. She was pregnant, but thanks to the help of associations and of a hospital favourable to the right to abortion, she was able to have an abortion in time. H. has agreed to talk to the police about her experiences but as she will soon be eighteen she is worried about her future. Will she be able to obtain residence status because she has been a victim of trafficking? In fact, nothing obliges the French authorities to grant her residence papers. Pressure from associations lobbying the government has led to a limited success in changing this situation. A law was passed by the National Assembly in January 2002 which promised to reinforce the struggle against different forms of slavery. The second article of this law stipulated that victims of trafficking who testified against a trafficker, would obtain a one year residence permit.[19] These limited reforms would have been well below the level of protection needed for trafficked women. However, this law was never passed by the Senate, and a new Assembly was elected in June 2002 with a new government which has pledged to introduce measures to deport foreign prostitutes.[20] The new government passed a law in March 2003[21] which increases repression against prostitutes and introduces measures to deport foreign prostitutes working in France. Victims of trafficking will receive a one-year residence permit on the condition that they testify against their trafficker.

As for women who are victims of modern slavery (working as unpaid domestic servants, without residence papers, without freedom of movement, and in addition suffering sometimes from sexual exploitation), they can also expect little or no protection from the French authorities and their fate thus also depends upon

[19] The conditions demanded by the law in order for such women to receive a residence permit are problematic, because these women often fear revenge attacks against their families if they testify against the traffickers. The protection that would have been afforded by this law was thus inferior to that suggested in certain international protocols protecting the victims of trafficking (Additional protocol to the Convention on Transnational Organised Crime, Vienna, October 2000; Resolution of the sub-commission of Human Rights of the UN, 15 August 2001).
[20] *Le Monde*, 10 July 2002.
[21] Law on internal security, March 2003.

the mobilisation of associations formed to defend them, such as the Comité contre l'esclavage moderne (Committee against modern slavery).

Unrecognised Workers

Women immigrants are rarely recognised as workers, who need a job and a salary to live on, or to support their relatives. Little account is taken of their personal projects which motivate their departure from their country of origin, such as the desire to free themselves from unwanted social and familial constraints. On a global scale we know that there has been a feminisation of migratory movements, due not only to economic inequality, but also to transformations in women's condition as they become (willingly or under obligation) more autonomous in an increasingly globalised world. But the attitudes of the French authorities have not always reflected these changes. Certainly, the residence cards which are attributed today on the basis of 'family and private life' give the right to work, unlike the 'visitors' cards which were often previously given to women. But immigrant women's place in the economy is still often ignored.

Middle-class and professional women in the countries of the North have created a demand for domestic labour. This demand is in large part filled by women who are maintained in situations of illegality and thus open to exploitation. Thus generally the assignation of immigrant women to domestic labour is reinforced, and they have little chance to receive any training or to make use of their competencies in other areas. Domestic workers find themselves isolated, and have great difficulty in obtaining the documents and attestations which allow them to prove the regularity of their employment and their income, or even the reality of their length of residence in France. It is thus increasingly difficult for them to obtain residence permits and to have access to any type of legal protection against their employers.

Other women work on the black market for small businesses (shops, restaurants or workshops), often managed by someone from their own community, or else they may find financial resources through the informal economy through work such as cooking or hairdressing, again usually in association with their own community.

A 'salaried' residence (sometimes given for seasonal work) is only attributed in exceptional cases, and the women who benefit from this status are rare. Male migrants have wider opportunities for finding work – in the building industry, agriculture, or in certain professions such as IT or research.

Conclusion

Female migrants and asylum seekers who do not manage to obtain a residence permit to live in France may live and work for years without papers, in a situation of illegality and precarity. These types of situation leave women particularly vulnerable to violence and sexual harassment (which they often experience when trying to find housing or a job), and some run the risk of falling into the hands of pimps. For example, at the exit of the Bobigny court where illegal migrants are tried, men try to pick up women *sans-papiers* and persuade them to become prostitutes. Further, many women have children to take care of, which places an additional burden on them and reinforces their insecurity and vulnerability. There has been some progress concerning access to social and health care services for those without legal residence status, but many of the women in these situations suffer from serious psychological problems (depression, anxiety) which are not treated. Sylvie M., a woman from Cameroon, explains the plight of a woman without residence papers who:

> ... has no rights, is dependent on a boss or a partner, has no existence as an autonomous individual, is continually anxious ... a woman *sans-papiers* is thus a target for exploitation from all sides. She has no real defence against this exploitation apart from her own internal resources. (RAJFIRE, 2001)

Separation from their relatives, sometimes even from their children left behind in their country of origin, is a particularly difficult experience:

> Without papers, we live as though we were in prison. It is impossible to leave France, to go for a holiday to visit our families, to see our children when they are at home in our country of origin. It hurts us to see others coming and going freely whilst we are trapped. We are prevented from doing everything: from working legally, from studying, from finding housing, from travelling. We cannot move around freely for fear of police checks, arrests, deportation. When women "sans-papiers" suffer from violence or attacks, they are too scared to report it to the police. We want to escape from this fear and this instability. (Femmes sans-papiers, 1999)

Despite all of these obstacles, however, some women do manage to overcome their problems and to lead a 'normal' life. They try again and again, usually without success, to have their residence situation regularised. Some are active in collectives of *sans-papiers*, but here they find it difficult to explain their difficulties as women. The blank refusal of the French authorities to negotiate collectively with the *sans-papiers*, and to consider the possibility of a general regularisation, together with continually more stringent immigration policies and a growing racism, means that immigrant women may well face a future of even more restrictive, violent and arbitrary treatment. A new law discussed by the National Assembly in the summer of 2003[22] will only serve to increase the difficulties and the dependent status of immigrant women. Under the terms of this law, women who enter France under family reunification will only receive a one-year residence permit for the first five years that they are in the country, with the possibility of obtaining a long-term residence permit only after five years. Spouses of a French national will have to wait for two years instead of the current one-year period to

---

[22] The Sarkozy law, named after the Minister of the Interior, Nicolas Sarkozy.

obtain a long-term residence permit. Increased controls and scrutiny will be introduced to prevent 'fake' marriages.

References

Bissuel, B. (2002), 'Divorcer ou vivre sans-papiers', *Le Monde*, 10 February 2002.

Collectif de soutien aux démocrates et aux victimes de la violence politique en Algérie (2001), *Identités Volées*, Lyon.

Femmes contre les intégrismes (1999), *Madame vous avez des droits*, Lyon.

Femmes sans-papiers (1999), *Manifeste*. Paris.

Freedman, J. (2003), *Immigration and Insecurity in France*. Aldershot: Ashgate.

Grosjean, B. and Rotman, C. (2003), 'Noces sans papiers. Le sort des épouses étrangères depuis les lois Pasqua', *Libération*, 5 May 2002.

Jama, C. (2001), 'Mariages forcés: quand les mots occultent les mots', in RAJFIRE, *Femmes étrangères et immigrées en France*, Paris.

Petek-Salom, G. (2001), 'Des gendres et des brus importés de Turquie par les familles', *Hommes et Migrations*, 1232, pp. 62-73.

ProAsile (2000), *Femmes réfugiées*. Paris: France terre d'asile.

RAJFIRE (2001), *Femmes étrangères et immigrées en France*. Paris.

Rochart, C. (2001), 'Le statut personnel des musulmans en France', *Hommes et Migrations*, 1232, pp. 35-48.

Chapter 4

Mechanisms for Colombian and Ecuadorian Women's Entry into Spain: From Spontaneous Migration to Trafficking of Women

Laura Oso Casas

In much of the contemporary discourse concerning immigration, in the media in particular, a distinction is made between trafficking and immigration of women. The term immigration is used to refer to women who leave their countries of origin to join their family in another country, or to come and work in domestic service industries, for example. Whilst on the other hand there is an almost symbiotic relationship which tends to be assumed between trafficking of women and prostitution. In effect, the term trafficking is associated in the collective imagination with what can be called the 'white slave trade', with the work of mafias which use criminality and violence to entrap women into migration for the purposes of prostitution. This distinction between immigration and trafficking can not be made in such a simple fashion however. Migration for sex work and prostitution is not always linked to trafficking of women. And on the other hand migratory flows which are involved in family reunification or in migration for work other than sex work, may be linked to networks or individuals which enrich themselves through the exploitation of human migration. Moreover, trafficking is not solely the preserve of mafia or large criminal organisations. In effect, small businessmen, other immigrants, or individuals, can and do act independently to profit from the exploitation of migrants (Campani, 2000).

In recent years, there has been a growth in the trafficking of migrants in the international context, and this phenomenon has characterised the migration to the countries of Southern Europe (Baldwin-Edwards, 1998). The trafficking of persons seems to have acquired an important dimension in this regional space, and has come in certain instances to function as a complement, even as a substitute, for the immigration of individuals who invest their own personal resources in a migratory project, or who are supported only by family and community networks ('spontaneous' immigration), without the intervention of criminal organisations, networks or businesses which have exclusively exploitative or lucrative ends.

This chapter will examine the strategies and modes of migration of Colombian and Ecuadorian women migrants to Spain. It will analyse the roles of different social actors involved in these migratory processes, distinguishing between 'spontaneous' migration which is fed solely by family and community migratory networks, and the various types of trafficking of migrants, from those involving small businessmen and individuals, to those large networks involving mafia and criminal organisations. The aim is to see how and why these women migrate to Spain, to examine the obstacles arising from particular political, economic and social conditions, and to analyse the insecurities that arise within their migratory strategies and projects.

The research for this chapter was carried out in Madrid, Pamplona and Galicia in 2000 and 2001. The research was conducted using principally qualitative methods : in-depth interviews and focus group discussions. The fieldwork was carried out with both immigrant and native Spanish women working in the cleaning and domestic service industries, as well as with NGOs working in the field of migration. In addition, research was carried out in Galicia with women working in clubs and brothels, as well as with clients of these women, with brothel owners and with representatives of NGOs. This second type of fieldwork was more difficult to realise successfully due to the delicate nature of the subject and to the fact that it was problematic for a female interviewer to gain access to these clubs and brothels. Table 4.1 below, summarises the interviews carried out with different groups of respondents during the course of the fieldwork.

What the research demonstrated was that the mechanisms for Colombian and Ecuadorian women's entry into Spain are complex, both in the case of women working in the sex industry, and in the case of women domestic workers. These mechanisms range from autonomous or spontaneous migration, to migration through large criminal organisations, with a whole variety of small trafficking networks in between. What this chapter thus aims to demonstrate is that many of the migratory strategies used by women working in sex clubs and brothels are very similar to those employed in domestic services. The differentiation between trafficking and migration is therefore not as simple as it might first appear.

Table 4.1   Respondents interviewed during fieldwork carried out with domestic and sex workers in Madrid, Pamplona and Galicia, 2000 and 2001

Country of Origin	Domestic Workers	NGO Representatives	Sex Workers	Clients, Husbands and Partners of Sex Workers	Brothel and sex club owners	Total
Colombia	23		29			52
Ecuador	37		3			40
Spain	17	18		11	3	49
Total	77	18	32	11	3	141

Migratory Strategies for Entering Spain

The use of the term 'migratory strategies' implies that the migrant has made a series of choices of action in relation to the mechanisms to be used to succeed in her migratory project. These choices relate both to the means of leaving the country of origin (initial investment, debt acquired, documentation obtained, contact with illegal networks or agencies ...), and to ways of entering the new country of immigration (means of transport, ways of avoiding border controls, initial integration in the host country ...). These choices and the conditions and limitation within which they are made will obviously vary depending on the countries of origin and destination. This study was carried out with women originating from Colombia and Ecuador. The inhabitants of these countries did not, at the time the fieldwork was carried out, require a visa to enter Spain fro three months as tourists. This was thus the most frequent method used by our respondents for entering the country. Most entered on a three-month tourist visa and subsequently illegally prolonged their stay in the country. This study is thus not one of clandestine immigration in the sense that the initial entry into Spain was not illegal. The immigration was in fact initially legal, and these women became illegalised immigrants by virtue of their outstaying of their tourist visa.

The fieldwork showed that there were three principal stages in these women's migratory strategies. In the first place, there was a need to find sufficient funds for the journey to Spain. In some cases the woman used her own economic resources to fund this – either through savings or in some cases redundancy payments. Those without sufficient personal economic resources turned to organisations, friends or family who could facilitate the raising of the necessary sums. The initial monetary investment was made up of the sum needed for preparation for the voyage – for obtaining a passport and other necessary documentation, buying sufficient clothing etc. – the price of the transport and the money for a 'bolsa' ie the dollars required by the Spanish customs officials for a tourist's entry into Spain.

The second stage involves a series of strategies necessary to avoid border controls and any other form of obstacle to entering into the host country. In the case of clandestine immigration by sea or by land, it is often necessary for the migrants to use organised trafficking networks to avoid detection at the borders. The situation in our case studies was different as the immigration involved was not clandestine (the women were entering legally as tourists and then staying in Spain illegally). However, even in these cases, strategies for avoiding border controls are necessary. Although it is legal to enter Spain for three months as a tourist, the Spanish authorities send to their countries of origin many immigrants who try to enter Spain as tourists. Thus the women we interviewed found it necessary to employ strategies consisting of a careful choice of routes for entering the country and of the type of aeroplane ticket used, as well as the acquisition of particular knowledge about how they should behave.

These women's strategies for entering Spain involved the use of non-direct flights, with a stop-over in another country within the Schengen area. This allowed them to enter the Schengen area through another European airport, and to

avoid arriving in the area first at the airport in Madrid where the authorities tend to be more strict given the arrival in massive numbers of immigrants from certain countries. Buying an aeroplane ticket from certain European airline companies involved a large intitial investment, but facilitated the women's entry into Europe and made the risks of being sent back to Colombia or Ecuador less likely. Another strategy for avoiding the attention of immigration officials at the airport was to buy a first class ticket, through which the women hoped to give the impression that they were rich tourists and not poor migrants looking for employment. The costs associated with these strategies have to be weighed against the penalties for failure:

> We risk losing everything if we're deported. So we've got to make sure that we get into the country and so we buy a first class ticket. It's our whole futures that are at stake. There are direct flights to Madrid or flights with stopovers. The more stopovers the better. I came from Quito via Amsterdam to Madrid. (Ecuadorian domestic worker, Pamplona)

The necessary 'savoir-faire' consists in being able to convince the authorities that the woman is travelling as a tourist, without any intention of remaining in Spain. This implies wearing a certain type of clothes which are unlike the traditional styles of Latin American clothing. The outfit chosen should not be too traditional, nor too short or tight – the woman aims to look like a dynamic businesswoman or a rich and elegant tourist. It is also advised that the women should dye their hair and wear jewellery and make up. They ought to carry a small handbag with a few strategic objects such as a tourist guide or map and a camera. One of the most important aspects of this self-presentation is the attitude the woman adopts when she is questioned at the border. These women must be convincing about the motives of their journey to Spain, and avoid making errors like that of a Dominican woman who was deported when she told immigration officials that she was coming to see the beach at Madrid. This famous anecdote resumes the need for all kinds of strategic knowledge to be avoid deportation at the frontier, and to be able to enter Spain as a 'tourist'. All of this planning and pretence obviously weighs heavily on the migrants who are already in a position of vulnerability having left their countries and their families, as the quotes below demonstrate:

> It's a horrible journey. You say goodbye to all of your family, you are sad, and then in addition you are stopped and interrogated at the border. You have to pretend, so that they think you're coming as a tourist. You have to have only a few clothes, you can't bring anything with you. (Ecuadorian domestic worker, Pamplona)

> You mustn't bring anything with you, no phone numbers, or photos of family. You just have to bring a suitcase, a wallet and a passport, nothing else. A very small suitcase with just three or four outfits. We're coming as tourists so we have to bring the minimum. (Ecuadorian domestic worker, Madrid)

The third stage of these migratory strategies necessitates finding a contact in Spain who will be able to help with the initial integration into society in the form of providing housing and food for the first few days and will help the migrant to find a job. The migrant domestic workers who were interviewed in Madrid and Pamplona revealed a series of different strategies for their initial social integration in Spain. For some, the easiest strategy was to find a job as a live-in domestic worker which meant that they would be provided with accommodation and subsistence. Others relied on finding a shared flat with other immigrants where they could stay until they were able to finance accommodation of their own. In some cases the women migrants would use migrant hostels which are run by NGOs as a means of finding food and accommodation for the first few days. The information about these means of social integration comes from the existence of networks of personal contacts which the immigrant may have, from contacts made whilst organising the journey to Spain, or from contacts made at job centres and hostels run by NGOs.

In the case of migrant sex workers, there were again several different types of strategy for integration into Spanish society. Some of the Ecuadorian women interviewed did not intend to work in prostitution when they came to Spain, but hoped to find work in the domestic service sector. Consequently, these women's strategies for integration were the same as many of the women working in the domestic service industry, often finding accommodation in a shared apartment with other migrants, or through family or friends already in Spain. These women ended up working in sex clubs or brothels after working in other jobs, or trying to find employment in other sectors.

Another group of women came to Spain independently with the idea of working in prostitution or sex work. These women did not have any contact with trafficking networks and were often able to find work in clubs through contacts with their compatriots who were already working there. Finally we interviewed some women who had entered Spain through means of organised trafficking. They had been enlisted for this purpose in their country of origin, their journeys had been financed by these organisations, and their integration in Spain was organised by the trafficking networks. These women were sent directly to sex clubs and brothels when they arrived in Spain, and stayed there until they had worked enough to pay off their debts to the traffickers. After they had paid their debts they often moved from club to club to find work.

Having examined the three principal stages encompassed by these women's migratory strategies, the rest of this chapter will analyse the different types of spontaneous migration and the diverse modalities of more or less organised trafficking which take place.

Spontaneous Migration

The First Stage: The Search for Money

The first type of spontaneous migration which we have identified is autonomous migration. This is where the individual gathers together independently the sum of money required to pay the initial investment in the journey. They may do this through a loan, mortgaging their house, or through the money received in redundancy payments. Amongst all of our interviewees, whether working in domestic work or in the sex industry, there were certain cases where their migration corresponded to this type of autonomous model. For example, sex workers from Colombia and Ecuador recount their decisions to migrate autonomously to work in the sex industry in Spain.

> I come from the middle classes in Colombia and I didn't like the idea of working in a house as a cleaner. A girl I knew had a contact for working in the sex industry. My sister gave me the money I needed for the journey and I arrived in Madrid. The girl who had the contact arrived too and we went to Pontevedra. Nobody brought me here or tricked me and I've never had any bad experiences. Nobody's ever hit me or anything. I look after myself. I've got private medical insurance. My working life has been calm, working in brothels. Girls like me have less need for a lot of money than those who have got to pay off debts. I took a free decision to come here and work in this industry. I'm not proud of what I do but it's a job. It's a quicker way of making money than cleaning. (Colombian sex worker, Galicia)

> I come from Guayaquil in Ecuador. I came to Spain in November last year because the situation is catastrophic where I come from. I worked in a business but I was made redundant. I had problems with the father of my children who mistreated me and threatened that he would throw me out of the house. I've got a sister living here in Spain and so I decided to come here using the money I got when I was made redundant. I came to Madrid first, and then to Galicia. (Ecuadorian sex worker, Galicia)

Another woman, Patricia, migrated autonomously but did not expect to work in the sex industry in Spain, coming to it as a last resort when no other employment was forthcoming. She left her four children at home with her mother in Colombia, sold the taxi that she had used to earn her living and invested the money in her journey to Spain. Once in Spain she found it hard to find work, particularly as employers demanded legal residence papers which she did not possess. In the end she had no choice but to go and work in a sex club:

> I had no more money. I'd knocked on all the doors, bought the newspaper and applied for all the jobs in the small ads. But everywhere they asked me for legal residence papers and a work permit. More and more papers. That went on for weeks. I couldn't find anyone to help me out or to give me an idea where to find work. When I had no more money I slept outside in a square. One morning I was in the metro and a Spanish woman asked me if I was Colombian and if I wanted to work. She explained to me briefly what kind of work it was, and I understood what was involved. She left me her number to contact her if I was interested. Another couple of weeks passed and I was completely desperate. I couldn't go back to Colombia after having spent all that money on the journey. And how would I feed my children? Finally I decided to call the woman. She gave me the address and I went to the club at about five o'clock in the afternoon. The club was closed and I had to get in through a bar next door. I asked a man in the bar what

time the club opened and he asked me if I worked there. I started to blush and said no. I was starting to cry. The man came with me and bought me a dress. He also gave me 20,000 pesetas. Afterwards I started working there. (Colombian sex worker, Madrid)

The same types of strategy for autonomous migration are found amongst migrant domestic workers. Marina, an Ecuadorian woman, decided to use her personal financial resources and savings to invest in migration to Spain. She believed that this investment in migration would be beneficial for herself and her children after a split with her partner in Ecuador. She contacted a friend in Pamplona who helped arrange the journey and helped her to find work looking after elderly people. Similarly Mercedes, Angela and Maria, who are all involved in domestic work in Spain, managed to make the journey thanks to their own private financial resources and savings, or to loans from family members. No third parties or profit-making networks were involved in their migratory trajectories:

In my case, it was my sister who lent me the money ....
Luckily, I had no debts, I had my savings and I spent them all to come here ....
When you've got family here there's no point in paying for a letter of invitation. You pay when you don't know anyone. There are lots of people who come without any family so they have to pay for their letters of invitation, but when you've got family, they arrange it for you .... (Focus group discussion amongst Ecuadorian and Colombian domestic workers, Madrid)

This type of immigration which stems from an initial investment from the migrant using their own financial resources, is the most independent type of migration which we found, although ti was not the most frequent amongst our interviewees. In both Ecuador and Colombia, potential migrants are those who are seeking financial stability and survival, and there are few in this category who have enough personal financial resources to finance the initial investment of the journey to Spain.

Thus a second type of spontaneous migration can be described as that which necessitates a loan from family or friends in the country of origin. The migrant in this case acquires the necessary resources for their journey by borrowing money from someone in the family or from a friend. In this case the migratory strategy involves new social actors. The loans that are given through these type of family or friendship networks do not implicate a market relationship in the same way as a loan from a bank or other financial institution. However these loans are not exempt from interest, and interest payments can be claimed in a more or less direct fashion. An investment in a third party's migratory project can, when this project proves successful, lead to a series of benefits including financial ones. The story recounted by this Ecaudorian woman is typical:

My sister and brother-in-law got a loan from one of the brother-in-law's brothers. They had to pay off their debt with interest. You always have to pay interest, usually its between 8 and 10 per cent – it depends on the person you borrow from. (Ecuadorian domestic worker, Pamplona)

These migratory strategies which imply borrowing money from family or friends, are less independent than 'autonomous' migration. There is a debt which much be paid, which means that the migrant finds herself in a more vulnerable situation. She may accept conditions of exploitation in order to make money to repay the loan she has received.

The third type of financial support for 'spontaneous' migration comes from loans given by migrants already installed in Spain, who have some kind of stability in their lives and who can thus afford to lend the money required for other migrants' journeys. This strategy provides a classic example of chain migration, whereby those who have already migrated feed the new waves of migration. This is a strategy which was used both by the women in our study who migrated for sex work and those who migrated to work in domestic services.

> There are some pimps who exchange women. There was a story in the press about a pimp who exchanged a woman for a horse, it's appalling. Nothing like that happened to me. My cousin lent me the money to come to Spain, she was already here and things were going well for her. I didn't come because I was bought or because I need to pay off a debt. I knew why I was coming. (Colombian sex worker, Galicia)

> I came thanks to a friend. I've got a friend here who is married. I was working in Colombia and the business went bankrupt, so I lost my job. My friend was on holiday in Colombia at the time and she asked me to come back to Spain with her. She lent me the dollars to pay for the journey and she gave me her address and telephone number so that I could say I was invited to stay with a friend. It's quite frequent in Colombia that people ask you to come and work in a sex club. The girls who came with me all came to work in clubs. A friend had told them that there was work here and they lent them the money to come. These friends, who are usually already married, lend you money for your ticket and to pay to get through customs. Then they tell you where to go and find the club. (Colombian sex worker, Galicia)

This migratory strategy which involves borrowing money from migrants already installed in Spain, is often part of a feeling of solidarity between migrants from the same country of origin, or else part of a larger strategy of family regroupment. This is clearly the case for many of the migrant domestic workers in Pamplona who manage to earn enough money to finance the journeys of other members of their families. This is also the case for migrant women working in prostitution. Véronica, for example, immigrated to Galicia in order to work in a sex club. A police raid led to her being placed in detention, and the fear of being deported incited her to lend money to her sister still in Colombia so that she could migrate in turn if Veronica was forced to return to Colombia. Her plan was that her sister's migration would save the family plan and would allow Veronica herself to come back to Spain at a future time. Veronica's sister told her story:

> My older sister always wanted to study ... She came to Spain first and she said that she wanted to help me so that I could come too. Then if she had a problem, if

she got deported, I would be able to stay and work, and eventually help her to come back to Spain ... We'd like to get a house together, a small base for our business, and like that we could pay for our little sister and my daughter to study. Then my big sister could study too. Her dream has always been to study. (Colombian sex worker, Galicia)

This financing of migration through migrants already arrived in Spain may also take place as part of a profit making project. This type of arrangement is not an organised business or a form of trafficking, but certain immigrants already living in Spain do manage to make a profit from investing in the migratory projects of others. A Colombian working in a sex club explains:

In my country if I asked someone to lend me money I'd pay them back with interest – that's normal. Now that I'm living in Spain legally, I can lend money to someone else and ask them to pay interest. I send them a letter of invitation and ask them to pay for it. You can do that for a friend if she wants to come and work in these clubs. But I wouldn't send out fifteen or twenty letters of invitation and make people pay loads of money for them, that's illegal. (Colombian sex worker, Galicia)

The Second and Third Stages: Getting Past Border Controls and Making Contacts in Spain

Those involved in 'spontaneous' migration – that which is autonomous in character as well as that which involves family or friends and that which depends on migratory chains – generally obtain the necessary 'savoir-faire' to get past border controls through community networks. These community networks also provide them with contacts to help their initial integration in Spain. These contacts in Spain do not always help new migrants to integrate for purely altruistic reasons. In fact they may do so in order to profit from them. The husband of a Colombian women migrant explains that:

My wife had money to come to Spain, she just had to pay for the letter of invitation. They made her pay 1080 euros for that letter. (Husband of Colombian sex worker, Galicia)

In Madrid and Pamplona, as in other cities, there is a very well organised Ecuadorian migrant community. This community is structured around shared apartments in which men and women working as domestic workers live. Those who work as live-in domestic workers use the apartments as secondary homes where they can spend their days off. These apartments may contain up to a dozen people and act as refuges during the initial stages of integration in Spain. Immigrants who have just arrived can find food and lodging there. The amount the immigrants pay for living in the apartments varies, and sometimes this means that those who are the legal tenants can make a profit from the vulnerability of those recently arrived. So these migratory chains can, in a less visible and less direct way, also contribute to the exploitation of immigrants into Spain.

Traffic of Migrants from the Countries of Origin: Banks, Loan Companies, and 'Travel Agencies'

Alongside these migratory strategies which depend on community networks and migratory chains, there is a whole layer of organisations in the countries of origin which participate in arranging the exodus of immigrants for purely profit-making ends. These types of organisation are not engaged in trafficking in that they do not arrange all the stages of the journey to Spain. Rather they function principally as a means of lending money to migrants to finance their journeys. Several of our respondents from Ecuador who were working in the domestic service industry had used a bank loan to finance their journey to Spain. A guarantee is needed to get a loan of this type, and in general it is family or friends in the country of origin who own property who serve as guarantors.

The money loaned will include enough to buy a ticket, as well as the necessary 'bolsa'. In general, the migrants try and pay as little interest as possible by repaying this money for the bolsa as quickly as possible once they arrive in Spain. This means that they have to find a job quickly to enable them to survive for the first few weeks without having to touch any of the dollars of the 'bolsa', and thus to send this money back to the bank as quickly as possible. This urgency in transferring the 'bolsa' back home in order to reduce the interest payments on their loans places the migrants in a particularly vulnerable situation where they have to take whatever job they can find. Often this means that they might end up in exploitative situations of employment.

For many, however, even obtaining a bank loan to finance their voyage is not possible. Frequently, therefore, they have recourse to the services of a 'travel agency'. These agencies act as lenders, but also participate in the organisation of the journey and in instructing the migrant in the necessary 'savoir-faire' for passing the border controls. The travel agencies also charge high rates of interest on the money loaned. In the same way as with bank loans, the money for the 'bolsa' has to be transferred back to the agencies as quickly as possible or else the rates of interest will rise considerably. These agencies also ask for the same types of guarantees as banks.

The work of these agencies comes closest, out of all the modes of organising migration that we have analysed so far, to trafficking of migrants, in so far as they participate in the organisation of the journey and the instruction of the migrant in how to pass border controls, in order to make a profit from this. However, unlike other trafficking networks they do not provide contacts for jobs or accommodation in Spain. Generally the women who use these agencies already have such contacts through community networks and the existing migratory chains. An Ecuadorian woman recounts her experience of an agency thus:

> Over there everyone thinks that only the travel agencies can get you over here. I came with my husband through an agency. They sell you a ticket at a much more expensive price – that's how they make money. Then they offer to lend you money necessary for the customs, so that you can come into Spain as a tourist. As there were two of us we borrowed 4000 dollars from them. There's a person who receives you at the airport and you give him back the money. Over there you leave a blank cheque in case you don't give the money back. (Focus group discussion with Ecuadorian domestic workers, Madrid)

In Colombia, the use of agencies to finance and organise travel to Spain is less frequent, and many of the women interviewed had used private lending companies. Like the travel agencies in Ecuador, these private lenders demand guarantees before lending money, and charge high rates of interest. Other women had mortgaged their properties to such companies in order to raise the money for the journey. These women explained how they had been forced to mortgage property in order to finance their migration to Spain to support their families:

> I've been in Spain for a year. I mortgaged my house to come here. I haven't got any children but I support my parents and I pay for my two brothers' studies. I looked for work everywhere but finally the only option left for me was prostitution. Everywhere I went to try and find work they asked for my papers. In reality, I came because a lot of friends told me, and I heard on the radio, that there was lots of work here in Spain. I didn't know anything about Spain, but I came. In Colombia I had never worked in prostitution. (Colombian sex worker, Madrid)

> I came after mortgaging my grandmother's house ... I didn't know what else to do to get money. What could I do to help my family? I came to Spain desperate to earn some money. (Focus group discussion with Ecuadorian domestic workers, Madrid)

> Most of the people who come have debts. They have a debt to the people who lent them the money and the interest rates are very high, whether its private loan companies or banks. The banks ask for lots of documents and papers to prove that you'll repay the money, and so because of that lots of people resort to loan sharks. But people get into debt because of the necessity of paying for the journey. They have to work here and send all the money that they earn back to Colombia to pay off the debt and the interest on it. They work just to send money and pay off debts. (Focus group discussion with Colombian domestic workers, Madrid)

The Migratory Chain and the Traffic of Migrants

For some of the women interviewed, the process of migration required the involvement of individuals who were neither friends nor family, and who, through a basically market based contract, participated in all stages of the migratory process. These women then had to pay off a debt either to other migrants who were already installed in Spain, or to Spanish citizens who in a private capacity had decided to invest in the migration of these women by lending them money for their journeys or selling them letters of invitation. Some of the people who finance the women's migration in this way are owners of brothels or sex clubs, who expect the money they have lent to be repaid either in cash or through the woman's work for them. The migration in these cases is organised by a person who travels from Spain to the women's country of origin, and organises the initial contacts with them and then the journey to Spain.

The people who are behind this particular type of trafficking are working more or less independently and are not part of large organisations or criminal networks. They lend money necessary for the journey and for the purchase of clothing and jewellery or perfume. They organise the journey and give advice on passing border controls. Finally, once the women concerned have arrived in Spain they receive them in an apartment or bed and breakfast, or take them directly to the place where they will work. The women then have a debt to pay off, which is usually large. The women in our survey talked about sums ranging from 3600 euros to 6000 euros, and sometimes the debt is even greater than this. This debt may be owed to the owner of a sex club or brothel, but it is equally likely that it is third person who will have arranged the traffic and to whom the woman will thus owe money. Several women recounted similar experiences:

> In Colombia there are people who contact girls to offer them a trip to Spain, and clothes and perfume. Three or four days later the girl is given a passport. You travel on a three month tourist visa. During those months you have to pay off your debt. Nowadays they're charging about 9000 euros. You're taken directly from the plane to the place where you'll be working. In my case, a friend of my sister-in-law came to Colombia and said that he needed two or three women to come to Spain with him. My sister-in-law told me about him. They told me that I'd be working in a club … The woman who brought me here told me that at the club they'd give me everything, food, lodging … I came with a few personal belonging. After eight days the woman came and asked me if I wanted to move to another club. I said no, but I didn't know how it would work with the debt, and who I would have to pay. Twenty days later the woman came back again to take all the money I had. She told me that the debt I had from having been brought here was 3000 euros. I didn't really realise how much money that was – I'd lost the sense of it moving from Colombia to Spain. I started to work it out and it seemed like a lot to me. The plane ticket had cost 1080 euros. The boss told me that he would give me the money I earned and I'd have to arrange with the woman what I was going to do with it. The boss of the club wasn't working with the woman who had brought me. In the end I had problems and I didn't pay anymore … What you get tricked by is the debt and the payment, not the work. We're scared to stop paying the debts because if not they can do something to your family. We're all scared that they'll kidnap one of our family in Colombia, so we keep paying. (Colombian sex worker, Galicia)

> I had a big debt. A Colombian gave me a ticket and 3000 dollars. He took me to a club where I paid 48 euros per day for food and accommodation. This man talked to the club owner and asked him to give him half of what I earned every day. One day, the man said to the club owner that he wanted more money, and the owner threatened me, saying that he would give him all of my money. The next day I ran

away to another club. I paid 3600 euros of the 6000 that I owed. (Colombian sex worker, Madrid)

In Galicia, there is a widespread practice whereby Colombian immigrants who are already installed in Spain and who have a certain legal status, invest financially in the migration of third parties. Some of the women interviewed had a freer and less dependent relationship with those who had lent them the money to migrate, although even in these circumstances there was a certain degree of abuse and exploitation taking place. The new immigrants are fearful of the consequences of non-payment of their debts and are therefore constrained to work wherever they can and earn as much as they can to pay it off. A Colombian woman recounts how her migration was financed by a friend of a friend in Spain:

> A friend suggested that I should come to Spain and she said she knew a woman who could bring me here. In Colombia there isn't any work and I wanted to leave. So I said to myself that I might as well get out any way I could. Over there they make you sign a letter proving that you've borrowed 4200 euros. They tell you that you should be able to pay it back through a month's work. I knew what I was coming to do. When you arrive you feel awful because the work is horrible and because you can't possibly pay off the debt in a month. You talk with the other girls and you work out that the debt you have is much greater than the cost of bringing you over here. I will pay it, although it's a lot of money. I owe the money to the girl who brought me here ... I want to talk to her and tell her that I'll pay what I can ... but I'm scared for my family in Colombia because if I don't pay they'll hold them responsible for my debt. (Colombian sex worker, Galicia)

Some of the women who have already migrated to Spain agree to get involved in the traffic of other women for profit. They can make a lot of money out of the vulnerability of these newly arrived migrants by charging them large sums to cover their debts and their costs for food and accommodation. Sometimes they enter into agreements with the bosses of sex clubs so that these bosses will keep back the new migrants' earnings and hand the money straight to those who have arranged the traffic. Carmen, one of the women interviewed, told us that it was another one of our respondents who had brought her to Spain, and that this woman had demanded a large sum of money, much greater than the real costs of the journey:

> It was X who brought me here – you know her, you've spoken to her too. X and Y both help to bring other girls over. They find girls in Colombia who haven't got any work. I had a big debt to them which I had to pay off. They knew exactly how much I was earning every night and I had to give it straight to them. My debt was 6000 euros. (Colombian sex worker, Galicia)

A focus group discussion amongst male club owners in Galicia, also highlighted the role of women migrants in recruiting other women, and exploiting them to make a profit. Although it can be argued that these club owners are eager to shift the blame for any exploitation that takes place away from themselves, it emerges from the discourse of both women migrants and club owners, that migrant women do play a part in recruiting and trafficking other women, and that they can profit considerably from this:

> Some of these girls do exploit the others. They pretend that everything is more expensive than it is. They'll bring girls over and if the ticket costs 1200 euros they'll charge them 6000 euros. And if the rent for the apartment costs them 250 euros in total, they'll make each girl who's living there pay 250 euros ...
> If it was a person who was just bringing over the women to exploit them I'd understand, but it's the girls themselves who are doing it to each other. I don't understand. They've already been through it all themselves, and now they're doing it to others. (Male focus group discussion, Galicia)

Spanish law punishes individuals who are implicated in the trafficking of women. So often the bosses of clubs do not want to get involved in this traffic given the risks it entails, and given that their profits come largely not from the traffic itself but from the work of the women in their clubs. So they prefer it to be another individual who organises the trafficking independently of them. In the focus group discussion with partners and clients of migrant sex workers, this separation between the operation of the clubs and the organisation of the trafficking was highlighted:

> It is not anyone who you know who brings the girls. It's just private individuals who want to make some money. There are complications involved in bringing the women over. And the club owners make more money from the work in the club than from the debt that the women have to repay. So they prefer it if someone else brings the women over and collects the debts. (Male focus group discussion, Galicia)

> In a really big club that's doing well, there's no need to get involved in trafficking women. If the club's doing well then the women will come and work there anyway. It's only when a club has got no girls that it's got to get involved in the trafficking to bring them over. (Male focus group discussion, Galicia)

Colombian women interviewed in Madrid pointed out that it was often a partnership between a Spaniard and a Colombian that would work to bring women over to Spain. Some of the women interviewed explained that they themselves had invested money in this trafficking, however, the experience was not always successful in terms of making a profit, as the experience of the woman below reveals:

> I agreed with a compatriot that I would help to bring girls over from Colombia and I invested money in it, hoping to make a profit on the interest. As I run a bed and breakfast I had room to put the girls up when they arrived, and then I would help them to find work. So I sent money for the tickets. I never heard any more from one of the girls, so it was me who had to pay off the debt and I didn't have anything left. And the man I was working with was with the mafia. So I paid him what I owed and I got out. (Colombian sex worker, Madrid)

Most of the women interviewed knew what type of work they would be doing in Spain. The trickery for them did not reside in the fact that they would be involved in sex work, but rather in the amount of debt that they accumulated, a sum which was far greater than the actual cost of the journey to Spain. Some only managed to pay off a part of their debts, whilst others, who were more scared of reprisals against their family in Colombia, paid it all. Once the debt has been paid off these women generally consider themselves as 'free' and mostly continue working in the sex industry in an independent fashion, moving from club to club.

There were, however, three cases where the women we interviewed had been deceived as to the nature of the work that they would do when they came to Spain. It is interesting to note that these women who had been tricked in this way had not bee trafficked by big networks or mafia, but had been brought over through contacts in their own families or through friends who had already migrated to Spain. Béatriz decided that she wanted to leave Ecuador and managed to do so thanks to the help of a friend who gave her everything she needed to get to Spain. In Ecuador this friend had told her that she would be working in an apricot growing plantation in Murcia, but when she arrived in Spain she was taken to a sex club in Léon:

> When I was in Ecuador, they told me that they were going to send me to Murcia to work in an apricot farm. Then, when I was in the taxi in Spain they told me I was going to Léon to work in a club. When I got to Léon I was forced to start working in the club, it wasn't the work that they had told me about. (Ecuadorian sex worker, Galicia)

A similar story is told by Vanessa. After splitting up with her partner Vanessa met some family members who had come back to Colombia on holiday, and who owned a so-called 'social club' in Spain. They lent her money to come and work in their club, but when she arrived in Galicia she realised that this 'social club' was in fact a brothel:

> They tricked me. When I arrived I started to rebel and to say I wouldn't work, but then the problems started. The first day they brought me downstairs and I had to sit on a stool whilst all these drunk men approached me. I just wanted to throw stones at them. But then they said to me that I owed them 1800 euros and that I had to pay them back by working. They said I could only leave when I'd paid them the money. (Colombian sex worker, Galicia)

Marta had a Colombian friend who lent her money to come to Spain and assured her that she had contacts for finding domestic work in Spain. She borrowed more money from a private lender to pay for the additional costs of her journey and left for Pamplona. When she arrived she was shocked to discover that her friend's contacts were in reality with a brothel where Colombian women were working as prostitutes:

> There was a friend who came to Colombia. She was Colombian but spoke Spanish really well. She said that she knew plenty of people who could find me work in

domestic service, cleaning or looking after children or old people. I got a loan and she said that I had three months to pay it back otherwise the interest rate would go up. The woman who brought me here told me not to worry because it would be easy to pay off the debt and that there was lots of work in Spain. But it was a lie. When we arrived in Pamplona she took me to a place where there were loads of girls in mini-skirts. I was scared and I started to cry. The woman told me not to be silly. She said I was nice looking and so I'd earn lots of money. I just told her that I hadn't come for that. (Colombian sex worker, Pamplona)

Sometimes, as has been pointed out, there is some form of association between the bosses of clubs and the individuals responsible for recruiting women and organising their travel to Spain. Certain of our respondents described how, in some cases, women are even sold to club owners by immigrants already living in Spain. Thus some club owners are directly implicated in the trafficking of these women, and in this case the situation of dependence and exploitation that emerges can be even more acute than in the case of those who have ended up working in the clubs as a result of spontaneous migration. A Colombian woman recounted her experiences of working in this type of exploitative situation:

A Colombian woman brought me here, she worked with the boss of a club in Galicia. I came in through Switzerland. A man met me in Berne and we came by car. When we arrived I saw what kind of a place it was. It was a terrible place, the men that went there were vile. But they told me that if I tried to escape they'd take revenge on my daughters in Colombia. There's such a pressure on you that in the end you resign yourself to it ... I had to pay the boss 7000 euros. In addition he made us pay 10 euros a day for meals. If you stayed in the room with a client for longer than you were meant to you had to pay for that too. It meant that there was no money left to send back home to Colombia. We asked to clients for tips so that we could get a bit of money to send home at the end of the week. We were like slaves. All we wanted was to get out of there. We were shut up in the club all the time and the boss spent all day shouting at us. If a friend wanted us to go out for a walk with them he shouted. Sometimes we were forbidden from talking to the clients in case we tried to escape. The boss thought that we belonged to him and that we had to work all the time for him. (Colombian sex worker, Galicia)

But trafficking does not only affect women employed in the sex industry. Our fieldwork revealed that trafficking of women to work in domestic service is also frequent. Some employers in the domestic service industry actively recruit and finance the migration of women from Latin America and from Eastern Europe in order that they will come and work for them (Oso, 1998). These women brought over to work in the domestic service industry can equally be tricked, forced to pay off large debts, and exploited in their relationships with their traffickers and their employers. A represeative of the charity organisation Caritas which works with migrant women, recounts the experiences of Eastern European women brought to work in domestic service in Pamplona:

The first women from Eastern Europe who arrived in Pamplona to work in domestic services were brough over by a Moldavian woman. She went back to her country to find some documents and a week later came back with other Moldavians and Ukrainians who were looking for work. They came by bus from Kiev, passing through Italy and France. This woman had promised to find them work, food and lodging. They paid for their journey and then when they arrived there was no work and no food. (Representative of Caritas, Pamplona)

Criminal Networks Implicated in Trafficking

A final mode of migration that emerged from our study is through the organised networks and criminal organisations and mafia involved in the trafficking of women. Caldwell et al. (1997), define an organised criminal group as a mafia when it is characterised by criminal activities orientated to profit, when it uses violence or the threats of violence to achieve this profit, and when it spends money to dissuade its members from cooperating with the police and to corrupt the authority of legitimate government (Caldwell et al., 1997). These mafia networks take charge of all of the process of recruitment/capture of migrants, transport of the migrants to Spain, reception and transfer to their place of work. Diverse methods of deception, violence and coercion are used to bring the women to Spain and to keep them working in the establishments to which they are sent.Often they are regularly transferred from one establishment to another, or sold to another 'owner'. The boss of two sex clubs explains how these mafia operate in Spain:

> In Saragossa there's lots of violence. The girls don't leave the clubs. If they leave, the owners would kill their family over there in their countries of origin. So they don't move. They've got about twenty clubs all over Spain. We don't really know who's behind it. But they have a monopoly in Eastern Spain. (Club owner, Galicia)

A Colombian woman, working in a sex club in Galicia, also told us about her experiences of the way the mafia work, calling it the 'white slave trade':

> The white slave trade really exists. They arrive in Colombia, they arrange papers for the women and they bring them to Spain to make them work. They tell the immigration authorities that they're bringing their fiancée to show them Spain. Then they take them to the clubs. The girls don't know what work they're going to do when they arrive, but they're taken to clubs and told exactly what they have to do. If they don't want to work they get beaten up. The women are taken from one club to another so no one can find them and help them. They're completely exploited. They work for men. (Colombian sex worker, Galicia)

Our fieldwork revealed two women who had been victims of this type of trafficking in its hardest form, where they were victims of relationships of domination with their traffickers. The experiences of these women are most similar to the traditional representations of trafficking portrayed by the media. The women are transferred from one club to another so that they cannot escape, locked up, sold and deprived of the most elementary freedoms:

I was already working in the sex industry in Colombia. I was told that I could make money coming to Spain, that I'd be able to send money back to Colombia and still have money for buying clothes and things. But they didn't give me any money at all. I arrived in a club in Pontevedra and then I was sent to another club in Lugo. We were watched all the time and they never let us go out. We were locked up. Sometimes we were treated all right, but sometimes we were beaten. Then they sent me out to work in the streets. I worked in Ovideo and Lerida. Finally they sold me to a club in Orensa for 4000 euros. In the end I did manage to escape and then I came to work in this club in Galicia. (Colombian sex worker, Galicia)

Conclusion

Table 4.2 presents an attempt at drawing up a typology of the migratory processes and strategies involved in Colombian and Ecuadorian women's migration to Spain. Like all migratory strategies, these are strongly shaped by the limitations imposed by Spanish immigration laws and policies. These policies mean that the women who come have to convince the authorities that they are coming as tourists. Once they have entered the country on a three month tourist visa they can only find work illegally which once again constrains their choices, and subjects them to insecurities, as can be seen by the examples of women forced to turn to prostitution and sex work because they could find no other way to earn money. The migratory strategies of these women are also strongly influenced by economic factors. The belief that they cannot earn enough money in their own countries leads them to risk borrowing large sums and incurring debts to migrate to Spain in search of employment. What the fieldwork demonstrated, was the complexity of the migratory processes and strategies of the women concerned. Our attempt at classification is limited because of the inter-connected and cross-cutting nature of these strategies. Moreover, the complexities revealed serve to deconstruct any simplistic division between independent migration and trafficking. The varying relationships of exploitation and dependency revealed in even some 'spontaneous' migratory situations demonstrate that not only women trafficked by organised criminal networks are vulnerable to this type of exploitation and insecurity.

Table 4.2   Typology of Colombian and Ecuadorian Women's Migration Strategies

Type of Migration	Autonomous Migration	Migration Using Loans From Organisations in Country of Origin	Migration Through Individuals in Spain	Migration Through Organised Criminal Networks
Decision to Migrate	Autonomous or familial decision	Autonomous decision, sometimes influenced by travel agencies	Autonomous or familial decision. Recruitment by individuals living in Spain	Enrolment by mafia using deception or force
Financing of Journey	Personal resources or loans without interest from family or friends	Bank loans, private loans, travel agencies, mortgages	Loans (with interest) from migrants already installed in Spain or Spaniards who invest in migration Investment of employers	Financed by mafia. Repayment through work in clubs
Organisation of Journey	Personal organisation or with the help of migrant networks	Personal organisation helped by migrant networks. Travel agencies may help in organisation	Personal organisation supported by the individuals providing the finance for the journey. Sale of invitation letters	Organised by mafia
Help in Crossing Border	Help of other migrants	Help of other migrants. Advice of travel agencies	Help and advice of individuals providing the finance	Organised by mafia
Reception and Initial Integration in Spain	Reliance on family and community networks	Reliance on family and community networks. Contacts through agencies	Initial reception and insertion facilitated by individuals implicated in finance	Organised by mafia

References

Acsur Las Segovias (2001), *Tráfico e inmigración de mujeres en España*. Madrid: ACSUR Las Segovias.

Baldwin-Edwards, M. (1998), Where Free Markets Reign: Aliens in the Twilight Zone, in M. Baldwin-Edwards and J. Arango (eds), Special issue on immigrants and the informal economy in Southern Europe, *South European Society and Politics*, 3, 3, pp. 1-15.

Caldwell, G., Galster, S., Kanics, J. and Steinzor N. (1997), Capitalizing on Transition Economies: The Role of Russian Mafia in Trafficking Women for Forced Prostitution, Illegal Immigration and Commercial Sex, *Transnational Organized Crime*, 3, 4, pp. 5-40.

Campani, G. (2000), Immigrant Women in Southern Europe: Social Exclusion, Domestic Work and Prostitution in Italy, In R. King, G. Lazaridis and C. Tsardanidis (eds), *Eldorado or Fortress? Migration in Southern Europe*. New York: St Martin's Press.

Catarino, C. and Oso, L. (2000), La inmigración femenina en Madrid y Lisboa: hacia una etnización del servicio doméstico y de las empresas de limpieza. *Papers*, 60, pp. 183-207.

Izquierdo, A. (directeur) (2000), *Mujeres inmigrantes en la irregularidad. Pobreza, marginación laboral y prostitución*. Madrid: Instituto de la Mujer.

OIM (1999), *Tráfico de migrantes: política y respuesta de la OIM*, MC/EX/INF/58. Geneva: OIM.

Oso, L. (1998), *La migración hacia España de mujeres jefas de hogar*. Madrid: Instituto de la Mujer.

Oso, L. (2001), Domestiques, concierges et prostituées: migration et mobilité sociale des femmes immigrées, espagnoles à Paris, équatoriennes et colombiennes en Espagne. Thèse de Doctorat. IEDES-Université de Paris I-Panthéon Sorbonne.

Oso, L. and Catarino, C. (1997), Les effets de la migration sur le statut des femmes: le cas des Dominicaines et des Marocaines à Madrid et des cap-verdiennes à Lisbonne, *Migrations Société*, 9, 52, pp. 115-130.

PART II
THE GENDERED LABOUR MARKET
AND ECONOMIC INSECURITIES

Chapter 5

The Globalisation of Domestic Work: Women Migrants and Neo-Domesticity

Francesca Scrinzi

An account of contemporary forms of re-productive work necessitates a reflection on the relationship between nationals and foreigners. In fact, paid domestic work, together with prostitution and sex work, constitute almost the only available forms of remunerated work for migrant women who represent half of the millions of people who are migrants today. Work in the unskilled tertiary sector, and in particular work for private households, constitutes one of the major sources of employment for such women. In the past ten years, the global demand for domestic labour, defined in general terms (services of care of families, children and old people, cleaning and maintaining houses and properties), has grown considerably, and this growing demand has pushed millions of women to offer their labour on the global market. The feminisation which has characterised migratory phenomena, particularly since the beginning of the 1990s, should be understood in the more general context of the transformations that have taken place in the post-industrial modes of production, and in particular, the massive development of the tertiary sector, most notably the unskilled service jobs which Sassen (1996) has defined as being a part of the necessary infrastructure of the global economy.

This chapter will examine some of the modalities of the setting up of a new domestic regime, and the implications as far as the re-composition of the workforce in terms of gender, class and nationality is concerned. To do this it will draw on ethnographic research carried out in the cities of Genoa and Paris. The chapter will begin by addressing changes in the theory and practice of activities classed as activities of 're-production'. It will then go on to consider the development of a global market for domestic services, and ways in which the development of the immigrant workforce in this area brings into question the notions of economic and social citizenship. Finally, it will examine the articulations between gender, class and nationality in the treatment of domestic workers in Italy.

The New Regime of Re-Production

The age of global migration is also one of feminisation of migration. According to Castles and Miller (1998), the four tendencies in recent migratory phenomena are acceleration, diversification, feminisation and globalisation. These new migrations are situated within the framework of a profoundly reconfigured capitalism, characterised by the tertiarisation of the economy, the deregulation of financial activity, the segmentation and ethnicisation of the labour market, the extension of informal sectors and the flexibilisation of work through increasing part-time work and sub-contracting. Certain authors have used these elements to define a model of immigration characteristic notably of the countries of Southern Europe (King and Zontini, 2000), but this model can be used more generally to talk about current global migration patterns. Further, many studies have already revealed the feminisation of poverty in global society and have analysed the effects of neo-liberalism from a gendered perspective. Women are particularly implicated in the economic and social dynamics described above, as 'heads of family' in migration (Bisilliat, 1996; Oso, 2000), as a low-cost workforce in free market zones, and as part of the relocation of work in developed economies (Terray, 1999). This latter function can be explained by the fact that many of the tasks which are necessary to the functioning of the economy and to the social reproduction of middle class households and which cannot be relocated to countries where they would cost less are carried out cheaply by women migrants working informally and flexibly. These women migrants are often overqualified with respect to the jobs that they carry out. To try and encompass all of these tendencies, Sassen talks about a 'feminisation of strategies of survival' in the global society, and shows to what extent the lives of households in the South depend more and more on the work of the women who are part of them (Sassen, 2000). In general, gendered analyses of globalisation and international migration tend to focus on households, which allows the articulation between macro and micro phenomenon connected with migration to become apparent, as well as taking account of the power relationships between men and women (Pessar, 1999). More precisely it is in the relations of household production and reproduction, and the current reconfiguration of these relations, that it is possible to seize some of the aspects of connection between the societies of origin and those of arrival.

The frontiers between the categories and practices of production and re-production are today the subject of tensions. These frontiers are in fact moving and becoming blurred, which raises certain questions regarding the effects of the globalisation of the work of re-production from the point of view of gender relations. The international division of labour and the status of migrant workers are at the heart of these questions. To a certain degree today's capitalist system seems to be able to dispense with a clear and explicit separation between the work of production and of re-production. The new forms of post-industrial domination respond to the demands of global production through the mobilisation of all available resources in a society. Thus the classic paradigm of a spatial, temporal and conceptual distinction between production and re-production is overcome. This paradigm whilst clearly a fiction useful to the functioning of the system, also constituted a point of departure for a gendered critique of economic relationships. This critique must now begin from a new point of view of understanding the implications of gender in the restructuring of the economy and of new forms of power. In the older form of industrial society, women were salaried producers on the one hand, and actresses of re-production on the other, accomplishing this work alongside State institutions which took care of education and health care provision to individuals (Chabaud-Rychter et al., 1985). Today, women are inserted in the new forms of production: on the one hand, de-localised production is undertaken to a great extent by women in the South, whilst on the other hand, the work of re-production in the North is more and more externalised by households and assigned to migrant women in return for very low salaries. A movement of delegation, externalisation and de-localisation regulates this new international division of labour which sees migrants as active protagonists.

Flexibilisation of Work and the Sub-Contracting of Re-Production

The flexibilisation of work allows businesses to adapt their productive apparatus, notably the level of employment, to evolutions in demand (Boltanski and Chiappello, 1999). They attempt to employ in fixed posts only the minimum number of people necessary, and to use external or flexible workers to carry out the rest of the work. Part-time work is an essential tool in the flexibilisation of work, as it allows employers to have access to a large number of personnel at busy times. This type of work is thus particularly frequent in service activities where it is not possible to 'stock' the product. Part-time working is very much prevalent for services cleaning offices, where the work cannot be carried out except at times when the office workers themselves are not there. It is also predominant in the industrial cleaning sector in general. A second tool of flexibilisation is sub-contracting. Sub-contracting is organised in chains whereby the large firms sub-contract work at a first level, and it is then sub-contracted again by these first level companies to second level ones, and so on. Each seeks to lower the costs of their activities, and to rid themselves of certain tasks by delegating them to sub-contractors capable of optimising cost levels. Permanent links are established between contractors and sub-contractors in order to enable the constant re-negotiation of charges and to exercise some control over production (through for example, the regular presence of someone from the contractor's company at the sub-contractors). To understand the role played by sub-contracting within the new organisation of labour, one must consider that the growth of the tertiary sector is one of the major evolutions in recent years, and that amongst this sector, services to companies have taken a large part of the growth. An important result of the growth of these type of services is the externalisation of such functions as cleaning, laundry, catering, transport, security etc. The job of cleaner is one of the rare unskilled jobs to have experienced a non-stop growth, and the cleaning sector is organised almost entirely around sub-contracting. In all of these 'employment transfers' the employer takes less and less responsibility and it becomes more and more difficult to establish that any relation of exploitation exists (Boltanski and Chiappello, 1999). Any relationship between employer and employee has to be traced through a long chain organised through a stack of sub-contractors where the different actors are often a long way from each other.

It was argued above that companies are more and more adjusting the number of hours worked by their employees to variations in the demand for work. As a consequence of this type of arrangement, workers in industries such as the cleaning industry find themselves in situations of an extremely precarious nature, and they are often forced to rush from one workplace to another, or from one employer to another, during their day's work, in order to gain a sufficient salary. When the company issuing the contract finds another sub-contractor who can do the work at a better price, the workers might find themselves transferred to a different workplace, or issued with different working hours, from one day to the next. But the increasing use of flexible work patterns does not just encompass part-time work, other types of solution have also been worked out by employers, and the mechanism can be used in the inverse direction. Amongst the migrant workers interviewed, many of those who worked in different industrial cleaning companies denounced the ways in which they were forced to work over-time for no extra pay. Their contracts did not define the number of hours that they were expected to work, but rather imposed on them a set number of tasks to complete within their working hours. For example, they were set a certain number of hotel rooms to clean on the basis of seventeen minutes per room. As seventeen minutes proved insufficient time to complete the cleaning of a hotel room, the workers found themselves working many extra hours to complete their allocation of rooms. However this extra-time was not paid, and when they failed to complete their allocation of rooms, they were recorded as being absent from work. As a result these women knew when they would start work in the morning, but not when they would finish, nor how much they would be paid at the end of the month (their basic hourly salary was only around 7 euros per hour). Other women migrants employed as hospital cleaners recounted that they worked on Saturdays for no pay. The dissolution of direct contacts and relationships between employers and workers means that this type of sub-contracting becomes a laboratory for all types of practices of evasion of employment rights, and that new forms of exploitation develop which rest on the employment of migrant workers with no legal status (Marie, 1999).

In general, it can be argued that one of the specificities of sub-contracting lies in the intensification of work through direct pressure of demand. The externalisation of the contract between employer and worker allows the intensity of work to be increased under the direct pressure of the market, which appears as an external, and uncontrollable factor. This external mode of control is more powerful and more 'legitimate' than that exercised by the direct giver of orders. 'Availability clauses' which ensure the continual availability of workers for employers and mean that they only have to pay them for the periods in which they actually worked, have become more and more frequent in recent years. Another commonly used practice is that of giving the 'cleaning agents' diverse tasks to do (e.g., warehouse work, equipment handling) which are not actually specified in their work contracts. Sub-contracting works in the cleaning industry through eating up workers time. As well as the types of contract mentioned above which force workers to carry out hours of unpaid work, it is also common to find that no time is allowed for breaks during the day, or that the time and cost of transport from one place of work to another are not covered by the employer.

Moreover, the use of sub-contracting allows employers to sidestep many of the constraints imposed by employment law, by making many of the legislative texts and regulations which refer to minimal conditions of employment inapplicable. For example, many of the companies which use sub-contracting actually employ very few people, and so their small size means that they do not have to have any union representation or workers' committees. In 1998 in the Paris region, for example, 38 per cent of the cleaning service companies had no permanent employees, and 40 per cent had between one and ten employees (INSEE, 2000). Externalisation has the result of liberating companies from the most difficult tasks of personnel management. Sub-contracting cleaning companies know this, and try to select workers who will be the most docile and easy to control. Employers choose preferably women immigrants, and if possible, those who are illiterate. When a woman applies for a job, she is often asked to write something on some pretext or another. Only those women who do not know how to write are chosen for the job. Women migrants are thus directly implicated in the flexibilisation of work, but also suffer the consequences. In effect, the use of sub-contracting and of temporary and part-time workers allows employers to pay only the hours actually worked and to leave unpaid all time spent in training, rests etc, time which was previously considered as part of a fair day's work. Companies which are searching for ever greater mobility and flexibility, rid themselves of tasks which do not concern the core of their business, and sub-contract them out to those who will offer the best price. Households externalise the work of re-production and turn to the market. The market tries to stimulate and to make profits from this demand.

Globalised Domesticity

The structure of immigrant women's employment in Europe began to transform at the end of the 1960s with a fall in the number of immigrant women employed in manufacturing industry and a parallel rise in the number employed in hotels, restaurants and domestic services. During the 1980s the work of women immigrants, particularly in the service industries, constituted a laboratory for the introduction of new forms of organisation of work, based on flexibility. These new types of organisation of work later spread to other parts of the active population such as other groups of women, young people etc. At the same time, the ageing of the European population increased the demand for personal services, particularly in the countries of Souther Europe where the rudimentary welfare state had always rested on the support of families, and where the level of market intervention in such services had previously been low.

Sassen's analysis of the global political economy aims to highlight the hidden interconnections between the global economy and its 'infrastructures' and between the global and national spaces. She also aims to restore visibility and rationality to the substrata of informal practices which characterise the economies of 'global cities' (Sassen, 2002). The informal economy provides cut price services to low income households which in turn provide workers prepared to work for low salaries in service industries. For example, migrant women work illegally as nannies to take care of the children of women working in the cleaning industry (Mozère, 2001a). Sassen reveals to what extent in many cities, the functions of support and service to the global elites are provided by women immigrants. Her analysis may not be applicable in its entirety to the European case, but the tendencies towards economic and social polarisation which she highlights are apparent throughout Western Europe. In particular, the gendered character of the relationships which link on the one hand the work of migrant women to the lifestyles of the global elite and the national middle classes, and on the other hand the informal or illegal sectors of the economy to the organisation of the national and international economy, are evident. A clear example of this is provided by the sex industry where a demand for entertainment which has been incorporated into the normal management and business practices of transnational companies has attracted many migrant women to work in prostitution and other sex work (Kofman et al., 2000). Another example which shows how the segregation of migrant women into unskilled services can result in a reproduction of the global distinctions of class, is that of the practice of using immigrant domestic workers to teach English to the employer's children. Whilst neither treated nor paid as teachers, certain migrant women, especially from the Philippines, are used to provide to the children of French and Italian families a social and professional resource (a grasp of the English language) which is central to the globalised definition of class (Mozère, 2001b). The value of this resource is clear both to the domestic workers and to the employers.

The Work of Migrant Women as a Laboratory for New Work Practices

The conditions of work for migrant workers in the global market seem, to some extent, to reflect changes in the general conditions of work, providing an exacerbated model of working conditions of all, both nationals and foreigners (Morice, 1997). The Italian example is particularly significant in this respect. The weakness of the Italian welfare state and the historical tendency of the Italian state to assign to women all work of social re-production, together with the size and importance of the informal economy in Italy[1] point to this fact (Palidda and Dal Lago, 2002). Neo-liberal economic policies are neither mediated nor regulated by the State, and are thus operated with considerable violence, particularly with regard to migrant workers. These migrant workers appear as flexible workers, par excellence, with no fixed housing, no family ties, no stable employment. These workers have little opportunity to denounce exploitation or violence on the part of their employers, as they lack the time and the social resources to support them in this type of endeavour. If these migrants are flexible workers par excellence, it is because of the general precariousness of their lives, their legal, economic and

---

[1] According to experts, 27 per cent of the Italian GNP comes from the informal economy.

social insecurity. Moreover, as a Trade Union leader from Genoa points out, these migrant workers who were often highly qualified workers in their countries of origin, do not perceive themselves as domestic workers or labourers and thus tend not to claim the rights due to them as such (Quadrelli, 1999). Today a migrant worker is often a highly qualified worker who is employed in an unskilled job. He/she will be paid little for this work, but can bring all of his/her unrecognised extra competencies to the job. In effect, in the space of a generation, Italy has seen a huge renaissance in the domestic service sector, and the arrival of domestic workers with high levels of education and qualification. During the 1960s and 1970s the number of women from the countryside of Northern Italy and from Southern Italy employed in domestic service gradually diminished, whilst at the same time the number of middle and upper class households with the financial resources to employ domestic help increased. These posts were taken by women who often did not recognised themselves as domestic workers, such as the headmistress from Lima who became a domestic worker in Genoa.[2] These workers have thus been 'displaced' in all senses.

The labour market experiences of migrant women show not only an experimentation in the increasing flexibilisation of employment, but also an increasing polarisation which is not only economic (in terms of differences in salaries), but also qualitative and symbolic. The migrant domestic worker does not simply become a substitute for the Italian housewife. An analysis in terms of gender shows that paid domestic work is actually the site of a symbolic polarisation which takes place between the roles of the maid and of the mistress of the house. For example, Anderson's research shows that migrant domestic workers are often expected to perform tasks that their female employers would not undertake themselves (Anderson, 2000). Many of these workers have the impression that they are carrying out tasks that their employers would not even consider necessary if they had to do them themselves. What counts here is the ability to choose which tasks to perform, an opportunity which is denied to some women and not to others. In this way, paid domestic work can be reduced to a question of status of citizenship (a status where class intersects with nationality).

The case of the domestic service sector in the city of Genoa demonstrates this same polarising articulation between gender, race and class, with some certain Italian specificities. Research carried out among recruitment and training agencies for domestic workers in Genoa (Scrinzi, 2001) shows the way in which the relational aspect of the job and the personalisation of the relationship of service, obscure the reality of non-choice (all of the interviews showed that migrant women do not choose domestic service), and at the same time allow the use of the paradigm of 'vocation'. This vocation is understood both in terms of gender – domestic work is a 'naturally' female type of work – and in terms of race/ethnicity – migrants have a cultural aptitude for this type of work. The attitudes of those in charge of recruitment agencies demonstrate the way in which the view of domestic service as a vocation encompasses a moralising and normative approach to social relationships. The research in Genoa allowed the verification at a micro-level of

---

[2] Interview with author.

the existence of practices that contribute to the social exclusion of migrant women and their construction as 'non-persons'. In effect, the research showed the ways in which such representations can result in the production of an ethnicised and racialised labour market. Practices employed in recruiting and training migrants are fixed within the confines of these stereotyped representations, and these stereotypes form an integral part of the daily work of recruitment agencies.

Moreover, in the majority of cases, the structures of recruitment and training of migrant workers are linked to the Catholic Church. In Italy the Church mobilised relatively early to respond to the arrival of migrant workers, whilst State intervention and legislation occurred much later. The religious orientation of these centres has an impact on the ways in which they respond to the needs of migrants. In virtue of their mission to protect single women, Catholic institutions have historically taken upon themselves the role of looking after domestic employees, women whom they see as morally at risk. The largest Italian organisations for domestic workers are thus of Catholic inspiration. Since the 1970s these organisations have dealt with the arrival of migrant domestic workers, who arrived at the start through the missionary networks of the Italian ex-colonies. Certain sociological characteristics of these centres favour a moralising approach to migrants and a familialist definition of the role of domestic workers. For example, these centres are often founded on the work of volunteers which means that the recruitment is often carried out through a charitable and personal approach. There is a common assumption that the migrant women being recruited are poor and deserving of help, but that at the same time they must merit the help given to them by Italian society. Moreover, most of these voluntary workers in the recruitment centres are women who are older than the migrant women who frequent the centres. This means that a maternalistic relationship is often established between them and the migrant women with whom they deal. The recruitment process is thus built upon an idea of giving a job to migrants in return for good behaviour. Migrant women may feel that they have to act out in some way their role of virtuous poverty: showing their modesty, patience, availability, and belief in the Catholic religion. This relationship between recruiters and migrant workers prefigures that between employers and migrant domestic workers. It reproduces the vision of domestic work as a service, a vision which obscures the reality of the work contract. In this vision, migrant women are in need of an Italian home and family, and this family will in turn protect and control them. Their job is perceived as a lucky opportunity for them, a concession for which they should be grateful.

Moreover, recruitment practices rest on the shared belief, common amongst the volunteers, that certain aptitudes for different tasks are associated with workers of different nationalities. In this 'culturalist' vision, particular ethnic and cultural traits become naturalised and it is believed that certain qualities necessary for the successful accomplishment of a task will naturally be associated to the 'culture of origin' of the migrant. Peruvian women are seen, for example, as more suitable than Nigerian women for looking after old people. Moroccan women, it is believed, like doing the cleaning. In Italy, the demand for domestic workers is shaped by stereotypes which attribute certain capacities and qualities to an individual on the basis of their nationality. At the same time, the way that recruitment happens in large part through word of mouth, favours the entry into the same sectors of workers of the same nationality, and thus perpetuates this division of the market by nationality. Such an ethnicising definition of the labour market also responds to a need to control migration and to exercise social control. The establishment of such distinctions and hierarchies between migrants of different nationalities is part of the political management of the presence of migrants in a society. In Italy, the division between the 'good' and the 'bad' migrant is incarnated in the figures of the Nigerian prostitute and the Filipino domestic worker.

Within the sector of domestic work there is also an enormous cross over between the circuits of recruitment and the social lives of migrants. The Catholic centres which take charge of recruitment also tend to try and exercise a control over the free time of migrant women, and stigmatise any social activity which is not connected to the parish. Moreover, the interviews show that in Genoa some of these centres consider it as an explicit goal to help the integration of migrants through the training of 'ethnic leaders' who are closely linked to religious institutions.

The research also shows the different ways in which training provided to migrant domestic workers attempts to suggest to migrants strategies and codes of presentation in relation to their Italian employers. Through the acting out of possible physical and discursive interactions between the domestic workers and their employers, models of conduct that immigrants should adopt in relation to Italians are proposed. These models are all based on the value of deference. The idea that deference and social invisibility are necessary characteristics of immigrants' conduct is based on an articulation between culture, nature and morality. Immigrant women are exhorted to maintain their cultural authenticity and moral integrity. The success of the migratory project as a project of social mobility, depends in this vision on the capacity of women to preserve their 'culture of origin'. Immigration poses a problem because there is always a risk that it will lead to criminality (for men) and to prostitution (for women). Training courses for migrant domestic workers thus tend to impose invisibility as a condition of normal life, because it is believed that it is only through this invisibility that successful integration can take place.

It is necessary to underline that this model of local management of immigration corresponds to a more general informal policy on the regulation of entry into Italy which seems to have been put in place by the Italian Ministry of the Interior. Since the end of the 1980s, Catholic immigrants into Italy have outnumbered those from Arab and Muslim countries. The immigration of young people outside of these Catholic networks has been discouraged. Research has shown the existence of an informal system of selection which rests on missionaries and on parishes, and which favours the entry and the regularisation of women coming from Catholic countries (Palidda, 2001). In Genoa, from the mid-90s onwards there was the start of migration from South America, first from Peru and then from Ecuador. This migrations profoundly changed the local context. The migrants who came from these countries were mainly women, and their numbers increased rapidly, based on personal contacts which built up 'migratory chains'.

The women also used the means of family reunification, despite the limitations imposed on this method of entry, to bring in husbands and family members. Within a few years, Ecuadorian women became the largest migrant group in Genoa. The crisis in the Ecuadorian economy which wiped out middle-class incomes, the relative facility of obtaining a tourist visa for Italy, and the availability of informal, black market, domestic work, all favoured their arrival.

The Genoese case shows the ways in which a moralising account of the relationship between employer and employee is reinforced when the employee is a migrant. The demand made on the domestic worker for social invisibility is reinforced by the lack of legitimacy of the foreigner in the midst of the national society. Women migrants are often represented in the media, in political discourse, but also in the associational movement, in a moralising light. Their presence in society is conceptualised through a gratitude due to them for their function as replacements for Italian women in the role of social re-production, and through the need that Italian women have for their work. Andall (2000) argues that in Italy those associations which make reference to the women's movement, as well as those associations of Catholic inspiration, have in fact ended up obscuring the real demands and problems of migrants by emphasizing the needs of Italian women (the need for domestic help, the lack of public services). The needs of Italians are thus recognised rather than those of foreign domestic workers. In order to analyse the situation of migrant domestic workers, it is also necessary to understand what symbolic resources may be mobilized by these women in defence of their rights. As argued above, the rhetoric concerning the needs of Italian families for domestic workers has for a long time constituted the frame of reference for any defence of the rights of migrant domestic workers. However, this situation may be in the process of changing. In Milan recently migrant women demonstrated against the Bossi-Fini law which had just been passed by Parliament. Their banners read: 'This time we won't pick up the pieces, we won't be docile, we won't take care of Bossi-Fini'.[3]

The fact that in Italy the previous law on immigration was associated with a regularisation of illegal immigrants concerning only those working as assistants to old people is significant. Italy has one of the eldest populations in Europe and the Italian welfare state is particularly insufficient so far as services to old people are concerned. This regularisation of care workers for the elderly showed that the government is aware of the need for migrant workers in such work of re-production, and that this type of regularisation does not enter into conflict with the fundamentally restrictive direction of the immigration laws. In fact this type of regularisation concerns only a limited number of workers, and the associated bureaucratic procedures for obtaining a regularisation have been increased and made more difficult. The limiting of the possibilities for family reunification and the fact that the granting of a residency permit is even more closely linked to the existence of a work contract whilst the offers of regular employment are few, means that there can only be a resulting increase in the number of irregular or

---

[3] Demonstration 14 June 2002.

illegal immigrants and workers, and that migrant domestic workers will become even more dependent upon their employers.

The Domestic Citizenship of Migrants

European integration has resulted in an increasing importance for national citizenship in terms of access to social rights, and it can be argued that the notion of post-national citizenship still has little real value in the political arena. Even the citizenship status of long term migrants who have access to social rights is reduced by the fact that they are still denied political rights. And these migrants who are long term residents have also found their citizenship status brought into question by the increasingly restrictive immigration policies which have made the status of all migrants more precarious. Social inclusion is more and more based upon the fact of obtaining a stable and legal employment, whilst at the same time the availability of this type of job is limited for migrants, and there are many more offers of illegal or informal work. The construction of European citizenship thus implies a proliferation of new divisions and a new stratification of social and political rights, with gender being one of the criteria upon which this stratification is based.

Parrenas (2000) discusses the 'international transfer of caretaking work' with reference to the chain which connects gender inequalities in the North and South. She describes the way in which women from the North who work outside of the home employ migrant women to take care of the domestic tasks in their place. These migrant women in turn, pay poor women in their own countries who do not have the financial resources to migrate, to take care of their own domestic labour. Different national policies, such as the development of a market in personal and domestic services which is presented as a means of normalisation of domestic service and of fighting illegal work; the cyclical regularisation of migrant workers involved in the work of re-production; and the use of quotas to ensure a sufficient workforce in the domestic service sector, are all policies which cannot be disassociated from the intensification of controls on migration and attempts of States to produce adjustments faced with the decline of welfare state systems. The totality of all of these types of evolution may lead us to talk about a 'new domesticity' which is the result of the development of a global market in the work of re-production.

Within this global market for domestic labour, migrant domestic workers seem to be caught in an impasse. On the one hand they are faced with the increasing segmentation and ethnicisation of the labour market, and the extension of the informal sector, which are very partially compensated by periodic regularisations, as in Italy. On the other hand they are confronted with the proliferation of insecure and devalued jobs in personal services. These jobs may be partially regulated by the law where paid domestic work has been in part normalised, as in France. The European Union has adopted as a model for the regularisation and control of paid domestic work the policies which France put in place in the 1990s. These policies consist primarily of fiscal controls of domestic work through employers' contributions. The major goal of the reforms carried out in France was to professionalize the domestic service sector at all cost. The results of this drive have been limited, however, and there are still a large number of migrant women working illegally and undeclared in the sector. As for Italy, available statistics indicate that there are 1 200 000 domestic workers currently employed and that of these 70 per cent are women and 50 per cent are migrants. Only 200 000 of the total are legally employed with a contract of employment (INPS, 1998). Evidently, in France and in Italy, as in all other European countries, it is almost impossible to measure the true scale of illegal employment in this sector. It is well known, however, that many migrants work as live in domestic helpers, who rarely leave the houses of their employers. There are also many cases of exploitation, violence and sexual harassment against migrant domestic workers – especially those with no legal residence papers – but these type of cases have a very low public visibility in Italy. Often the employer will obtain sexual favours from a domestic worker not through direct physical threats or violence but through forms of exchange which push the victims into giving such favours in return for the promise of a work permit, for example. Although it is technically possible under the law for any victim of exploitation to obtain a residence permit if they testify against their employer, in practice this applies only to those who have been involved in trafficking and working in prostitution (Fondazione Internationale Lelio Basso, 2001).

In these conditions, the representations of the positive value of the domestic work of women migrants are shown to be purely rhetorical. Domestic work undertaken under these type of conditions cannot contribute to any re-assessment of social relationships and identities, beyond that of reinforcing relationships of inequality between 'citizens' and 'migrants'. In this sense, rather than talking about new forms of 'domesticity', it might be more accurate to talk about new forms of 'servility' (Ongaro, 2001). In this sense, it may be interesting to undertake a historical analysis of the transformations in paid domestic labour, and to compare the construction and representations of paid domestic work in an era when it was carried out mainly by local women from the lower classes, to the current period when it is carried out generally by migrant women. It seems that paid domestic work is even less valued than it was in the past: not women's work, but migrants' work (Piette, 2000).

Conclusion

A study of globalised domestic work raises questions relating to the function of migrants' labour in a post-industrial economy, to the process of ethnicisation of the labour market, and to the transformations taking place in gender relations in European societies. A reflection on the discourse used in the most recent Italian law on immigration can bring some insight into these subjects. The Bossi-Fini law introduced a new term into the language on migrant workers. Those migrant workers given the task of looking after old people were defined as *badanti*. The word *badante* means literally someone who looks after something in a very minimal sense. The verb *badare* may well be used, for example, to describe the activity of keeping an eye on something which is cooking. It is odd to use such a minimalist description of the work of those who are caring for dependent people. It might be argued that the Bossi-Fini law is in fact denying the important role played by migrant domestic workers, a role which has previously constituted the justification for the presence of these migrants in Italy. What is taking place is thus a certain transformation in the normative definition of the role of migrants domestic workers in Italian society. It seems that the government is no longer prepared to recgonise that immigrant domestic workers constitute a pillar without which the ageing society could not function, nor could the Italian family remain as it is today. The invention and use of the term *badanti* to define migrant domestic workers sweeps away the sentimental and moralistic representations which have surrounded these workers and reveals the xenophobic essence of Right-wing policies on immigration. The clear message aimed at both migrant workers themselves and the voters of the Northern League is the following: the government is obliged to regularise a few thousand migrant workers, but these will be strictly controlled. As far as the status accorded to migrant domestic workers is concerned it seems that the instrumental and racist views of the Right-wing coalition have prevailed over the more universalist vision which characterized sections of Italian Catholic thought. When migrant domestic workers are needed they are treated as indispensable replacements for Italian mothers and housewives. When it is a question of recognising the rights of migrant domestic workers, even only the limited rights of granting them a residence permit and a work contract, they are reminded that they are only very poor substitute for Italian women and that Italian society is doing them a great favour by allowing them in.

References

Andall, J. (2000), *Gender, Migration and Domestic Service: The Politics of Black Women in Italy.* Aldershot: Ashgate.

Anderson, B. (2000), *Doing the Dirty Work? The Global Politics of Domestic Labour.* London: Zed.

Bisilliat, J. (1996), *Femmes du Sud, chefs de famille.* Paris: Karthala.

Boltanski, L. and Chiappello, E. (1999), *Le nouvel esprit du capitalisme.* Paris: Gallimard.

Bribosia, E. and Rea, A. (2002), *Les nouvelles migrations. Un enjeu européen.* Paris: Editions Complexes.

Castles, S. and Miller, M. (1998), *The Age of Migration.* Basingstoke: Macmillan.

Chabaud-Rychter, D. et al. (1985), *Espace et temps du travail domestique.* Paris: Meridiens.

Dal Lago, A. (1999), *Non-persone. L'esclusione die migranti in una società globale.* Milan: Feltrinelli.

Fondazione Internationale Lelio Basso (2000), *Il lavoro domestico in Italia e le forme di sfruttamento parachiavistico*, research report.

INPS (1998), *Istituto Nazionale della Previdenza Sociale*, Statistics for 1997.

INSEE (2000), *Les services aux enterprises en Ile-de-France.*

King, R. and Zontini, E. (2000), The role of gender in the South European immigration model, *Papers*, 60, pp. 3- 34.

Marie, C-V. (1999), Emploi des étrangers sans titre, travail illegal, regularisation: des débats en trompe-l'oeil, in P. Dewitte (ed), *Immigration et integration, l'état des savoirs.* Paris: La Découverte.

Morice, A. (1997), Quand la lutte contre l'emploi illegal cache les progress de la précarité légale, in D. Fassin et al (eds), *Les lois de l'inhospitalité: Les politiques de l'immigration à l'épreuve des sans-papiers.* Paris: La Découverte.

Mozère, L. (2001a), Petits metiers urbains au feminine ou comment échapper à la précarisation? Research Report. Université de Rouen: GRIS.

Mozère, L. (2001b), La Philippine ou la Mercédès-Benz des domestiques. Entre archaïsme et mondialisation. *Sextant,* 15 – 16, pp. 12-31.

Ongaro, S. (2001), *Le donne e la globalizzazione. Domande di genere all'economica globale della ri-produzione.* Soneria: Rubettino Editore.

Oso, L. (2000), L'immigration en Espagne des femmes chefs de famille, *Cahiers du Cedref,* 8-9, pp. 25 – 52.

Palidda, S. (2001), *Migrazioni: tra vecchi e nuovi pardigmi.* Unpublished research report.

Palidda, S. and Dal Lago, A. (2002), L'immigration et la politique d'immigration en Italie, in E. Bribosia and A. Réa (eds), *Les nouvelles migrations. Un enjeu européen.* Paris: Editions Complexes.

Parrenas, R. S. (2000), Migrant Filipina domestic workers and the international division of reproductive labour, *Gender and Society,* 14, 4, pp. 36-48.

Pessar, P. (1999), The role of gender, households and social networks in the migration process: a review and appraisal, in C. Hirschman et al. (eds), *The Handbook of International Migration.* New York: Russell Sage Foundation.

Piette, V. (2000), *Domestiques et servants: Des vies sous condition.* Bruxelles: Académie royale de Belgique.

Quadrelli, E. (1999), Rapporto di ricerca sulla devianza e la criminalità nel territorio genovese. Università di Genova.

Sassen, S. (1996), *La Ville Globale.* Paris: Descartes & Cie.

Sassen, S. (2000), Women's burden: Counter-geographies of globalisation and the feminization of survival. *Journal of International Affairs,* 53, 2, pp. 503-524.

Sassen, S. (2002), La métropole: site stratégique et nouvelle frontière, *Cultures et Conflits,* 33-34, pp. 76 – 98.

Scrinzi, F. (2001), Consumi cul.turali. I processi di etnicizzazione delle donne marocchine a Genova, in A. Torre (ed), *Non sono venuta a scoprire le scarpe. Voci di donne immigrate in Liguria.* Cuneo: Edizioni Sensibili alle foglie.

Terray, E. (1999), Le travail des étrangers en situation irrégulière ou la delocalisation sur place, in E. Balibar (ed), *Sans-papiers: l'archaïsme fatal.* Paris: La Découverte.

Chapter 6

The Integration of Immigrant Women into the Spanish Labour Market

Colectivo Ioé[1]

Introduction

This chapter presents some results of the research conducted by Colectivo Ioé on the integration of migrant women from the 'third world' in Spain into society and employment (Colectivo Ioé, 2001).

At times, although we do not intend to, we can be led to consider the integration of immigrants into society and employment from a nationalist and standard point of view. The starting point that we are adopting in this article is quite different. On the one hand, we understand that integration into society and employment will always be plural and, on the other hand, that this plurality involves many people, who are affected by it. Not only does it define the boundaries between natives and immigrants, but in each case it unveils a wide range of personal and social aspects that it affects. Our aim is to encourage our readers to be open to this subject and, above all, to continue thinking about the various views involved, as it is easy to move from one topic to the next without a break, in other words, from a negative view of immigration to a positive one without even thinking about it.

Forms of Economic Exchange Beyond the Paradigm of the Market

If we wish to explore the ways that immigrants are integrated into employment in Spain and its complex social and human reality, we find that, on the one hand, official statistics are partially hidden and, on the other hand that it is often the subject of clichés and simplifications that influence public opinion.

To start with, employment statistics do no adequately reflect the presence of workers from third world countries. Work permit figures only refer to non-Community workers who are assigned to the General System for Foreigners (they

[1]Colectivo Ioé is a sociological research team specialised in migration and the labour market. It is made up of the sociologists Carlos Pereda, Walter Actis and Miguel Ángel de Prada. Information: e-mail: ioe@nodo50.org and www.nodo50.org/ioe/; tel. 915310123. C. Luna, 11, 1° Dcha. 28004 Madrid, Spain.

exclude illegal workers and also those under the Community System); the figures for the Working Population Survey refer, in principle, both to the employed and the unemployed, regardless of their administrative situation, but its coverage is clearly inadequate, and finally, the Social Security figures of people entering work do not include illegal workers or those who are naturalised or unemployed. However, most importantly, employment that is paid in money is only part of the work done by immigrants, especially women, which is also through reciprocal exchange, redistributing all sorts of goods and services within the home and the community. These forms of exchange, like commercial exchange, do not take place in a neutral context between free and autonomous individuals, as is the intention of the neo-classical economy, but rather they are predetermined by the existing power relationship between social groups, which are marked out by particular differences which give them their social identity and place them in their respective positions.

Adhering to the proposals of a theoretical trend that is critical of mercantilism, which reduces work to paid employment, we have tried to explore the various forms of productive activity of immigrant women based on three types of economic exchange:

Reciprocal relationships: exchange of work or its products (goods or services) between private individuals, which does not involve money but is based on a feeling (real or assumed) of cooperation, belonging or participation in a common project or one that benefits those involved. The main form of reciprocity in current society is domestic work, which includes all those tasks that members of a household carry out in the home or in its immediate context in order to satisfy their own needs; more hours go into this type of activity than into paid work, and it is mostly women who do it. Secondly, reciprocal exchange also takes place in non-paid jobs that are done outside the home between relations, neighbours or friends, shared interests, etc.; this type of activity, as we will see, features strongly among immigrant women.

Commercial relationships: exchange of work between private individuals involving money (or agreed exchange of goods and services of a determined value). This is the most valued form of work, and the only one recognised by national accounting, employment law and, in general, by public opinion. The most frequent method is the capitalist company although there are also other forms of independent or collective employment structure. In the domestic sphere there are three types of commercial employment: domestic employment, which involves the same tasks as 'domestic work', but on the basis of a salary relationship between members of the family and external employees (this is the most common occupation of immigrant women from the third world); working at home, in which the members of the household, sometimes along with people from outside, do work that they later sell on the market (this was the predominant form of work in Europe until the 18th century but has since been in decline), and home-help services, either public or private, or more frequently semi-public through agreements between the local administration and non-governmental companies or organisations.

Redistributive relationships: exchange of work, whether or not it involves money, between public agents, i.e., involving exercising citizenship, in order to administrate power and manage economic and social policy. This work may be carried out by the public sector or through the participation of citizens in voluntary, political and union organisations, etc., which aim to influence the general structure of social institutions.

Levels of Reciprocal Exchange

In general, paid work by immigrant women refers in the majority of cases to another area of production, the home or domestic economy, to which they contribute with their dedication and affection, by contributing their salary and/or in the form of money sent to relatives that are still in their country of origin. In reality the subjects of emigration are not individuals but family groups, whose needs and expectations are behind the decision both to emigrate and to undertake commercial employment.

Migratory Chains

Family links are particularly strong between spouses and towards children (particularly if they are minors). According to surveys, more than two thirds of workers from the third world are married and 59 per cent have children;[2] a considerable number of single women also have children, especially Dominican women (more than 60 per cent), which frequently results in single parent families in which the mother is the only head of the family. Emigration itself causes a serious split in family life, when it separates wives from their husbands (which is the case for 33 per cent of the women who are married) and mothers from their children (38 per cent of those with children). These situations, which mainly concern women who have been living in Spain for a shorter period, and in general live-in domestic workers, result in a dual displacement: first of all, the maternal function is passed on to other family members (spouse, grandparents, aunts and uncles, older children, etc.), who take on that role as part of family reciprocity, or an external domestic employee is taken on (undoubtedly with a much lower salary than that earned in Spain); secondly, the separation of spouses will probably mean that their emotional and sexual needs will not be satisfied, which may be compensated for by establishing new relationships (and the eventual separation of the previous couple) or by using commercial services, etc.

   The separation of spouses and of mothers and children 'frees' immigrant women from part of the domestic work that was assigned to them; which explains why their commercial working days are longer (an average of 46 hours per week)

---

[2] The data on female migrant workers from the third world was obtained from five surveys conducted by Colectivo Ioé in 2000 in the following employment sectors: domestic service, hotel and catering, cleaning companies, offices and freelance workers (aggregate sample of 1 579 cases).

than their native peers (28 hours per week),[3] as they spend half the amount of time on domestic tasks in their own home (10 hours/week compared with 19 hours/week among Spanish women). What happens is that a large proportion of the domestic work of immigrant women is done by their relations in their country of origin, without whose contribution the emigration of women would not have been possible. In return, the female immigrant workers provide a substantial proportion of the family income in the country of origin. 23 per cent of their total salary is sent home, with an average of 24 600 pesetas/month in the second quarter of 2000 (higher than the average salary in the majority of the originating countries), and this figure increases according to the number of relatives remaining in the country of origin. Dominican women, for example, have the most children in their country of origin and, as a result, send the largest percentage of their income home.

Family and friendship networks are also behind the decision to emigrate, insofar as they inform, encourage and fund the initial trip. Later, when the migrant arrives in Spain, they help the person who has recently arrived to obtain accommodation and employment, or to keep afloat during the critical periods that tend to arise. The results of the surveys fully confirm that, for all of these functions, work carried out through reciprocal exchange between relations, compatriots and friends is the most decisive factor in the integration of migrant women into society and employment. In 54 per cent of cases their first trip to Spain was funded by family savings, including on occasions the sale of property; also, many of those who had to take out loans (43 per cent) did so by mortgaging family property, as a guarantee that the money borrowed would be paid back. Over time, the migrant women become a bridgehead for further influxes of migration, enabling other relations, neighbours and friends to come to their country. For example, 80 per cent of foreign women who work in domestic service say that they have encouraged or enabled others from their family to travel to Spain. In this way, although others play a part in migration networks (such as those who loan money and travel agencies, whether legal or illegal), the main and decisive driving force behind travel is the family itself and its capacity to invest in order to improve the standard of living of all of its members in the medium and long term.

New Family Structures

Once they have settled in Spain, immigrant women also find their main support in family and friendship networks within their community. Aside from those who 'live in' at their employers' homes, it is usual for the women to live with people from the same country that they have some knowledge of, either family members or not, the latter giving rise to households made up of compatriots that are not related to each other but play the role of substitute families (this is the situation of 11 per cent of the women that we surveyed, along with 14 per cent who live with relatives and other compatriots). In the households in which there are few or no

---

[3] The data on native workers is based on surveys conducted in parallel with those on immigrants in four employment sectors (domestic service, cleaning, hotel and catering and offices). The aggregate sample of Spanish workers is 934 cases.

family ties (beyond relationships with spouses or children), it is likely that the reciprocal exchange will become commercial, ranging from contributing to the cost of staying in the house to paying outrageous rents, even above the usual market prices for the area (taking advantage of the ignorance of the newly arrived woman). In these cases, the (supposed) reciprocity can be used as a tactic or ploy to attract more profitable clients.

In the majority of cases the splitting of family nuclei is forced upon them (survival (for survival and/or to improve the material living conditions of the whole family) and is not an option freely chosen by those concerned. The most extreme situation is in the sector of live-in domestic employees, for whom fulfilling the financial objective of emigration means reducing almost their entire life (reciprocal and redistributive exchange, and leisure time) into the space of (commercial) work: 'life' is elsewhere, weekends, holidays, retirement.

The amount of time that the community has been established in Spain only partly accounts for the consolidation of families in the country of immigration (homes in which all the members are related). This is the case of Moroccan and Argentinean women, a large number of whom have managed to regroup their families or create a new family (sometimes with a Spanish spouse), unlike other more recent immigrants, such as Ecuadorian or Colombian women, who tend to share their homes with compatriots who are not from their family. However, there are other long-established communities, such as Filipino, Dominican and Chinese, who hold on more firmly to the expectation of returning to their country and therefore are more resistant to family regrouping in Spain.

The majority of female immigrant workers who are married are married to someone of their own nationality, although there are 15 per cent of mixed couples in which the husband is Spanish. The endogamy is most pronounced among Chinese and Ecuadorian communities (less than 2 per cent with a Spanish partner). The case of Ecuadorian women is explained by the fact that the group has only recently arrived in Spain, as in the first few phases of migration the predominant links are among the migrant population and there are few with the rest of society; however, the cases of Chinese women could be attributed more to the fact that they belong to a different cultural and religious world, which is reinforced by the fact that they specialise in a particular niche of employment (restaurants and shops within their ethnic economy, although they do have the opportunity to meet Spanish customers). At the opposite end of the scale, the longest standing Latin American communities (Argentinean, Chilean, Dominican and Peruvian) and other more recently established communities (Colombian and Cuban) have above-average percentages, as their cultural proximity to Spain results in mixed couples (unless the relationship began in the country of origin as the result of a Spanish man visiting that country). Among Moroccan women there is very pronounced endogamy among those who work in domestic service (2 per cent mixed couples) while there are 50 per cent mixed marriages in the office sector. The latter proportion is explained by the fact that in this employment sector there is a high number of second generation young people who have grown up in Spanish society and gained their qualifications for work in Spain.

Social Relations with Compatriots and Friends

In their free time, immigrant women mainly interact with compatriots from their country of origin (52 per cent), which confirms the importance of networks within each community. Mono-ethnic links are most common among domestic service workers and surpass 65 per cent among women from the Chinese and Filipino communities, while Dominican, Ecuadorian and Moroccan women are close to that figure. The relationship is particularly strong with people from the same town or region (in one third of cases, and more than half among Dominican women), while the majority interact with compatriots from any of the different regions in their country. The tendency to interact with people of the same origin, which is typical in some communities that are relatively long-established in Spain, such as the Chinese and Filipino communities (to a lesser extent the Dominican and Moroccan communities), seems to point to a segmented model of integration according to which those groups prefer not to dilute themselves through open relationships with the other communities as a strategy for maintaining their own culture and capitalising on work skills and resources that are more valued in relationships within their own community (contacts, doing the shopping or caring for the children, sharing a flat, etc.). Out of all immigrant women, 37 per cent interact equally with compatriots and Spanish friends, which is the turning point towards a third group, which mainly interacts with people from the majority population. Finally, a smaller sector of domestic service workers say that they do not interact with anyone (13 per cent of Peruvians, 9 per cent of Ecuadorians, 7 per cent of Moroccans); this situation is largely among live-in employees.

The main places for meeting up with friends are, for 75 per cent of immigrant women, private homes; the domestic sphere stands out as a hub of relationships, not only with close family but with friends in general. Next come bars, cafés and discotheques and public areas (such as gardens and squares) that are used by 41 per cent and 30 per cent of female immigrants respectively; public areas are preferred by women working in domestic service and cleaning, bars and cafés by administrative workers and freelance workers, and discotheques by hotel and catering workers. Much lower come churches or mosques (17 per cent) and immigrants associations (10 per cent). In all of these locations reciprocal exchange relationships predominate.

Seeking employment is another activity in which family members, friends and acquaintances play a decisive role: two out of every three working women (almost 100 per cent in the case of Chinese women) say that this is their main route for integration into the labour market, far ahead of other methods such as adverts in the press or public (INEM – National Employment Office) or private job shops (immigrant associations, NGOs, religious organisations, etc.). Here the active role played by employers of female domestic service workers should be highlighted, who have 'placed' 12 per cent in their friends' homes. This is the case of a dually mutual exchange, although it involves people linked by a commercial relationship: the domestic employee does a favour for a compatriot and the employee for a Spanish friend.

The majority of immigrant women (86 per cent) say that they have not had serious disputes with their employers in the various posts occupied. If we only look at those who have had disputes, the two mains sources of support have come through reciprocal exchange: family members and friends (44 per cent) and work colleagues (28 per cent). Much further behind comes commercial (private advice) or redistributive support (unions and support associations). Along the same lines, up to 86 per cent of the women surveyed say that during their time in Spain they have experienced periods of financial difficulty (no work or no money). In such situations, their main source of help was once again family and friends (65 per cent), will other redistributive support comes far behind (the main source was the respective churches – parishes or mosques – in 6 per cent of cases). It should be pointed out that 11 per cent of immigrant women did not receive any support during those periods, which in many cases did not prevent them from overcoming the problem.

Participation in the Monetary Economy

In absolute numbers women from the third world with paid employment are a small group, 70 000 contributors to social security in 2000, although the trend is towards growth, as two thirds of them began to contribute during the last three years. This figure should be extended to include categories of workers not registered by that source: those who are naturalised, who are counted as Spanish (around 30 000), and the illegal or non-contributing workers (which at the beginning of 2000 we estimated at a minimum of 75 000 people). Among hidden workers the two largest sectors are women who alternate between temporary or casual employment with varying periods of unemployment[4] and those who work in the so-called 'sex industry', the numbers of which are unknown but undoubtedly high in the light of the information available. Taking into account that according to the LFS there were 5.3 million 'employed' women in Spain in the second quarter of 2000, the 175 000 immigrant women in paid employment from the third world represented 3.3 per cent of female employment in Spain at that time. If the comparison is made with 'working' Spanish women (6.7 million) the proportion of immigrants drops to 2.6 per cent.

Given the limitations of the official statistics, we decided to conduct monographic studies of the main employment sectors. In order to do this we selected the five sectors which, according to the most reliable source in terms of the formal economy (statistics for people joining social security) provide employment for 81 per cent of immigrant women from the third world. We also

---

[4] In the five occupations that were the subject of monographic studies alone we detected 33 000 illegal female workers, to which should be added those who were unemployed at that time, as well as illegal workers and the unemployed of other professions. The reason for including the short-term unemployed in the general calculation of women in unstable employment is that from the point of view of a changing labour market, both groups refer to the same people.

conducted an initial examination of another group of immigrant workers, those employed in sexual services, which are entirely absent from the statistics but which represent a volume of employment only exceeded by domestic employees.

Main Occupations of Immigrant Women in the Formal Economy

According to the statistics for joining social security, the five main occupations provide employment for 81 per cent of women from the third world. As can be seen from the Table, those five occupations only provide work for 33 per cent of immigrant men from the 'third world', 67 per cent of women from the 'first world' and 52 per cent of the total number of women working in Spain. This already represents a threefold specialisation of women from the third world: when women are compared to men (immigrants or natives); when immigrants are compared to Spanish or native citizens; and when women from the third world are compared to those from developed countries.

Out of the five segments selected, domestic service particularly stands out, providing employment for just over half of the non-Community women who contribute to social security, and for the majority of them is clearly the 'gateway' to the Spanish labour market. This circumstance justifies the need to look in greater detail at the operation of this branch of employment in order to find out what role immigrant women from the third world are playing in it, as well as men of the same origin, the proportion of which (14.3 per cent) compared to the total number of men employed in the sector is higher than that represented by the women (10.4 per cent) in proportion to the whole of their gender.

The four other occupational sectors provide employment for 28 per cent of women from the third world. In the case of cleaning companies and the hotel and catering trade, it again stands out that there is a greater specialisation of men, the proportion of which in the corresponding gender sector is almost three times higher in cleaning (8.8 per cent compared with 3.5 per cent for women) and almost double in hotel and catering (2.5 per cent compared to 1.6 per cent). However, it should not be forgotten that although in the whole of Spain domestic service, cleaning and hotel and catering are clearly female-oriented occupations (they employ 18.4 per cent of women and only 6.7 per cent of men), that difference is accentuated in the case of immigrants from the third world of both sexes. Along with gender specialisation there is discrimination due to ethnic or national origin, although that should be qualified in that it has a negative effect on those from the third world and a positive effect on those from the first world.

Out of the five occupations given, the three that are greatest in the corresponding labour markets are in the services sector: domestic employees, cleaners and hotel and restaurant staff (10.4 per cent, 1.7 per cent and 1.6 per cent, respectively of the whole female working population in Spain in these areas).[5] Below are two cross sections of female workers which are present in all the

---

[5] We used the LFS in this case and not social security registration, as a general reference, as it is a more faithful representation of the true scope of the Spanish labour market, including many illegal workers (especially in the case of domestic service).

branches of employment: those who are self-employed[6] and administrative workers; these two occupations have greater professional status and although the number of immigrant women from the third world working in them is significant, the proportion is low in the corresponding occupational sectors (0.5 per cent in each case, far below the average of 1.3 per cent). We therefore see an overspecialisation of immigrant women from the third world in three branches of low-qualified services from a professional point of view; 68 per cent of the group is in that category (i.e., nearly four times more than working women in general, which represent 18 per cent in these three branches). The proportion of foreign women from the first world doing these jobs is even lower than that of Spanish working women. However, those women from developed countries are highly specialised in the two qualified occupations in our selection (self-employed and office work) to the extent that more than half of them work in those occupations (compared with only 13 per cent of women from the third world and 33 per cent of the total working women in Spain).

Hidden Employment for Female Immigrant Workers

Naturalised and illegal workers. A realistic approximation of the employment situation of women from the third world should take into account, as well as those who are registered, at least two other types of workers that are not included in the official classifications: naturalised workers (who feature as Spanish for administrative purposes) and illegal workers. The first case involves immigrant women who, usually following several years of residence, have obtained Spanish nationality; the second case involves those who for various reasons (not having a residence or work permit, refusal of the employer to register them, lack of interest from the employee, etc.) do not contribute to social security as workers. In the surveys that we conducted, these two sectors represented varying proportions depending on each occupation.

Women from third world countries that are registered as foreigners with social security in the five occupations selected (55 857 contributors) represent less than half of those who are actually working in those markets, according to our estimates (112 743). Those who are naturalised represent 22 per cent of the group and illegal workers represent 29 per cent. The proportion of naturalised workers increases for high status occupations (self-employed and office) and decreases in the lower-qualified services (especially cleaning and domestic service). For illegal workers, the highest rates are among domestic workers (32.5 per cent) and the self-employed (28.7 per cent), in this case due to the high frequency of 'family helps' who do not contribute to social security because they consider themselves to be covered by a close relative (spouse, parent, etc.).

Due to the inclusion of the new categories (naturalised and illegal workers) the overall proportion of immigrant women from the third world in the five sectors is 4 per cent, which is greater in domestic service (20.6 per cent),

---

[6] We excluded from this group domestic workers who are 'self-employed', which we classified in the same sector as domestic workers who are employed.

considerably lower in the other branches of services (2.9 per cent and 2.8 per cent in cleaning and hotel and catering) and much lower in higher-status occupations (1.2 per cent in offices and 1.3 per cent in self-employed). These proportions are reversed in the case of immigrant women from the first world, who are scarcely present in domestic service and cleaning companies. Overall, foreign women working in Spain in the five sectors examined (without considering naturalised and illegal workers from the first world) amount to more than 145 000, which represents 5.3 per cent of women workers in those sectors.

Marginal markets, jobseekers and non-commercial work: The case of sexual services. As well as the occupations recorded in the official statistics there are others that are marginalized, if not illegal, which have no social or legal protection, although they are capable of providing 'financial success'. These activities, despite their significance, do not tend to receive the necessary attention, even from researchers. We should also take into account those women who are unemployed in commercial terms and therefore do not appear as workers in the statistics and estimates of the working population.

One of the marginal occupations par excellence is sexual services, in their various forms, which were also considered in the study. The association between immigrant women and prostitution is one loaded with ideological and moral stigmas which have so far made it difficult to deal in a calm and detailed manner with its magnitude and implications. The phenomenon is seen almost exclusively through the media consequences of police action (especially cracking networks of traffickers of women), which generate scandal among the public and reinforce the stigmatisation of women working providing sexual services. The result is a simplistic label, which sees one part as representing the whole and prevents us from having a balanced knowledge of the sector. However, in other countries there are studies that demonstrate the financial significance of the 'sex industry' and, in particular, of the presence in that industry of migrant men and women. In order to not once again deny or forget the existence of those people, we wish to present an initial, exploratory analysis of this employment sector, although the results that we arrive at cannot be compared with those of the other sectors studied. We do not have accurate figures on women working in sexual services, however, from the partial information supplied by various studies[7] it can be deduced that the proportion of female immigrants from third world countries in that labour market is much higher than in any of the other occupations, perhaps with the exception of domestic service.

---

[7] According to a study conducted by the Civil Guard (2000) 90.8 per cent of prostitutes registered in street clubs in rural areas were foreigners, mainly from the third world. The Spanish partner in a survey conducted by Tampep (2000), Médicos del Mundo, estimated that the proportion of foreigners was 50 per cent, but only in street prostitution in Madrid. In Castilla y León, a survey found 41.5 per cent foreigners (which in the sub-sample of clubs was 85.5 per cent). A study conducted in the South of Galicia (1996) calculated the percentage of foreign prostitutes at 80 per cent (12 per cent Portuguese). Finally, an older survey (1992), conducted in Asturias, recorded 22 per cent foreign women.

Another group of immigrant women that is barely known about which should be added to those covered so far is unemployed women seeking work. The position of the most subordinated sectors of the labour market is characterised, among other things, by higher rates of unemployment. Across the whole Spanish female working population the rate of female unemployment is much higher than that of men. In the case of immigration, so far only the LFS (which has considerable gaps in coverage) provides unemployment figures for foreign workers: in 1998 the rate of unemployment among foreign female workers was 25.3 per cent, double that of male immigrants (12.1 per cent[8]). Our aim was to access the registers of the National Employment Institute in order to find out about the progress and characteristics of foreign women seeking work and those receiving benefits, but the negotiations were unsuccessful. Therefore, this is an important area which needs to be researched.

Lack of Redistributive Exchange

Redistributive exchanges, in the case of immigrant women from the third world in paid employment, can be considered from two points of view: as individuals in the economy, they contribute money (through taxes and social security contributions) and receive benefits and services from the Spanish public sector, but also contribute, through sending money, to sustaining the economies and balances of payments of their countries of origin; as political individuals, they have a specific place in the institutions and power practices of Spanish society.

Contributing More than They Receive

Female immigrant workers contribute a considerable amount to the public treasury through their social security contributions and direct taxes (I.R.P.F. – personal income tax) and indirect taxes (when they buy products on the market). Based on our surveys we can estimate that salaried immigrant women contributing to social security contribute nearly 21 000 million pesetas per year to the public coffers, broken down as follows: 10 500 million from domestic employees; 1 500 million from cleaners; 3 600 million from hotel and catering workers; and 5 200 million from administrative workers. Due to its greater level of complexity, we cannot even estimate the amount received through personal income tax or indirect taxes, but altogether it is very probable that the contribution made by immigrant women in the four sectors examined is more than 30 000 million pesetas. To this figure we should add at least 2 200 million pesetas contributed by self-employed workers

---

[8] It appears that the situation particularly affects Moroccan women (50.7 per cent) and women from elsewhere in Africa (41.6 per cent). However, in terms of the difference between the sexes, there is more unemployment among women than among men among Moroccans and non-Community Europeans, while male unemployment appears to be higher in the other groups. See INE (National Statistics Institute), *EPA. Encuesta de Migraciones 1998*, Madrid, 1999.

who contribute to social security, and an unknown amount in other direct and indirect taxes, particularly corporation tax.

In terms of benefits from the public sector, immigrants and their families receive a set of general services including health and education. However, there are very few who have received specific benefits for unemployment (4 per cent, domestic employees do not have access to this benefit), subsidised housing (1.3 per cent), educational grants (9 per cent) or income support (1.3 per cent). Also, only 1 per cent say that they used the INEM to find work while 2.7 per cent used public institutions to resolve serious financial difficulties.

This balance of contributions and services contrasts with that of Spanish working women in the same employment sectors as the immigrants. Applying the same criteria to estimate the amount of contributions to social security, they add up to 16 000 million pesetas per year, 23 per cent less than that contributed by the foreign women. The difference arises from the majority sector of domestic service (-68 per cent) due to the fact that the majority of Spanish women do not contribute to social security; in the other three sectors, where the rate of registration of Spanish women is higher, they contribute more (+19 per cent in cleaning and hotel and catering, and +23 per cent in office work). However, regarding specific benefits, Spanish female workers have received more benefits in almost all areas (unemployment, subsidised housing, educational grants, mediation from INEM, etc.), with considerable fluctuations depending on nationality and the amount of time spend in Spain (Moroccan and Argentinean women, for example, have had greater access to these benefits).

From a macro-economic perspective we should also consider the contribution of immigrant women from the third world in terms of the use that they make of the net income from their work, which we estimate at around 185 000 million pesetas (1 110 million euros) for all of the five occupational sectors surveyed (not including the sex industry). This represents a modest but significant financial injection into the economy in terms of private consumption (92 000 million pesetas), savings (35 000 million, controlled by Spanish banks) and payment of debts (21 000 million, partly in the country of origin and the remainder in Spain). Also, they send 23 per cent of their income (36 400 million pesetas) to their country of origin. This distribution of expenditure, compared with that of female Spanish workers in the same occupational sectors, is characterised by a smaller proportion of consumer and credit expenditure (which is a form of advance consumption) and a greater proportion of savings and money sent home. Female immigrants from the third world therefore have a more austere day-to-day life in Spain (less immediate consumption) for the benefit of the general well-being of their families in their country of origin (money sent home) and as an investment for the future (savings).

Money sent home by immigrant women helps to alleviate international inequalities, inasmuch as it generates an increase in demand and investment in the countries of origin, for some of which it is one of the main sources of income. For example, in Ecuador income from money sent from emigrants (mainly in the United States and Spain) amounted to 1 100 million dollars in 1999, which in that year represented 8 per cent of the gross domestic product and was the second largest source of income for the balance of payments, after oil.

Apart from the five occupational sectors studied monographically, we do not have accurate information on the contribution made to the Spanish economy by the other sectors. Taking into account our general estimate of 175 000 women workers from the third world, the sum of net income must be more than 300 000 million pesetas per year (less than 1 per cent of the total of all salaries in Spain, 38.5 billion pesetas in 1998, according to Banco de España).

Immigrant Women as Political Individuals

The integration into the labour market of immigrant women and the economic role that they have in Spanish society is not adequately reflected in the recognition and exercise of their employment and citizenship rights. Without dwelling on the effect of fluctuations in migration policy over recent years, the analyses that we have conducted enable us to outline three considerations: first of all, the majority of female immigrants have suffered from and/or suffer from various limitations to exercising their employment and political rights on an equal footing with the rest of the population; secondly, among the natives who have most contact with them (employers and work colleagues) there are frequently discriminatory attitudes, speech and practices; thirdly, the foreign women themselves have a very low level of group structure and therefore, limited powers of negotiation in the employment and political spheres. However, there are also indications to the contrary, pointing to greater recognition of the rights of female immigrants, as workers and as citizens.

Immigration policy has had, at the very least, a twofold discriminatory effect on female immigrants: first of all due to its shortcomings, as there is not an active admissions policy facilitating legal employment from the outset; secondly due to excess as since 1993 it has established a limited quota of jobs, which are mostly precarious and female-oriented, according to the criterion of preference for national labour. The former increased illegal employment, which was already considerable in Spain; the latter caused domestic service to become the main and almost obligatory gateway for 63 per cent of non-Community foreign women. In the former case, illegal employment means a lack of employment rights and possible abuse in contracting and working conditions; in the latter case, domestic service could become a segregated and fragmented employment niche for many immigrant women, which they have entered into out of necessity and not by free choice, and which is difficult to get out of, (one in every five has managed to, but the vast majority stay in it, in spite of their aspirations). The limitations generated by state regulation are even more acute for the sector of women who work in the sex industry who simply stay outside of employment legislation.

Regarding the discriminatory speech and practices that we have detected among the native population towards foreign workers, the attitudes range from explicit rejection ('Well I see a loud black woman and I don't want to have her in my house') to implicit rejection, placed in the mouths of others ('I don't mind, but the children... or the elderly people... my parents, for example...') or the affirmation that generalised racism is the norm ('They are as racist as we are. There is racism in every culture'). Immigrant women are frequently stigmatised and seen as inferior, as potential social individuals: on the one hand by suspecting them questioning the patriarchal order (when they are freed from the social control of men), but also, paradoxically, when they are considered 'irresponsible' and as a result, victims of the actions of others. The result of this type of speech is that certain differences are compared, such as national origin and gender, the practical results of which are the creation of a hierarchy and exclusion – strong over weak.

Gender oppression has distant origins in the institution of patriarchy and recent origins in the recent change in male and female roles which brought capitalism with it, coinciding with the industrial revolution. The split between the public (political) and private (home) spheres and the allocation of the former to men, resulted in women being relegated to the pre-political sphere so that they were not considered as having full rights; the fight foe gender/sex equality occupied a large proportion of political debates in the 19th and 20th centuries. The recent entry of women into the public sphere across the board (both employment and politics) in so far as it is not combined with men working in the home or with the provision of sufficient redistributive services (crisis in the welfare state), is having different repercussions depending on the social roots of families: in the more well-off families there is a deprivatisation or commercialisation of the domestic sphere, through the use of various external institutions and services (domestic employees, home services, private kindergartens, etc.); on the contrary, families with limited resources have to increase domestic work, which is focused around the women in the house, which tends to result in the dependent members of the family being neglected (children, the elderly, the sick, etc.) and/or an increase in family stress. Between these two extremes, there are broad sectors of families that can partly use external services. In order to deal with the demands of the new family model (the woman who 'goes out' of the home and the man who does not 'come in') 'other women' will have to fill in the gap left by them. We therefore encounter the paradox of an increase in the demand for personal and domestic services while there is a reduction in supply, an extreme which has been resolved due to the influx of female immigrants from the third world. These women help to avoid both the inherent contradictions in an unbalanced change in family roles and the lack of social commitment from the State, which could increase the quantity and quality of the network of redistributive services in the home.

Finally it is worth referring to the lack of structure among immigrant women, as a group within the power structure of Spanish society. From an individual point of view, they see themselves above all as working women who find a source of personal independence and public recognition in their economic activity; this position is far from the stereotype of 'servitude' which was predominated by elements such as loyalty and personal subordination to employers. Although 'serving positions' (domestic service, cleaning, hotel and catering, etc., and sexual services are not experienced as a vocation, or even as jobs desired by the majority, they are the only employment opportunities that they have in order to stay afloat in emergency situations and find a way into Spanish society. This is why individual social integration strategies prevail, which aim to take advantage of comparative advantages that they can offer compared with native workers (greater geographical mobility, accepting lower salaries or worse working conditions, a more 'generous' deal, etc.).

Conclusion

The day-to-day experience of immigrant workers from the third world – in employment and in terms of employment legislation – shows them that they are in an environment in which there are practically no social rules to protect them and that the most important area is personal contacts. This is the reason behind the importance of reciprocal relationships, even within employment, and the mistrust of and distancing from the established channels of group representation, such as political parties and unions (only 3 per cent of foreign salaried women are members). However, membership of immigrants associations (13 per cent of those surveyed) and churches or mosques is usually with compatriots (18 per cent) as well as the demonstrations that took place following the recent legislative changes (sometimes with considerable support from the Spanish public) are some indicators that are pointing to the possibility of moving forward in the development of collective links and the defence – both institutional and political – of their employment and citizens rights.

References

Colectivo Ioé (2001), *Mujer inmigración y trabajo*. Madrid: IMERSO.

Chapter 7

Women, Migration and the Labour Market: The Case of France

Sabah Chaib

An analysis of the issue of the place of immigrant women in the French labour market and of the factors explaining their insertion into as well as their exclusion from this market necessitates an examination of certain basic assumptions. Firstly, there is the question of whether or not there has been any manifest interest in this issue from the different public and private actors involved (public authorities, Trades Unions, associations etc). And secondly, the question arises of what qualitative and quantitative data will allow us to recognise and determine the various factors that impact on immigrant women's labour market insertion, and evaluate the impact of these various factors. In a report for the European Union, Colette de Troy (1987) argues that the primordial element which should guide public action in this area, is the production of knowledge of the subject and the deconstruction of stereotypes through the production of both quantitative and qualitative data which would allow a better comprehension of the complex realities of the professional situation of migrant women. One might argue, in fact, that one of the first signs of the integration or the exclusion of migrant women in the host society is to be found in the level of interest in their situation and in the nature of knowledge produced on this subject, as well as in the public policies which are engaged in their direction. However, in France their has been a relative lack of interest in this question both on the part of the public authorities and of academic researchers.

The question of the insertion of migrant women in the labour market has become an object of interest relatively late in France. Whilst it might be assumed that France as a country with a long history of immigration should be in possession of up-to-date knowledge of these issues, paradoxically it is comparatively behind other European countries in these terms. This situation may be explained by the fact that despite statistics which show that migrant women now play a large structural role both in the total migrant population (women made up 47 per cent of the total migrant population in 1999) and in the labour market, it is still not considered as evident that migrant women will work. Instead it is often assumed that migrant women will remain economically inactive, or that if they do work it will just to earn a bit of extra money, not in order to support themselves or their families. Thus, whilst male immigrants have become an object of interest of economic studies which seek to determine their role in the national economy, the same is not true of women immigrants. Most studies carried out on the subject of women migrants have been directed principally at their cultural and familial roles. These social representations of women immigrants as economically inactive and financially dependent on their (male) partners, has also been perpetuated by the definitional difficulties encountered in studying a population so heterogeneous in terms of their countries of origin and of the timescale of their migration to France.

The little information which there is relating to immigrant women's labour market participation reveals above all their vulnerability. Whilst a hard core of migrant women remains economically inactive, those that do work are employed in unskilled professions and are usually employed in the private sector where they have little job security. Often they work in part-time or temporary jobs. Their labour market participation is often fragmented, affected by the precariousness of their employment situation and their vulnerability to unemployment.

Some elements of convergence may be seen between the situation of immigrant women and French women in the labour market. But this convergence is hampered by the existence of structural obstacles for immigrant women. These obstacles are linked to differences in human capital which may pose a disadvantage in times of economic depression; direct and indirect legal barriers; and discrimination visible both in educational orientation and the availability of training, and in illegal discriminatory practices in employment.

Women Immigrant's Labour Market Participation: An Absence of Research

One of the reasons for the absence of research on immigrant women's labour market participation can be seen in the way in which research on immigration in general has developed in France. Whilst immigration has become an object of greater interest to researchers in recent years, women have occupied a marginalized and predetermined place in these studies – kept within the domain of the family. Further, the way in which such studies tackle the subject of women is often in terms of the dominant problematic for talking about immigrant families, that of adaptation, or of the passage from tradition to modernity. The predominance of this problematic explains the frameworks for interpreting the economic activity of immigrant women. These frameworks often rely on a psycho-social approach which tends to show the ways in which immigrant women achieve emancipation through paid employment or through the fact of achieving some degree of economic independence. It is interesting that the concept of emancipation which has been widely criticised by feminist researchers in other contexts because of its vague and undefined use, is still used rather uncritically when writing about immigrant women. A second framework of analysis, linked to the first, is the perception that migrant women's work is an attack on 'group integrity'. For example, the image of the Maghrebi woman who transgresses communal codes of honour by leaving the house to go and take paid employment in the public sphere (Abrous, 1989).

Thus, rather than a total absence of interest in immigrant women's employment, we can see research which has privileged a cultural approach to the subject, based on assumptions about cultural specificity in gender relations. This culturalist approach assumes the existence of patriarchal families, privileged sites of masculine domination, and lends them a major explanatory role in examining migrant women's place in the labour market. Migrant women themselves are represented in their 'traditional' roles as passive women both inside and outside of the family sphere.

A series of studies commissioned by the Social Action Fund (FAS) in 1995 on the theme of immigrant families have contributed to put into question existing social representations of these families and of the gender relations within them. These studies have, therefore, provided a basis for the reconsideration of the place and the role of immigrant women both within the family and in society in general. Although there are still few such studies concerned with the sociology of migrant families, they demonstrate the dynamic nature of migrant family structures, and the heterogeneity of family configurations. The example of women who have taken over the role of head of the family shows by itself that family structures and gender roles do not conform to a unique schema which can be assumed in advance. Further, there is a clear dynamic of evolution in the relationships between family members over time. The same can also be said of the decisions of mothers in these families to take up professional activities. These decisions emanate from a whole range of very heterogeneous social, economic and cultural conditions. Similarly the impact of women's professional activity on the gendered division of labour within the family will be very variable. One notable convergence which emerged, however, between all women, those who had taken up paid employment and those who had never had a salaried activity, was the insistence on the necessity of their daughters working. The importance accorded to the fact that their daughters should enter the labour market was explained by the worries about the precariousness of couples and the problems of divorces and separation (Chaib, 1997).

The studies that have been carried out, however, are far from exhausting the research themes that deserve to be examined. The rare socio-economic studies which were undertaken on the basis of the census results of 1968, 1975 and 1982 (Morokvasic, 1974; Taboada-Leonetti and Levi, 1979; Silberman and Moulier, 1982), have not been repeated, and theories on immigrant labour have not been applied to migrant women, reinforcing the idea that only male labour is a worthwhile subject of research. It is significant that a fairly recent report on 'immigrants in the labour market' did not mention women at all (Lautman and Coutrot, 1993).

The rarity of research in the area of immigrant women is coupled with a lack of gender disaggregated statistics on migratory flows and on professional activity. These lacunae are reinforced by methodological difficulties linked to the production of statistical data which do not give enough information on the characteristics of the jobs undertaken nor on the sociological background of the women doing the jobs (legal status, education and qualifications, migratory experiences etc.). Moreover, different forms of employment other than salaried employment – independent, informal, illegal or domestic work – and the different objective and subjective motivations and experiences attached to these types of work are studied very little. In the 1990s, research which was done showed the structural presence of women in migratory flows and the heterogeneity of migrants. However, whilst the concept of heterogeneity is highlighted more and more in studies of migrants, in many studies there is still insufficient attention paid to the different migratory experiences and varying social, economic and political conditions for migrants. The difficulties in defining the category of immigrant women and in apprehending the growing heterogeneity within this category has only added to the perpetuation of social representations of immigrant women as economically inactive and dependent on their partners.

Characteristics of Immigrant Women's Economic Activity

The characteristics of immigrant women's labour market position reflect above all their vulnerability. They are frequently restricted to unskilled and low paid jobs and are badly affected by job insecurity and unemployment.

In 1999, statistics revealed that there were 2.1 million immigrants who were economically active in France. Immigrants thus made up 8.1 per cent of the total active population. Of these economically active immigrants, 634 000 were women. The number of economically active women immigrants had increased from less than 600 000 in 1996 (INSEE, 2000a). More than one million foreigners between the ages of 20 and 60 were employed in the private sector. They remain in the least qualified jobs, particularly those of unskilled workers. However, as the demand for unskilled manual labour has been reduced over the past fifteen years because of technological innovations and because of the crisis in the manufacturing and construction industries, many migrants now find work in the tertiary sector. The tertiary sector is a particularly large employment sector for migrant women (INSEE, 2000b). Migrant women are affected more than migrant men and more than French women by insecurity in employment, but this does not seem to affect their desire to enter the labour market as their rate of employment is increasing faster than the average national rate.

Statistical data confirms the growing labour market participation of immigrant women, but also demonstrates important differences according to their country of origin. Women originating from Portugal, Spain, Sub-Saharan Africa and Asia have a comparable rate of labour market participation to French women of the same age (more than 75 per cent of these women between the ages of 30 and 39 are economically active). Women originating from Algeria, Morocco and Turkey have lower rates of labour market participation: 61 per cent, 44 per cent and 39 per cent respectively between the ages of 30 and 39. The large variations in the rates of economic activity at this age reflect above all differences in the age at which the women entered France. Of the Algerian women aged between 30 and 39, many more had come to France before the age of 16, and the activity rate for those who have arrived at an earlier age is much higher.

Another important factor in analysing immigrant women's labour market participation is the date at which a woman entered into the labour market. Generally, the longer that a migrant has been in the labour market, the greater their protection against instability and job insecurity. Women immigrants who have generally entered the labour market later than men are thus disadvantaged in this respect. They are also at a disadvantage compared with male migrants in that they have had to integrate themselves into the labour market at a time when the socio-economic environment is less favourable. Many women entered the country at a time of economic crisis in the mid-1970s, whilst many male migrants entered France in the period of economic growth in the 1960s.

An analysis of the significant variables determining the probability of an immigrant woman entering the labour market in France and occupying stable employment, shows the importance of a variety of factors: the length of labour market participation, their fluency in French and the reasons that they came to France (in other words whether or not coming to find work was one of the principal reasons for migration).

Determinants of Labour Market Participation: A Convergence between French Women and Migrant Women

When considering the determinants of labour market activity there is a clear element of convergence between the trajectories of French women and immigrant women. The list of tendencies established by Maruani (1999) in relation to French women's labour market participation, can be applied perfectly to immigrant women of certain nationalities. Maruani points one the one hand to a re-equilibration of the sexes within the labour market, a feminisation of the workforce, a transformation in female employment behaviours and a rise in the levels of education. On the other hand, she also notes a re-growth of inequalities, concentration, segregation, bipolarisation, inequalities in salaries and a growing number of low salaries (Maruani, 1999). The negative elements of this tableau confirm that there is no natural progression towards gender equality in the labour market irrespective of national origin. However, these elements do point to a fundamental shift in gender relations in employment, and the same elements can also be used to illustrate a convergence between the employment patterns of French and migrant women.

One of the major points of convergence between French and migrant women in the labour market is connected precisely to their growing economic activity. The activity rates for some groups of foreign women are approaching those of French women. In 1973, for example, only 30.7 per cent of Portuguese women worked, in 1995 the figure was 64.4 per cent. Similarly, the activity rate of Maghrebi women has quadrupled in the past twenty years, going from 8.4 per cent to 36.6 per cent. At the same time as we can remark a general growth in immigrant women's economic activity, it is also interesting to note a modification in the composition of the active foreign population in terms of national origin. The most notable part of this modification is a growth in the proportion of women from outside the European Union in the workforce. Portuguese women still remain the most numerous amongst the foreign women in the labour market, but the proportion of Portuguese women compared to that of women of other nationalities is falling. At the same time the proportion of Algerian and Moroccan women in employment is growing, as is that of Asian women, who are rapidly catching up with French women in terms of rates of labour market participation.

A second element of convergence between French and migrant women which impacts upon their economic activity is related to their birth rates. Migrant women have birth rates which are intermediary between those of the women in their country of origins, and those of French women. By the second generation the convergence with French birth rates is total. Studies have shown the positive impact of having a child on women's decision to migrate (in order to improve their child's chances of having a better quality of life), and also in women's decisions to enter the labour market (Echardour, 1996). Many women wait until their child has reached a certain age before re-entering the labour market, but it seems that a continuous economic activity, is becoming a more and more generalised phenomenon amongst women of immigrant origin in France today.

Immigrant women's rates of economic activity are in general determined more and more by the same variables which affect French women's economic activity – level of education/training, family responsibilities, partner's level of income etc. However, despite these elements of convergence, it would be wrong to think that it is merely a matter of time before immigrant women occupy exactly the same place in the labour market as French women. In fact, there are continuing specificities in the place occupied by immigrant women in the labour market, and the difficulty in explaining these specificities in terms of the usual factors determining labour market participation points to various forms of discrimination which may occur. Thus it might be more accurate to talk about an evolution rather than an amelioration in immigrant women's labour market position. An in-depth analysis of economic activity and the determinants of labour market insertion reveals that immigrant women are discriminated against both in terms of equality of treatment and of freedom of movement within the labour market.

Labour Market Discrimination

The issue of discrimination in the labour market is a complex one. The lack of research which provides a systematic comparison between the situations of men and women of both French and immigrant origins aggravates the difficulties which arise in the analysis of discrimination and its particular causes, such as the distinction to be established between the role played by personal behaviour and that played by more structural factors linked to the functioning of the labour market. Discriminations may be linked to law and the legal status of migrants. But as migrants who obtain the nationality of their country of residence may also be faced with obstacles in their access to the labour market it is important to consider also factors such as the prejudices and institutional practices of employers. As Georges Tapinos remarks:

> The difficulties encountered by foreign and immigrant women stem from both their situation as a woman and/or a foreigner and from discriminatory dispositions resting upon a legal basis. A continuum of situations exists from those where a direct and effective discrimination takes place to those where a woman will be the victim in a particular incidence of a more general discriminatory disposition. (Tapinos, 1992: 54)

Legal Discriminations

To say that legal discriminations are well known is in fact not completely exact, it is necessary to recall both direct and indirect forms of legal discrimination (the latter being more difficult to apprehend). These two forms of discrimination create obstacles and situations of blockage for migrants (Boyd, 1991). Direct legal discrimination can be observed, for example, in the closure of access to certain forms of employment for which French nationality is required (this applies to about seven million jobs in total). Indirect discrimination is observable in restrictions relative to a migrant's ability to obtain a job – a refusal to deliver a work permit for example.

Today, the impact of legal discriminations can be seen particularly through the legal entrance and residence status given to a migrant. It is clear that the legal status of a woman migrant will have a huge impact on her insertion into the labour market. In this respect, the fact that before 1984 residence permits issued to women who had come to join family in France did not permit them to work is highly significant. Women in this situation could, after a certain time, go to the police prefecture and ask for a work permit, but this might be refused depending on the employment situation at the time. In 1984 a single ten year residence permit was introduced which granted the right to work and thus gave a relative legal security to permanent residents. However, the measures in place before 1984 have still had an impact on women's labour market participation. Those women who were not legally allowed to work were not diverted from the labour market altogether but rather were pushed into informal or illegal work. This pressure has particularly marked the professional histories of Maghrebin women.

Further, the different statuses accorded to immigrants other than those of workers (refugees, students, asylum seekers etc.), are a way of managing the stock of migrants in terms of the employment and labour market situations. Not all of these different legal statuses confers the right to work, and if they do so, it may be under very particular conditions e.g. students have the right to work only for a certain number of hours per week. For many, the right to work is only a precarious one. Many highly qualified immigrants receive only a provisory work permit, for example the 8000 foreign doctors in France are only allowed to work in public hospitals and then only in a position of relative precariousness. And whilst confirmed refugees receive the right to work, since the early 1990s asylum seekers have been debarred from employment. The majority of these asylum seekers thus end up swelling the ranks of those employed illegally.

The restrictive legislation and policies in place regarding the entry and residence of immigrants, have an important effect on the selection of candidates for migration and on their forms of professional and social insertion in the host country. Immigration policies which are becoming more and more convergent at a European level as far as restriction and selection of migratory flows is concerned, have made autonomous female migration more difficult. In effect, the risk of legal insecurity is higher for women immigrants than for men: the fragility of their conjugal situation (for example in a situation of divorce), can have a negative impact on their rights of residence and consequently on their right to work. The recognition of bilateral conventions on personal status further weakens the situation of immigrant women (in particular the family codes of Algeria and Morocco which are unfavourable to women).

The existence of such legal barriers (both direct and indirect) has led some to denounce the instrumentalisation of legal insecurity as a means of controlling the flexibility of the immigrant workforce (Morice, 1998; Marie, 1998). The vision of immigration in terms of a stock of labour to control and regulate, rests in part on the acceptance of the unfounded principle that in an unfavourable economic context, 'immigration equals unemployment'. This type of vision justifies the existence of legal discriminations and contributes towards a justification of illegal discrimination by employers.

A Place Assigned to Immigrant Women?

The question of discriminations in the labour market leads us to a reflection on the differentiations that occur within this market, and on the particular place that may be assigned to immigrant women. Examples of discrimination may lead us to believe that beyond the occurrence of prejudice and 'ordinary racism' there is an over-riding logic of complementarity, that is to say an idea that the immigrant workforce should not provide competition to the native workforce. This characteristic can be found in the processes of recruitment of many cleaning agencies, a large number of which were started up with a workforce that was essentially female and immigrant. Observations from fieldwork carried out in the sector of industrial and domestic cleaning, by Philippe Bataille amongst others (Bataille, 1997), demonstrate a modification in the nationalities, positions and roles of the female immigrant workforce. Many small cleaning businesses have been set up and developed rapidly in response to a market demand. The most dynamic of these companies have been gaining larger and larger contracts, both in terms of the financial rewards and in terms of the social status of clients – such as hospitals, clinics, public administration – which call upon their services. Parallel to this growth one can observe a selection being operated in the way in which the workforce is classified in terms of working hours, organisation of work, distribution of particular tasks. For example, in the case of a cleaning organisation in the Savoie region, there were no selection criteria in place for cleaners to be sent to industrial warehouses, empty or newly built buildings. However, where the contract was for cleaning a doctor's surgery, lawyer's offices etc, there were strict selection criteria for the cleaners to be sent there. These criteria, as described by Bataille, match exactly with those for other organisations, those who are sent to work in doctor's surgeries, administrative offices etc, are more likely to be or European origin. The arguments employers use to justify this type of selection relate to the employee's mastery of written French necessary for the accurate use of certain products, the need for good 'general presentation'. These criteria are particularly stressed when the work involves direct contact with a client. Thus women of African and Asian origin working for such companies are far more likely to be sent to do the dirtier, industrial cleaning jobs, and jobs where they are unlikely to come into contact with clients. Those jobs which involve cleaning smart offices, surgeries etc, and where the cleaner will come into contact with clients are delegated to employees of European origin. These examples tend to demonstrate a clear discrimination which is being operated in the labour force between women of European origin and immigrant women of African and Asian origins.

Employment of Immigrant Women: A Source of Labour Market Flexibility

The tertiarisation of the economy has resulted in a double dynamic in the labour market. On the one hand the level of qualification of the workforce has been rising, and on the other hand there has been the creation of greater insecurities for those at the lower end of the workforce, linked to unemployment, less job stability etc. For the female workforce, these trends seem to be pointing in a negative direction for the future. Certainly it seems that the trend for increased female labour market activity will not be reversed, but at the same time there will be greater and greater job segregation and bipolarisation between qualified and non-qualified women. There is also a tendency for increased individualisation in terms of employment history, and as many sociologists have pointed out, all these elements imply the necessity of a move away from analysis in terms of class to a more micro-analysis in terms of individual trajectories through the workforce.

Within this picture, the female immigrant workforce occupies a particular place. The fact that women immigrants have encountered the types of discrimination described above has contributed to a particular type of trajectory with immigrant women being involved in many of the new type of work practice which are evolving as a result of the increasing bipolarisation of the workforce. Many immigrant women have thus been involved in home-working, selling from home, working flexible hours, different types of contracting work. Qualitative research on immigrant women's employment has shown how much contractual and flexible work are a major part of their workforce participation. Many of these women's professional careers show no social or professional mobility but rather a variation in different types of contract (informal, part-time, temporary) or a diversity of different types of job, moving from industry to domestic services for example. Unemployment amongst women of immigrant origin is less a product of redundancy and more the result of the ending of one temporary contract and inability to find another one. Any training that these women might experience is usually undertaken during periods of forced inactivity through unemployment, and often as a means of filling time rather than of acquiring a qualification which would permit them to advance their careers.

As Annie Gauvin has highlighted (1994), developments in women's professional trajectories can be seen as an indicator of general evolutions in the labour market. And within the category of female employment, the labour market activity of immigrant women, usually at the bottom of the employment ladder, prefigures particularly the evolution of the labour market for non-qualified workers. In particular the tendencies of increasing job insecurity, prolongation of periods of unemployment, discontinuities in the career trajectories are representative of a recomposition of the bottom end of the labour market. The tertiary sectors within which immigrant women have typically found employment are today becoming the site of greater competition as the number of active members of the workforce grows at a greater rate than the creation of new jobs. This sector of the labour market which was considered as marginal and socially under-valued has now become central both to a category of economically active but little qualified women workers, and also to public authorities who would like to stimulate the creation of extra employment in this sector. However with a lasting employment crisis in this sector (despite an economic upturn not all employment sectors have benefited equally), it has been difficult to stimulate the creation of new jobs in this area. Whether politicians will be successful in reinvigorating this sector of employment and in reducing the instability of this section of the workforce remains to be seen. In the meantime it seems that immigrant women will continue to be governed by the same labour market processes and pressures and to play a similar role to that they have traditionally occupied – that of a flexible workforce which can act as a shock-absorber for the labour market. This role is similar to that played by male immigrants with one major difference – immigrant women's work is concentrated more than ever in less visible and less heterogeneous sectors of the labour market making it even more difficult to define strategies for aiding their labour market integration.

References

Abrous, D. (1989), *L'honneur et le travail des femmes en Algérie*. Paris: L'Harmattan.
Bataille, P. (1997), *Le racisme au travail*. Paris: L'Harmattan.
Boyd, M. (1991), 'Les femmes immigrées et les politiques d'intégration', *Conférence Internationale sur les Migrations*. Paris: OECD.
De Troy, C. (1987), *Les Femmes Migrantes et L'Emploi*. Brussels: European Commision.
Echardour, A. (1996), 'La vie professionnelle des immigrés originaires du Portugal', *Espaces, Populations, Société*, 3: 11 – 24.

Gauvin, A. (1994), Les trajectories d'emploi des femmes: une composante essentielle des marches du travail contemporains, *Cahiers du GREC*, 11, pp. 6 – 21.

INSEE (2000a), 'L'emploi des immigrés en 1999', *Insée Première*.

INSEE (2000b), 'Les salaries étrangers: loin des secteurs porteurs et des positions valorises', *Premières Synthèses*, 46, 1.

Lautman, J. and Coutrot, J. (1993), *L'intégration des immigrés et le marché du travail: état de savoir et questions*. Paris: GRETSE.

Marie, C-V. (1998), A quoi sert l'emploi des étrangers, in A. Morice et al. (eds), *Les lois de l'inhospitalité*. Paris: La Découverte.

Maruani, M. (1999), 'La feminisation du monde du travail', *Les Cahiers Français*, 291: 35-57.

Morice, A. (1998), Trafic de main d'oeuvre et emploi illegal, les irréguliers dans l'étau des textes et des pratiques, *Hommes et Migrations*, 1214, pp. 35-57.

Morokvasic, M. (1975), 'L'émigration des femmes et quelques unes des transformations sociales qu'elles entraînent, envisages du point de vue des femmes yougoslaves', *Migration*, 5: 125-138.

Silberman, R. and Moulier, Y. (1982), 'La montée de l'activité des femmes étrangères en France: une tendance qui ira en s'accentuant', *Travail et Emploi*, 12: 73 – 84.

Taboada-Leonetti, I. and Levi, F. (1979), *Femmes et immigration: Insertion des femmes immigrées en France*. Paris: Documentation Française.

Chapter 8

Selling Sex: Trafficking, Prostitution and Sex Work amongst Migrant Women in Europe

Jane Freedman

An area of growing concern both for public opinion and for policy-makers in the European Union, is that of the trafficking of women and children for sex work within Europe. In terms of European policy making, the issue of trafficking is closely linked to those of illegal migration and trans-national crime networks and so is seen as a threat to the security of the European populations which the EU wishes to protect. Thus, trafficking has increasingly been seen as a matter for increased police action and co-operation at the EU level. At the same time there is concern for the growing insecurities faced by many women who are trafficked into Europe to sell sex. However, there is an argument that whilst attempting to repress trafficking, policy-makers have not paid enough attention to the insecurities and vulnerabilities of the 'victims' of this practice, and have not addressed the real causes of the problem. Further, in concentrating solely on the victims of trafficking and on separating those trafficked to sell sex from other migrant women who sell sex 'voluntarily', it may be argued that a false distinction is established which rests on a rigid interpretation of the 'market' for prostitution, and ignores the very pressing reasons which weigh on migrant women in their decisions to enter prostitution or sex work. A fuller understanding of the global conditions surrounding women's migration and labour force participation is necessary in order not to place the issue of trafficking in its full context. In trying to separate the 'innocent victims' of trafficking, from the increasingly 'criminalized' migrant prostitutes and sex workers, governments have merely increased many migrant women's insecurity and vulnerability to exploitation and violence.

It might be argued that the enormous concern surrounding the issue of trafficking is in fact based on an incomplete understanding of the phenomenon which means that policy measures designed to combat it may either not work or may have unintended side effects (Salt, 2000). Increasingly, European governments have responded to trafficking through tightening immigration controls, but increasingly restrictive immigration policies and border controls could in fact be seen to be increasing the likelihood that would-be migrants will be trafficked and also mean that those who have been trafficked are likely to be returned to their countries of origin, exposing them to the same conditions which persuaded them to migrate in the first place, often with increased vulnerability as they will remain under threat from the persons or organisation which trafficked them. As Pearson comments: 'This fails to give trafficked persons opportunities for recovery and redress, and further deprives them of access to justice, through the possibility of criminal or civil action against traffickers' (Pearson, 2002: 2).

This chapter will examine the debates surrounding trafficking and prostitution within the more general context of the growing market for migrant sex workers within Europe, and will argue that only by understanding the forces that push migrant women to work in the sex industry globally, will governments be able to formulate policies which reduce rather than increase the vulnerability and insecurity of these women.

The Difficulties of Definition: What is Trafficking?

There are two major difficulties in any analysis of the issue of trafficking in Europe. Firstly the lack of any generally agreed definition of what trafficking consists of, and secondly, the paucity of research and reliable statistics on the phenomenon. To take the issue of definition first, the problems lie firstly in what exactly constitutes trafficking of persons (whether and how it is different from human smuggling, for example), and secondly in the immediacy of the linkage between trafficking and prostitution. A very narrow definition of trafficking would contrast it with human smuggling by arguing that force is used in trafficking, whereas a person consents to being smuggled into a country. However, although there are circumstances where women are literally kidnapped or abducted and brought into Europe to work in the sex industry, in many other cases a woman will agree to be smuggled into the EU, even paying those who agree to get her across the borders. Further, in all cases of human smuggling those being smuggled surrender some degree of control to the smugglers and may well end up being exploited in some way. In such cases a woman might believe that she is entering Europe to take up a legitimate employment offer that does not involve sex work, or she might be aware that she is migrating to work in the sex industry, but may nevertheless end up being deceived and exploited by those who brought her into the country (Kelly, 2002). Which of these situations should be defined as 'trafficking', and the degree of coercion or exploitation involved in trafficking is open to disagreement, as is the element of sexual exploitation which is involved in a trafficking situation. For some trafficking only involves smuggling people in to a country to work in prostitution, others extend the definition to include all types of sex work, or even non-sexual forms of slavery and exploitation. The multitude of definitions which might be applied to trafficking is reflected in the very broad definition adopted by an optional UN Protocol to Prevent, Suppress and Punish Trafficking in Persons, Especially Women and Children, became open for members signatures in Palermo in December 2000. The protocol defined trafficking thus:

(a) 'Trafficking in persons' shall mean the recruitment, transportation, transfer, harbouring or receipt of persons, by means of the threat or use of force or other forms of coercion, of abduction, of fraud, of deception, of the abuse of power or of a position of vulnerability or of the giving or receiving of payments or benefits to achieve the consent of a person having control over another person, for the purposes of sexual exploitation.

Exploitation shall include, at a minimum, the exploitation of the prostitution of others or other forms of sexual exploitation, forced labour, or services, slavery or practices similar to slavery, servitude or the removal of organs;

(b) The consent of a victim of trafficking in persons to the intended exploitation set forth in subparagraph (a) of this article shall be irrelevant where any of the means set forth in subparagraph (a) have been used.

So far the protocol has been signed by at least eighty countries (Hynes and Raymond, 2002), but even signatories to the protocol may have differing definitions of what trafficking is in their national laws and these national definitions are what will be used in compiling any data on trafficking (Kelly, 2002). The debate over definitions seems likely to continue with some pressing for such wide-ranging definitions that they will cover any foreign or migrant woman involved in sex work or prostitutions, whilst others exclude any situation where force has not been used to bring a person into prostitution. Although such debates over definition may seem abstract or irrelevant when faced with the real exploitation and vulnerability of many women and children, in fact, the definitions adopted are important in shaping government policies towards illegal immigrants and sex workers and too narrow a definition of trafficking may result in a failure to understand the different pressures (not only physical force) which push women to migrate in search of work in the sex industry, and a blindness to the levels of exploitation which can exist within this industry.

The second difficulty identified above involves the lack of detailed data or research into the scale and nature of trafficking of women into Europe. Difficulties in researching this area are obvious. Trafficking is illegal and is often linked to networks involved in other illegal activities so that access to traffickers themselves is almost impossible and may be dangerous. Similarly victims in destination countries will often try to escape detection as they have a status of illegal immigrants and fear deportation back to their countries of origin, and even if this hurdle is overcome many will be unwilling to reveal details of their experiences for fear of reprisals against themselves or against their families. As Kelly explains: 'Their fear of both the traffickers and the local law enforcement and immigration officials is likely to affect what they will say, including whether they identify themselves as victims of trafficking' (Kelly, 2002: 7).

What research and data there is on trafficking seems to reveal a situation in which the inequalities and poverty created by globalisation and economic restructuring, have left many women with little choice other than to engage in sex work to ensure their survival or that of their families. It would be simplistic to say that it is just poverty which forces women into the sex industry, but it seems true that growing inequalities in income have in many cases reinforced gendered divisions of labour and gendered discriminations which often leave women with few alternatives in their countries of origins, and in addition their options for migration are limited by the increasingly stringent controls imposed by EU countries. Estimates as to the number of women trafficked into and within Europe each year range from 300,000 suggested by the IOM to 120,000 put forward by the European Commission. Women trafficked come from developing countries in Asia, Africa and Latin America, and there are also a growing number of women who are trafficked from Eastern Europe and the former Soviet Union. The Ukranian Ministry of the Interior estimate, for example, that 400,000 women were trafficked from the Ukraine in the ten years from 1999-2000 (Hughes, 2002).

Causes of Trafficking: Increasing Gender Inequality?

Although the phenomenon of trafficking is not exclusively a female one and men are trafficked too, the majority of 'victims' of trafficking are women. It seems then that the cause of the growth in trafficking may be found not only in the growing global inequalities of wealth, but also in increasing and changing forms of gender inequalities in many countries. Having identified that trafficking in women for prostitution and sexual exploitation seems to be a growing problem in Europe, as elsewhere in the world, it must then be asked why? It seems that at the root of this phenomenon are growing inequalities in wealth both between and within countries, and also continued and worsening gender divisions and inequalities. Poverty is clearly part of the problem although it would be over-simplistic to attribute the growth in trafficking and in the number of migrant women working in the sex industry to the result of poverty alone. In fact, the growing employment of migrant women in the sex trade in Western Europe, whether as a result of trafficking or of 'voluntary' engagement in the sex industry, can be seen as part of a global pattern of increasing inequalities in wealth, both between and within countries. These growing inequalities in wealth and status have in many cases only served to exacerbate existing gender inequalities and divisions, and have in some cases, created new ones. In addition, it may be argued that globalisation has provided the conditions for the establishment of a global market in sex, of which migrant women form an integral part. In this respect, trafficking has also been linked to the growth of the sex tourism industry, which takes European men to Asia, Africa and Latin America with the specific intentions of finding prostitutes in these countries (Leidholdt, 1996).

Some analyses of the increase in trafficking and prostitution have highlighted the feminization of poverty as a major cause of this increase. However, as argued above it is overly simplistic to attribute this phenomenon merely to poverty, and the very concept of the 'feminization of poverty' has itself come under question, as it is argued that a more sophisticated approach to gender inequalities in poverty must be adopted (Cagatay, 1998). The widening inequalities caused by globalisation can be seen as causing greater gender inequalities in that it becomes harder for women to transform their capabilities into incomes or well-being (Kabeer, 1997). Across a wide range of cultures, women are assigned the greater part of the unpaid domestic and caring work. This limits their opportunities to engage in paid work – also, the financial burden of children might fall on them – many prostitutes had children to support. The gendered division of labour which results in women doing most of the unpaid caring work also makes women more vulnerable to transient poverty resulting from personal, familial, or general social, economic and political crises. One of the principle responses to such crises is the mobilization of women's and children's labour (Moser, 1996, 1998), yet where few opportunities for women to engage in paid labour exist they may be forced to migrate to seek work where they can find it. And in the present global situation, there are a plethora of vacancies for women to work in the sex industry in Western countries. As Scrinzi points out in chapter 4, the European sex industry is a case where there has been a normalization of the demand for immigrant women's labour, and where the distinctions of race, ethnicity and class upon which this demand are based, are concealed or suppressed.

In the case of Central and Eastern Europe from where many of the women working in the Western European sex industries now come, a UNDP report pointed to the rise in human poverty in these countries, and noted that women have been particularly affected by this impoverishment and by the growing inequalities of wealth in particular (UNDP, 1999). Women in these countries have been particularly badly affected by the transition to a market economy, suffering both economic and physical insecurity. Women have found themselves progressively pushed out of public life and many of the economic sectors in which women's labour was concentrated have suffered substantial job losses and reductions in pay. Various studies of the Russian Federation indicate that women account for between 60 and 80 per cent of the registered unemployed, and that in some regions this figure may rise to 90 per cent (Maughan, 1996; Hughes, 2002). At the same time, cuts in social services have placed the burden for domestic and caring work more and more onto women. As the UNDP report suggests: 'Having been deprived of paid employment, many women now resort to low-paying and insecure work in the informal sector in order to supplement their families' meagre sources of income.' (UNDP, 1999: 7). Women's personal security has also been affected by the rising threat of personal violence, both within and outside the household. Several studies have made the link between poverty and gender violence. In a recent World Bank study of experiences of poverty, for example, respondents from more than 90 per cent of the countries under review identified gender violence as a serious problem. The greatest increases in violence were reported in Eastern Europe and Central Asia where they were perceived to be linked to economic decline and breakdown of state institutions (Narayan, 2000).

Thus it becomes harder to draw a line between women who are forced into sex work and women who engage in it 'voluntarily', as the choices of the large majority of the migrant women working in the Western European sex industries can be seen to be fairly limited. There are a variety of ways in which women are drawn into prostitution and sex work. In some cases the strictest definition of trafficking will apply ie they are kidnapped and brought by force to work in prostitution. For many others, they are tempted to leave their countries of origin through the promise of a job in the EU, and leave unsure as to what that 'job' might be. Take the case of Irina, who left Moldova after her friend's boyfriend promised to find her work in Paris. Imagining that she would work as a machinist in a clothes factory, it was not until she was left on the pavement in a Paris suburb with instructions that she must earn 200 euros before the next morning, that Irina really understood the full extent of the insecurity of her situation (*Le Nouvel Observateur*, 23 January 2003).

A survey carried out by the Russian Ministry of Internal Affairs found that approximately 50 per cent of women who are trafficked are offered other types of employment in a foreign country. About a quarter of these women believe that they will work as waitresses or bartenders, whilst others are offered jobs as fruit pickers, models, nannies, cooks or saleswomen. The majority of the jobs offered are unskilled labour, although a smaller minority of women who have some skills such as knowledge of a foreign language, or secretarial or nursing qualification, may be led to believe that they will find skilled positions in the country to which they are going (Hughes, 2002).

National and EU Responses to Trafficking

As mentioned in the introduction, the trafficking of women and children for sexual exploitation has become a major cause of concern for many European governments and for policy-makers in the European Union. In a speech at a European Union information event on trafficking in March 2001, the Commissioner for Employment and Social Affairs, Ana Diamantopoulou, highlighted the importance of this issue for European policy-makers:

> Western Europe must face up to an uncomfortable fact: it is at the heart of a modern-day slave trade. This is not an over-dramatisation. It is estimated that up to 120 000 women and children are being trafficked into Western Europe each year. Many of these are bought and sold into forced prostitution, beaten, imprisoned, raped and sometimes killed. The trade is international, well organised and growing. It is brutal and highly profitable. A CIA report estimates that traffickers make up to a quarter of a million dollars with one woman trafficked and re-trafficked. Or as one London-based pimp put it: 'She cost me £800. And I can sell her for £250 an hour.' But, today, slavery is illegal. It is an affront to the universality of human rights including the rights of women. The sexual exploitation of trafficked women, marketed like cattle and thrown away when they have outlived their usefulness is a frightful reminder of how little we have progressed in the past fifty years. (Diamantopoulou, 2001)

This concern with trafficking has meant that during the 1990s, EU institutions developed a range of policies concerned with the issue (Wijers, 2000). The European Parliament, for example, adopted four resolutions on trafficking.[1] The

---

[1] Resolution on the Exploitation of Prostitution and the Traffic in Human Beings, April 1989 (OJ 120, 16.5.1989); Resolution on Trade in Women, September 1993 (OJ 268, 4.10.1993); Resolution on Trafficking in Human Beings, January 1996 (OJ 32, 5.2.1996); Resolution on the Communication from the Commission to the Council and the European Parliament on

importance of the fight against trafficking was also explicitly mentioned in article 29 of the Treaty of Amsterdam of 1997. Most recently, the Council adopted a framework decision on combating trafficking in human beings in July 2002,[2] whose objective was to try and ensure a common approach to the problem of trafficking amongst all EU member states and to try and fill the gaps in current legislation on the issue.

All of these initiatives have been hampered, however, by definitional problems described above, and by the fact that the varying definitions of trafficking reflect differing interests and policy objectives. In particular, the connection of the issue of trafficking to that of immigration and asylum policies in Europe has affected the ways in which governments have framed this policy issue, and might be seen to have hampered any attempts to aid those women who have been victims of trafficking. The assimilation of the issue of trafficking with that of illegal immigration is particularly evident in Europe, and has led from a shift of focus away from the problem of violence against women to that of illegal entry and residence in a European country. Thus the violation of the rights of the women who have been trafficked becomes a secondary problem to the violation of the laws of the state into which they have entered. As Wijers points out:

> In this perspective the state, rather than the women involved, is the 'victim' – namely of migrants who want to enter the country illegally and of smugglers who help these migrants. The women concerned are transformed from victims to outlaws or collaborators, and are, thereby subject to penalization and expulsion, regardless of the risk to their safety and livelihood. (Wijers, 2000: 214)

This emphasis on the penalisation of trafficking as a form of illegal immigration means that although European member states have made efforts to introduce policies and legislation to protect the 'victims' of trafficking, often these forms of protection are linked to the co-operation of the 'victim' in the prosecution of their trafficker. The way that these policies are implemented often means that there still remains little incentive for women who have been trafficked to cooperate with police. They fear that testifying against their traffickers will increase the risk of reprisals against them if they are repatriated. And as many countries offer no guarantee of protection or of permanent residence permits to these women, the benefits of helping to prosecute the traffickers may seem minimal, especially as many of the traffickers belong to large family networks who will continue operating even if one of them is prosecuted and imprisoned. As a counsellor from a German group helping trafficked women to testify in court explains, the women are afraid because they know that the network to which their trafficker belongs still exists and often they have been explicitly warned that even if the trafficker is imprisoned, other members of the network or family will pursue them (cited in Caldwell et al., 1997). The resilience of trafficking networks is demonstrated by

---

Trafficking in Women for the Purpose of Sexual Exploitation, December 1997 (OJ C14, 19.1.1998).
[2] COM (2000) 854.

the number of women who are eventually re-trafficked following repatriation. A report for UNICEF estimates that between 30 and 50 per cent of trafficking survivors are eventually re-trafficked following repatriation to countries in Eastern Europe (UNICEF, 2002).

Even where a state will offer some degree of protection to a woman who has been trafficked, there is also the fear of reprisals against relatives left behind in their country of origin. In particular, children that trafficked women have left behind with other family members are often the targets of those seeking reprisals against women who have given evidence against them (Demir, 2003). The protection both of repatriated trafficked women and of their families relies on the government and police forces of their country of origin. But in many cases these governments are either unwilling or unable to offer such protection. As a report for the Italian Ministry of Foreign Affairs suggests, local police are often unequipped or unwilling to offer the necessary protection to repatriated victims of trafficking or to their families (IOM Rome, 2000). And a study by UNICEF revealed that 70 per cent of women trafficked from South Eastern Europe do not trust the local authorities to provide adequate protection for them if they return home (UNICEF, 2002). In some cases local police and officials are not only uninterested in the protection of trafficked persons but have also been found to be directly or indirectly involved in the organisation of prostitution and trafficking (Hughes, 2002).

These issues of re-trafficking and reprisals against women and families have led to increasing pressure throughout Europe for the introduction of new strategies for protection of victims of trafficking and of their families. However, even where such measures exist, the implementation of such protection relies largely on the discretion of local officials who first encounter the trafficked women. The women themselves are rarely aware of the legal framework that might exist to protect them (Demir, 2003).Some countries in the EU have introduced specific legislation targeted at protecting the victims of trafficking. Belgium and the Netherlands, for example, both have specific legislation aimed at protecting the victims of trafficking. However, in both cases the granting of residence permits to those who have been trafficked is conditional on their willingness to testify in court against their trafficker, and even if they do testify, most will receive only a temporary residence permit, which gives them little long-term security. In addition, poor coordination between police, prosecutors and immigration officials means that women who have been trafficked are often unable to access the rights to which they are entitled (Pearson, 2002).

Italian legislation has gone further than that of Belgium or the Netherlands towards the protection of the victims of trafficking, with residency permits being available to trafficked persons who are considered in danger as a result of leaving their situation of exploitation and who are willing to engage in a social integration programme (Pearson, 2002). The granting of a residence permit is not dependent on the 'victim' making a formal legal complaint against the trafficker, although they must submit some information about the details of their being trafficked to the authorities. This legislation, which separates the process of criminalisation and prosecution of traffickers from the needs for protection and social integration of the trafficked person, may be seen as a good example of the ways in which European states might best act to promote the security of trafficked persons, and to end the cycle of violence and exploitation within which they have been trapped. However, the reality of the situation in Italy, is that despite the existence of this legislation, there is still pressure for trafficked women to act as witnesses against their traffickers in order to ensure the granting of a residence permit. An Italian judge estimated that about 80 per cent of residence permits issued under this legislation were given to those who had testified against traffickers, whilst only 20 per cent were granted to those who had not testified but had only enrolled in social integration programmes (cited in Pearson, 2002).

In addition, in many cases the police who arrest a trafficked woman involved in prostitution, may not consider the possibility of her having been trafficked, and will concentrate on her status as an illegal immigrant. Many women who have been the victims of trafficking may thus be deported without being aware of their rights to protection under the law. The IOM reported, for example, that in most cases Italian police were continuing with immediate deportations of Albanian sex workers whom they arrested (IOM Rome, 2000). Similarly, Anti-Slavery International reports the case of Sylvia, a 17 year old who was trafficked from Nigeria to Rome. She believed that she would have the chance to study when she arrived in Italy, but was instead forced into prostitution. When arrested by the Italian police for failing to have the required visa she was immediately deported back to Nigeria without any attempt to discover how she had come to be working as a prostitute in Italy. Following her deportation, the man who had arranged her trafficking to Italy visited her family and threatened to kill them if she did not repay her debt to him. So in order to protect her family, Sylvia agreed to be re-trafficked (Anti-Slavery International, 2003). Thus it can be seen that the emphasis on the speedy deportation of illegal immigrants, in Italy, as in other European countries, in many cases continues to override and policies or legislation that may be in place for the protection of trafficked persons. It can be argued therefore, that in order for European states to introduce real protective measures for trafficked persons, it is necessary for this issue to be separated more clearly from that of governments' attempts to clamp down on illegal immigration.

The Growth of the Transnational Sex Work Industry

The high profile of recent debates over trafficking may have served to obscure other realities relating to migrant prostitution and sex work within Europe. Whilst media reports and policy interventions have highlighted the plight of the 'victims' of trafficking, far less attention has been paid to the situation of women who have migrated 'voluntarily' to seek work in the sex industry in Europe. The debates over trafficking have framed the issue in terms of women from poorer countries falling 'victim' to unscrupulous male traffickers, but have ignored the wider racial, ethnic and gendered aspects underlying the global patterns of migration and sex work. What is clear, however, is that trafficked women make up only a minority of those migrant women working in the European sex industry. Although it is again difficult to accurately gauge the number of migrants working in the European sex industry as many of these women are working illegally, estimates suggest that the proportion of migrants finding work in this sector is growing rapidly. Studies from Holland suggest that about 60 per cent of the country's sex workers are migrants, and the figures from Germany indicate that the figure there is between 50 and 70 per cent. Most of these migrant sex workers have no legal residence status in the country in which they are working, and are thus increasingly vulnerable to exploitation and violence. In many countries a two-tier system of prostitution may be seen to be developing, with differing conditions for prostitutes with legal EU residence status and those without. This distinction, based on the legal/illegal division, has an underlying racialized aspect which is often overlooked in the discourses surrounding prostitution.

Transnational prostitution and sex work can be understood in terms of larger global migratory systems within which millions of people migrate for a varying and highly complex number of reasons, including the need to escape poverty or repression, and to find work in another country. The phenomenon of migrant prostitutes is not new, Walkowitz reports, for example, that during the 1880s, British women worked as prostitutes in Belgium and other parts of Europe (Walkowitz, 1980). However, current global economic conditions have shaped the particular way in which the transnational sex industry operates today. The sex industry is one of the contemporary 'growth industries'. Prostitution and other types of sex work have become big business for many countries where the sex industry has become 'an integral part of tourism' (Phizacklea, 1996: 167).

At the same time, the effect of globalisation on women's lives, especially in poorer countries has been well-documented. In particular, the pressures of Structural Adjustment Programmes have been implicated in creating greater gender inequalities. The insecurity that often accompanies restructuring becomes an additional burden that bears on women most severely. Indeed, it has been argued that gendered divisions of labour and gendered inequalities have been worsened under the terms of SAPs as women's workload is increased firstly as the burdens of social reproduction and welfare are shifted more and more on to women under an implicit assumption that women can take over services of care formerly provided by the state, and secondly by the demand for women's increased labour market participation in order to earn extra income to sustain their household (Purewal, 2001). The growth in global inequalities of wealth has served to exacerbate existing gender inequalities in many instances. As discussed above in relation to trafficking, poverty compounds and magnifies sets of unequal gender relations within which women have little or no power in negotiating sexual encounters and relationships. When faced with poverty, sex becomes a commodity which women might trade or sell in return for material support, thus making themselves vulnerable within both private and commercial sexual relationships. For increasing numbers of women, paid sex work may be the only source of income. In many cases sex workers are young girls or women who have been sent by their families to earn money to support the household. It has been reported that thousands of young girls from rural areas in Cambodia, for example, have been sold to the commercial sex trade (Subramaniam, 1999). As well as creating conditions of poverty and gender inequality which have supported the growth of the sex industry in poorer countries, globalisation has also encouraged many to migrate to seek better opportunities in richer countries. As noted in the introduction to this volume, one of the tendencies of contemporary patterns of migration is feminisation (Castles and Miller, 1993), and within this feminisation there are an increasing number of women who become involved in sex work abroad (Kempadoo, 1998). Some of these women will have been involved in the sex industry in their own countries before migrating, others migrate to find employment, and enter the sex industry once they are abroad. In either case the legal system in place regulating migration and prostitution often combine to create 'highly complex and oppressive situations' for these women (Kempadoo, 1998).

Empirical studies of migrant women working in the European sex industry support this view of transnational prostitution as part of a global system of labour migration which entrenches gendered inequalities. A study of Thai women working in the sex industry in Germany, for example, found that the majority of them were single mothers who had to support their children, and that this was a major motivation in their migratory processes. Others who did not have children felt economically deprived and saw no possibility of improving their economic situation if they stayed in Thailand. Many of these women had previously worked in prostitution in Thailand, often migrating firstly from rural to urban areas within the country to find employment, and then as a second step moving to Germany. In summary:

> Economic deprivation, the dual factors of social expectations and control over women with respect to their responsibility to the family in Thai society, and the transitions in the lives of Thai migrant women on one hand, combined with the attraction of better economic conditions in Germany on the other hand, are factors influencing the emergence of transnational prostitution and marriage migration. (Pataya, 2002: 81)

The study of Thai women working in the German sex industry reveals the general shape of migratory patterns involving women moving to Europe and becoming involved in the European sex industry. Since most European countries have closed their borders to labour migration, the ways that migrant women can legally enter the EU are limited, and so migrant sex workers, like other migrant workers, have to find different ways to enter Europe. Some enter through marriage to a European citizen, others arrange to migrate to Europe through transnational social networks, or through the use of commercial networks or agents. Apart from those who marry a European citizen, most of these women have no legal residence status which leaves them open to exploitation and violence. Those who enter Europe through the services of commercial networks may end up indebted to these networks. Their situation is thus not very different from those of women trafficked into Europe as described above. However, as these women have supposedly chosen to enter the sex industry 'voluntarily', there is little sympathy for them in the political discourses surrounding prostitution.

Analyses of the place of migrant women in the European sex work industry have pointed to the transformations that the influx of a large number of migrants have had on this area. Lazaridis points to the example of Greece, where the massive influx of migrant women has led to a modernization and rationalization of the system of prostitution on the basis of the huge profits to be made (Lazaridis, 2001). One of the results of this 'modernization', and of the organized search for potential profits, has been an increase in violence and exploitation of women working in the sex industry. In particular, migrant women are the targets of this violence and exploitation, as a two-tier system develops between native and migrant sex workers. This two-tier system is based on racialized and ethnicized perceptions and stereotypes, and is underpinned by the discourses of the state on prostitution.

The New Moral Discourse: Increasing Restrictions on Migrant Sex Workers

Whilst it is undeniable that there has been a growth both in the trafficking of women for sexual exploitation, and of the number of migrant women working in the sex industry in Europe, there is a divergence about how to tackle these issues. One of the problems that has been identified in European states responses towards prostitution and migrant sex work is that in differentiating between trafficked women, and those who choose to work in prostitution, governments are ignoring systems that abuse the rights of the 'voluntary' sex workers (Doezema, 1998). This new moral discourse and distinction between voluntary and forced prostitution is also used by governments to justify increasingly restrictive policies against migrant women 'voluntarily' engaging in sex work. Differing responses to prostitution stem from varying attitudes towards prostitution in general, and towards the status of sex work as employment. Different European governments have historically had varying responses to the issue of prostitution, ranging from strictly abolitionist policies, to efforts at regulation of the industry. Abolitionism is rooted in a moral opposition to prostitution, refusing to recognise it as legitimate work. Whereas regulationist approaches stemmed from concerns over public order and the threats that prostitution was perceived to pose to public health. These concerns over public health have been given a new urgency in recent decades by the emergence of the AIDS epidemic which has led to a growth in the number of health promotion projects aimed at sex workers (Day, Ward and Kilvington, 2000).

In some European countries, the fight against trafficking has been conceived as part of a more general attempt to control prostitution in general, and in particular the number of migrant sex workers in a country. This type of attempt at control can be seen as a development of the historical regulationist approaches which is combined with a contemporary emphasis on eliminating illegal immigration. In addition, as argued above, new 'moral' discourse has emerged in the debates over prostitution in recent years. This new moral discourse differs from historical moral discourses around the abolition of prostitution by its focus on the issue of trafficking and the separation of this issue from those emerging from more 'traditional' debates over prostitution. In fact, the emergence of a moral discourse around trafficking has in some ways paved the way for reactionary policies around prostitution. Coupled with an intensifying policy agenda to repress illegal immigration, this can lead to increased insecurity for all migrant prostitutes and sex workers, as the discourses and policy agendas ignore their real situations. In February 2001, for example, British police raided brothels in Soho, London, and arrested 40 women. The justification for the raids was that the police were acting to 'liberate' victims of trafficking. The English Collective of Prostitutes who protested against the raids argued, however, that most of the immigrant women working in the sex industry in Soho were working voluntarily (Kantola and Squires, 2002). And the women who were 'liberated' in the raid received little subsequent protection from the police, being detained, and in some cases summarily removed from the UK. Nina Lopez-Jones of the English Collective of Prostitutes, argued that these raids constituted an abuse of power by the police and policy-makers, an abuse made possible by the construction of a moral discourse against trafficking:

> Women were led to believe that they could expect protection, only to find themselves and deported. This raid lays the basis for trafficking legislation which would give the police greater power of arrest, while the women on whose behalf they are supposedly acting would no longer need to give evidence – the police, not the victim, would testify about the truth of her situation. (*The Guardian*, 22 February 2001)

In other European countries also, the emergence of a new moral discourse surrounding prostitution, a discourse which is entwined with debates over illegal immigration, has led to particularly repressive measures against migrant women working in the sex industry. In France, for example, migrant sex workers have become a prime target for the new government's attempts to restore internal security – but the aim of these policies is clearly not to provide added security for those engaged in sex work. The new internal security bill, which was presented to the Council of Ministers by the Minister of the Interior, Nicolas Sarkozy on 10 July 2002, and received its first reading in the National Assembly on 17 July 2002, brought together the two issues of prostitution and immigration, with a clause stating that 'Those responsible for actively or passively soliciting will be liable to systematic removal from French territory and to a definitive withdrawal of all rights of residence when they are of a foreign nationality' (cited in *Le Monde*, 7 August 2002). As a result of the government's determination to reduce prostitution and their linking of this issue specifically to immigration, prostitution support networks have reported increasingly frequent police raids which target immigrant sex workers. Cabiria, an organisation which promotes community health amongst prostitutes in Lyon, kept a 'diary' of the violence experienced by migrant sex workers in the city at the hands of the police. Their report highlights the ways in which these women are being pushed into greater and greater insecurity because of the way that they are targeted by the police under orders from both the Ministry of the Interior, and the Mayor of Lyon. Although these actions are portrayed as part of a drive against prostitution in general, one of the police commissioners of Lyon apologised to a French prostitute for having taken away her car, explaining that the police had thought that it belonged to an African woman, and that French women were not being targeted by the police (Cabiria, 2002). Another prostitute, one of whose clients is a policeman reported that:

> He had warned her that there would be a growing repression of prostitutes and that this time all of the immigrants would be expelled, and that even those women who had French nationality but were of immigrant origin would suffer repression. The 'traditional' prostitues [ie white French women] would be offered places in retraining workshops. (Cabiria, 2002: 6)

Legalisation or Criminalisation? The Examples of the Netherlands and Sweden

Recent analyses of differing approaches to policy on prostitution have frequently focused on the examples of the Netherlands and Sweden which have each recently enacted policy reforms relating to prostitution. The differing reforms enacted in either country reflect two opposing views of prostitution, seeing it either as a legitimate form of work or as a type of sexual exploitation which should be outlawed. In each of these cases, the particular ways in which the reforms were framed have had important implications for migrant sex workers, often highlighting the differing status of migrants and nationals in the sex work industry.

The recent policy changes in the Netherlands show a move towards legalisation and regulation of the sex work industry. In 1997, the Minister of Justice put forward a proposal to legalise brothels. The bill was passed by the Dutch Parliament in 1999, and the new law came into effect in 2000. This law can be seen as a radical departure from previous discourses on prostitution, recognising sex work as legal work like any other. Proponents of this approach to prostitution have argued that this type of legalisation and regulation would allow for a greater defence of the rights of women working in the sex industry. However, some have argued that the legislation actually worsens the position of migrant women sex workers in the Netherlands, rendering their position even more insecure than those of their colleagues in other European countries (Van Doorninck, 2002).

The status of non-national and non-EU prostitutes was one of the issues that was prominent in the Dutch parliamentary debates on the prostitution bill. However, the majority of MPs opposed any moves to legalise the status of the estimated 10,000 to 15,000 foreign sex workers working illegally in the Netherlands. The underlying racial distinction between legal and illegal prostitutes was suppressed in the debate. Only a few MPs from the Green Party drew attention to the underlying racialization of the issue, mentioning the fact that the 'illegal' prostitutes were mainly black women catering for the demands of white men (Outshoorn, 2000). The issue of whether or not to legalise migrant prostitutes merely served to frame the parliamentary debate even more in terms of the need to stem illegal migration. As Outshoorn points out, 'the main discourse in the debate was in terms of what has been called the "hydraulic metaphor": describing migration as a "flood" or "tide" against which dams or dykes should be erected' (Outshoorn, 2000: 14).

The resulting decision not to legalise the thousands of foreign sex workers currently in the Netherlands has meant that in effect a two-tier system of prostitution has emerged. Those prostitutes who are EU citizens may obtain a license from the local council, and with this license comes a series of regulations aimed a protecting the prostitutes and ensuring safe and health working conditions. Sex workers will have the same labour rights as any other workers in Dutch society. For those sex workers without EU citizenship, however, the conditions are very different. They cannot get a license to work legally, and any brothels which employ them will be subject to prosecution for employing an illegal immigrant. These sex workers will effectively have to move underground and become effectively invisible to the authorities (Day et al., 2000). This obviously poses risks for these women who will be unable to claim any of the protection offered to the other prostitutes, and may be placed in increasingly vulnerable situations where they have no recourse to the law if they suffer from violence or abuse.

A completely different approach to prostitution has been adopted by Sweden, which has recently taken a strongly prohibitionist stance and has criminalised the buying of sexual services from a prostitute. The new law which makes it a criminal offence to buy any sexual services was passed by parliament in 1998 and became law in 1999. Whilst the Dutch law treats sex work as a legitimate form of employment, the Swedish law takes the stance that selling sex is a form of exploitation and that those who do it need to be protected. The pressure for such a law, which criminalises the clients of prostitutes but not the sex workers themselves was strongly influenced by a concern for the pursuit of gender equality and for the defence of women's rights. In addition, however, a discourse around immigration entered into the debates over the law. One of the arguments used to support the adoption of this 'sex-buying' law was that of the threat of migrant prostitution to Sweden. Members of the Commission set up to investigate the issue of prostitution specifically cited the fact that they did not want Sweden to become a market for prostitutes from abroad as a reason for legal reform (Gould, 2002). The threat of migrant prostitutes was linked to the spread of disease, specifically HIV in Sweden. As an interview published in the *Expressen* newspaper claimed that:

> Without exaggeration one can say that there is an invasion of foreign girls ... They are exploited by pimps, mistreated by their clients and spread life-threatening diseases ... Girls from the East have no tradition of using protection. Condoms are simply too expensive in their own countries. They are used to unprotected sex and bring this tradition further into Sweden. (Quoted in Gould, 2002: 206)

The first visible effect of the new legislation in Sweden has been a tenfold decrease in the numbers of women working visibly on the streets in major cities (Day et al., 2000). However, the fact that prostitution has become less visible does not mean that it has disappeared altogether, and critics of the law point to the fact that it may have merely driven prostitutes underground, into less safe working conditions. Moreover, in terms of the effect on migrant women, the law could, like its Dutch counterpart have particularly negative effects. The law is theoretically to apply evenly to the sex industry, but the discourse around the threat of migrant prostitutes, particularly in terms of their threat to public health, as revealed in the citation above, may well mean that these migrant women and their clients are particularly targeted. As a result these migrant sex workers may be forced to move from Sweden, and Swedish men who wish to purchase the services of sex workers may choose to do so more and more abroad. Thus the problems associated with sex work will not be solved but merely displaced. As Day et al. comment: 'Abolitionist policies may apply evenly to the industry but early indications suggest that a two tier system could develop which distinguished local from migrant workers and the purchase of sex in Sweden from its purchase abroad' (Day et al., 2000: 7).

An analysis of both the Dutch and Swedish approaches to prostitution shows that although seemingly diametrically opposed, these new laws may in fact have similar effects, especially concerning the status and position of migrant sex workers. In both cases, the debates around prostitution made explicit reference to a distinction between national and migrant sex workers, and by making this distinction allowed for a discriminatory treatment of the two groups. The fact that a discourse on illegal migration prevailed in both countries, and that migrant sex workers were perceived as a 'threat', has meant that these groups of migrant sex workers have been increasingly stigmatised and forced underground into increasingly insecure positions. Whilst the debate over the merits of legalisation and abolition of prostitution continue, the position of migrant sex workers will not be improved unless the prominence of the division between national and non-national/legal and illegal women is diminished.

Conclusion

As the above discussions have shown, the issue of trafficking is merely one aspect of the contemporary discourses surrounding prostitution and sex work in Europe. However, the prominence given to this issue, and the moral discourse that has arisen surrounding it, has in some cases served to obscure the exploitation and abuses suffered by other migrant women who have 'voluntarily' entered into prostitution in Europe. Moreover, the continuing emphasis given to the fight against illegal immigration, and the pressures to speedily deport illegal immigrants, have meant that even where measures have been put in place to protect 'trafficked' women, the reality of the protection afforded has been very limited. Neither the regulationist nor the abolitionist approach to prostitution typified by the recent legislation in the Netherlands and Sweden respectively have overcome the underlying distinctions between forced/voluntary prostitution and between national and migrant sex workers. Whilst these distinctions remain in place, it can be argued, that there can be no progress in establishing policies that protect all sex workers from exploitation and abuse.

References

Cabiria (2002), *Journal de repression. Violences faites aux prostituées à Lyon*. Lyon: Cabiria.

Cagatay, N. (1998), *Gender and Poverty*. UNDP.

Caldwell, G., Galster, S. and Steinzor, N. (1997), *Crime and Servitude: An Expose of the Traffic in Women for Prostitution from the Newly Independent States*. Washington: Global Survival Network.

Castles, S. and Miller, M. (1993), *The Age of Migration*. Basingstoke: Macmillan.

Day, S., Ward, H. and Kilvington, J. (2000), *European Prostitution Policy: A Time of Change?* London: European Network for HIV/STD Prevention in Prostitution.

Demir, J. (2003), The trafficking of women for sexual exploitation: a gender-based and well-founded fear of persecution?, *New Issues in Refugee Research*, 80. Geneva: UNHCR.

Diamantopoulou, A. (2001), Poverty to Slavery: The Misery Behind the Fantasy, speech given at an information even on trafficking in women, 8 March 2001, Brussels.

Doezema, J. (1998), Forced to Choose: Beyond the Voluntary v Forced Prostitution Dichotomy, in K. Kempadoo and J. Doezema (eds), *Global Sex Workers: Rights, Resistance and Redefinition*. London: Routledge.

Gould, A. (2002), Sweden's Law on Prostitution: Feminism, Drugs and the Foreign Threat, in S. Thorbek and B. Pattanaik (eds), *Transnational Prostitution: Changing Global Patterns*. London: Zed.

Hughes, D. (2002), *Trafficking for Sexual Exploitation: The Case of the Russian Federation*. Geneva: IOM.

Human Rights Watch (2002), *Hopes Betrayed: Trafficking of Women and Girls to Post-Conflict Bosnia and Herzegovina for Forced Prostitution*. New York: Human Rights Watch.

Kabeer, N. (1997), Agency, Well-Being and Inequality: Reflections on Gender Dimensions of Poverty. *IDS Bulletin*, 27, 1, pp. 11-21.

Kantola, J. and Squires, J. (2002), Discourses Surrounding Prostitution Policies in the UK, Paper presented at the Political Studies Association Annual Conference, Aberdeen, April 2002.

Kelly, E. (2002), *Journeys of Jeopardy: A Commentary on Current Research on Trafficking of Women and Children for Sexual Exploitation within Europe*. Geneva: IOM.

Kempadoo, K. (1998), Globalizing Sex Workers' Rights, in K. Kempadoo and J. Doezema (eds), *Global Sex Workers: Rights, Resistance and Redefinition*. London: Routledge.

Lazaridis, G. (2001), Trafficking and Prostitution: The Growing Exploitation of Migrant Women in Greece, *European Journal of Women's Studies*, 8, 1: pp. 67-102.

Leidholdt, D. (1996), Sexual Trafficking of Women in Europe, in R. Amy Elman (ed), *Sexual Politics and the European Union*. Oxford: Berghahn.

Maughan, J. (1996), *Women's Work: Finding a Place in the New Russia*. Ford Foundation Report, Spring 1996.

Moreno, G. (1999), *Violence against women, gender and health equity*. Cambridge MA: Harvard Center for Population and Development Studies.

Moser, C. (1996), *Confronting Crisis: A Comparative Study of Household Responses to Poverty and Vulnerability in Four Poor Urban Communities*. Washington: The World Bank.

Moser, C. (1998), The Asset Vulnerability Framework: Reassessing Urban Poverty Reduction Strategies, *World Development*, 26, 1.

Narayan, D. (2000), Voices of the poor : Can anyone hear us? Washington: The World Bank.

Outshoorn, J. (2000), Legalizing Prostitution as Sexual Service: The Case of the Netherlands, paper presented at the ECPR Joint Sessions, Copenhagen, April 2000.

Pataya, R. (2002), The Transnational Prostitution of Thai Women to Germany: A Variety of Transnational Labour Migration? in S. Thorbek and B. Pattanaik (eds), *Transnational Prostitution: Changing Global Patterns*. London: Zed.

Pearson, E. (2002), *Human Traffic, Human Rights: Redefining Victim Protection*. London: Anti-Slavery International.

Phizacklea, A. (1996), Women, Migration and the State, in S. Rai and G. Lievesley (eds), *Women and the State: International Perspectives*. London: Taylor and Francis.

Purewal, N. (2001), New Roots for Rights: Women's Responses to Population and Development Policies, in S. Rowbotham and S. Linkogle (ed) *Women Resist Globalization*. London: Zed.

Salt, J. (2000), Trafficking and Human Smuggling: A European Perspective, *International Migration*, 38, 3, pp. 13-44.

Subramaniam, V. (1999), The Impact of Globalization on Women's Reproductive Health and Rights: A Regional Perspective, *Development*, 42, 4, pp. 145-149.

UNICEF (2002), *Trafficking in Human Beings in South Eastern Europe*.

Van Doorninck, M. (2002), A Business Like Any Other? Managing the Sex Industry in the Netherlands, in S. Thorbek and B. Pattanaik (eds), *Transnational Prostitution: Changing Global Patterns*. London: Zed.

Walkowitz, J. (1980), *Prostitution and Victorian Society: Women, Class and the State*. Cambridge: Cambridge University Press.

Wijers, M. (2000), European Union Policies on Trafficking in Women, in M. Rossilli (ed), *Gender Policies in the European Union*. New York: Peter Lang.

PART III
NEGOTIATING SOCIAL AND
POLITICAL IDENTITIES

Chapter 9

Living with HIV: The Experiences of Migrant Women from Africa in the UK

Jane Anderson

In many ways AIDS encapsulates the global body politic. Global inequalities of class, gender, and ethnicity are revealed as poverty, powerlessness and stigma propel the spread of HIV. The bodies on which states and wealthy leaders inscribe both their power and their powerlessness are those of women, youth and poor men. (Schoepf, 2001: 335)

Introduction

Any chronic progressive incurable medical condition imposes insecurity and uncertainty on life. This has been especially prominent in the case of HIV and AIDS. Despite the exponential rate of progress in technical and medical knowledge on the subject, much remains unknown and cures and vaccines remain elusive. The associated weight of stigma and fear impacts on social interaction and colours both personal and social identity. For any individual the repercussions of HIV infection will depend on their circumstances, the other areas of peril in their lives and the range of resources that can be brought to bear. Women who are migrants are frequently caring for others as well as for themselves in a strange land, increasing the complexity of their lives. In the UK women of African backgrounds shoulder much of the burden of the HIV epidemic. Recent data on HIV infection shows that Recent data shows that the proportions of non-nationals amongst those living with AIDS in the UK is 22 per cent (Del Amo et al., 2001), and 74 per cent of those heterosexually infected with HIV in the UK between 1997 and 2001 were of immigrant origin (Del Amo et al., 2001). These figures are clearly disproportionate to the numbers of migrants in the population as a whole. This shift of the disease into marginalized communities, particularly migrant communities has affected women particularly, as both physiological and social and economic factors heighten their vulnerability to infection. Moreover, once diagnosed with HIV, numerous other problems arise.

For African women in the UK, HIV may be only one element in a life beset with other difficulties. Many are in a very precarious situation frequently facing serious economic and social problems. Growing xenophobia and discrimination and a hostile media only add to these problems. These women frequently have responsibilities for others, especially children, often without support from family or friends. Such challenges are complicated by the very different cultural backgrounds from which most have come. It is in this context that African women have to manage the reality of a potentially fatal illness.

Project Nasah, an action research project exploring the treatment information and other needs of Africans with HIV in the UK reports that the largest differential between African and white British people with HIV is the extent to which basic, practical needs are problematic, especially access to money, housing and employment. In comparative terms African people with HIV are likely to need more than other populations with HIV and yet are probably likely to get less (Weatherburn et al., 2003). Although the literature on the reality of living with HIV is increasing, most is written about the experiences of men. As the proportion of women living with HIV increases, it is important to analyse the experiences of these women as well, to understand the gendered impacts of the disease. This chapter is based on research carried out amongst African women living with HIV in London (Anderson and Doyal, 2003; Doyal and Anderson, forthcoming). It aims to reveal the insecurities that they face not only because of their HIV positive status, but because of the many interlinked discriminations and difficulties which compound their illness.

Black African Populations Living in the UK

Data from the 1991 census showed that Africans account for about 0.4 per cent of the UK population, 32 per cent of whom were born in Britain. Approximately 85 per cent of all Africans in the UK live in Greater London, although current government policy on the dispersal of newly arrived migrants will cause this to shift. Africa is a vast and varied continent. This is reflected in the African Diaspora in the UK, although modified by the differences in ethnic and social origins of those who choose to migrate.

Important areas of similarity exist within African communities in the UK, in particular the shared experiences of immigration regulations, low income and treatment of black and ethnic minority groups living in Britain (Elam and Chinouya, 2000). The African population in the UK is one of the most highly educated with high levels of university and professional qualifications. Despite this it is also a group with one of the lowest rates of employment and a high experience of social exclusion (Fakhouri, 1996). Some Africans have described London as 'the great leveller'. It is here that African people with a university education will be working alongside unskilled people in low paid, low status occupations (Elam, 2001).

Diversity within African communities is reflected in varying migratory experiences and reasons for settling in Britain. These are further characterised by differences between the generations, gender differences and family structures. Markers of difference between African communities exist in terms of the size of the community in the UK, the extent to which English is spoken, the migration history of the community and the religious affiliations of various groups (Elam and Chinouya, 2000).

The African population in Britain is the result of successive waves of migration. From the early 1950s families and students came predominantly from West Africa, in particular Nigeria and Ghana to work and to study. Increasing numbers of refugees and asylum seekers, especially from Uganda, came to the UK in the 1970s and 1980s. Within this group there are separate waves reflecting the course of the conflict in Uganda over twenty years. The migration patterns of the last decade reflect the political instability and conflict in Africa with increasing numbers of asylum seekers and refugees leaving West Africa, Zimbabwe, Zambia, Congo, Angola, Somalia and Ethiopia. The recent difficulties in Zimbabwe have resulted in a substantial influx of people to the UK.

Recent changes in the immigration and asylum laws in the UK have subjected asylum seekers to increasingly insecure conditions (Clarence, this volume). Many of these changes have directly affected the welfare of asylum seekers and have had a specific impact on their health, and on their ability to access and receive effective care and treatment for a range of illnesses, including HIV/AIDS. Although asylum seekers are entitled to medical care from the National Health Service, a range of conditions makes the organisation of this care and its effectiveness problematic in some cases. In a survey carried out in 50 UK organisations providing support for asylum seekers, 98 per cent felt that it was impossible to maintain good health under the voucher scheme and 70 per cent described asylum seekers experiencing regular hunger (Refugee Council, 2000). The Greater London Authority has described major concerns about the health of people arriving in the UK to seek asylum (GLA policy support unit, 2001). These problems can only compound the difficulties of those asylum seekers living with HIV/AIDS. Any treatment they receive for their illness will be undermined by lack of proper nutrition. Similarly the difficulties in obtaining milk vouchers that women asylum claimants have experienced could undermine medical efforts to prevent mother to child transmission of HIV (McLeish, 2002).

In addition the policy of dispersal has provoked difficulties for the health care of asylum seekers. Most asylum seekers initially arrive in London and Southeast England. In an attempt to reduce pressure on local services in se England a policy of no choice dispersal to locations across the UK is in operation (Audit Commission, 2000). The impact of this on the continuity of medical care is a topic of much concern and has particular relevance for the provision of complex multidisciplinary care of the sort required in HIV infection.

HIV Infection and its Patterns

Human immunodeficiency virus (HIV) has spread throughout the world with a variety of epidemiological patterns emerging in different areas reflecting different populations and risks. In Britain patterns of HIV infection have changed over the past few years. Although men who have sex with men constitute a majority of the people with HIV in the UK, since 2001 more new HIV diagnoses have resulted from heterosexual sex than from sex between male partners, reversing the pattern seen since the start of reporting in the mid 1980s. A majority (67 per cent) of these heterosexual infections are occurring in people from African backgrounds. Amongst Africans diagnosed positive in Britain women outnumber men by two to one, which is in sharp contrast to the overall UK average figure of 0.6 to one. The overall proportion of women in Britain living with HIV who are of African origin is increasing. Of the 1730 new HIV diagnoses reported in women in Britain in 2001 almost 70 per cent occurred in Africans, of whom 204 (18 per cent) were pregnant at the time of diagnosis. In 2001 in specialised Genito-urinary medicine clinics in London 4.8 per cent of African born men and 7.7 per cent of African born women were HIV positive. This compares to figures of 0.2 per cent of UK born men and 0.2 per cent of UK born women (Unlinked anonymous surveys Steering Group, Department of Health, 2002).

The epidemic has had a devastating impact on the African continent. United Nations statistics estimate that, worldwide, at the end of 2002 there were 42 million people with HIV, of whom 30 million (71 per cent) were in sub-Saharan Africa (UNAIDS, 2002). The majority of infections are acquired via heterosexual intercourse. There are a variety of data sets of variable accuracy, estimating HIV seroprevalance across the continent. These provide figures, amongst others, ranging from 80 per cent seropositivity amongst soldiers in the Zimbabwean army, 60 per cent in the Angola and Congolese army, almost 40 per cent in attendees at antenatal clinics in parts of South Africa and approximately 36 per cent in the general population of Botswana. Although West African figures have been lower than those for the East and South East of the continent these are now rising with at least 5 per cent HIV positivity in Nigeria (Barnett and Whiteside, 2002; Buve et al., 2002).

In most parts of sub-Saharan Africa, women are quickly becoming the majority of those infected by HIV/AIDS. Indeed Peter Piot of WHO described AIDS as a 'women's epidemic'. More women than men are infected with HIV (UNAIDS, 2002) and the burden of care for others who are infected, both at a community and family level falls largely to women (Ankrah et al., 1996; Baylies, 2000). A recent report from cities in Kenya and Zambia demonstrated a six-fold greater HIV prevalence in young women aged 15 to 19 in comparison to men of the same age, and three times higher in women aged 20 to 24 years (Glynn, 2001).

Vulnerability of Women to HIV Infection

Women's liability to HIV is a consequence both of social and biological factors. In various ways socio-economic position, gender, age, and marital status all intertwine to create a complex web of vulnerability (Baylies, 2000). A fundamental imbalance of power and control between men and women within many societies has been recognised as central to the issue (Baylies, 2000; Baylies and Bujra, 1999; Berer and Ray, 1993; Doyal et al., 1994; Schoepf, 1998). Baylies (2000) describes the ways in which the same cultural notions that operate in society as a whole influencing the gendered relationships of power and control also operate in and regulate intimate relationships. In the sexual setting these frequently translate into relative passivity for women and the passing of sexual decision making and initiatives to men. There may also be a greater tolerance of sexual mobility in men, both before and after marriage. Women's ability to exert control over sexual activity is frequently less than that of their male partners and is an important factor in the dynamics of HIV transmission. In situations of rape or coercion negotiation is not even a possibility and the increase in rape both as a weapon of war and within many societies generally is of particular concern for onward transmission of HIV. Within marriage women are frequently dependent on the behaviour of their husbands. The desire for children makes issues of protection complex. Recent studies in Africa have suggested that the age differential between men and women in sexual relationships is important. Women with male partners older than themselves have higher rates of HIV infection (Gregson, 2002; Kelly et al., 2003).

Physiological factors that influence enhanced female susceptibility to HIV include larger amounts of virus being transmitted during ejaculation in semen than are passed in vaginal fluids, and, and longer contact times for infected fluid in the vagina than in the male urethra. Coexisting sexually transmitted infections serve to enhance HIV transmission in both sexes, however in women these may frequently be asymptomatic, making them less likely to be treated. Infections associated with genital ulceration such as chancroid, herpes and syphilis are particularly strongly associated with increased risk of HIV transmission and acquisition. Herpes Simplex type 2 has been shown to be more prevalent in young women than young men and may be an important factor (Glynn, 2001).

HIV Prevention in African Communities in Britain

Although it has been largely assumed that most of the African people living with HIV in the UK have acquired their infection in high prevalence countries, as the pool of infected people in the UK increases so the opportunities for acquisition and transmission will grow. The escalating burden of the HIV epidemic in the UK on the African community has lead to government policy focusing on HIV prevention for Africans as a priority area (Department of Health, 2001). However to date there is little data on the sexual behaviour of Africans in the UK to inform such a programme. Johnson et al. (2001) in a national survey of sexual behaviour noted that Black African men described significant levels of high-risk sexual behaviour. The largest study to date has been a participatory community based exercise – the Mayisha project – which gathered data on almost 750 Africans living in inner London (Chinouya et al., 2000). Approximately equal numbers of men and women were recruited. Less than 40 per cent regarded themselves as being at risk of acquiring HIV and about one third reported ever having had an HIV test although a quarter had previously had a sexually transmitted infection diagnosed at some stage. Despite the assertion by the majority that condom use with new partners was acceptable within the group, less than one third actuality reported using condoms with their most recent partner. Of those who travelled back to African countries 17 per cent of men and 9 per cent of women reported having a new sexual partner in the visited country. The Padare project, a community study in central London, is a preliminary investigation of sexual behaviour in 214 HIV positive Africans in the UK (Chinouya and Davidson, 2003). In this study 73 per cent of respondents were women. About three-quarters of the sample reported penetrative sex within the previous month with 40 per cent reporting either no or only occasional use of condoms. About half the sample thought that it was difficult to use condoms with new sexual partners. Eighteen per cent of the women participants reported having had a baby since receiving their HIV diagnosis.

The investigators working on both the Mayisha and Padare projects have emphasised the importance of developing collaborative partnerships between researchers, sexual health promotion teams and local communities. The Mayisha project demonstrated the benefits of such collaborative working in tackling the issues of talking about difficult or taboo subjects. In terms of HIV prevention programmes the need for specific interventions aimed at the African community does not necessarily indicate higher risk behaviours in this group but rather reflects the difficulties in reaching a diverse community with specific cultural, religious and linguistic characteristics. Similar points have been made by workers in other European countries, e.g. Switzerland, where specific sexual health projects aimed at migrant communities have been established (Burgi and Fleury, 1996).

HIV Diagnosis and Management

Studies in Britain have found that African patients with HIV come to medical attention consistently later in the course of infection than white UK born patients (Barry et al., 2002; Saul et al., 2000; Del Amo et al., 1998). Compared with the UK average, a higher proportion of black Africans has a diagnosis of AIDS within 3 months of their first HIV diagnosis (PHLS, 2001). Research looking at ways in which people access HIV testing services in the UK has found that Africans frequently describe a low self-perceived risk of HIV (Fenton et al., 2002; Erwin et al., 2002). The majority are diagnosed when ill health, either that of themselves or a close family member, intervenes. The implications of these results are that opportunities for early intervention and therapy that may preserve good health are being lost. Although there are many possible explanations for this state of affairs there are almost no studies that explore the experiences of African people living with HIV infection in the UK.

Vertical transmission of HIV from mother to baby can be substantially reduced by the use of antiretroviral drugs in pregnancy, delivery by caesarean section and avoidance of breast-feeding. These interventions are routinely offered to pregnant women with HIV in the UK. However issues around caesarean section and bottle-feeding may be culturally difficult for African women. Bottle-feeding may be construed as poor mothering ability and in some situations caesarean section is seen as a surrogate marker for HIV infection. To maximise appropriate interventions it is necessary for women to be aware of their HIV status whilst pregnant. Since 1998 all pregnant women in Britain are offered HIV antibody testing in antenatal clinics. A substantial proportion of new diagnoses of HIV in women of African backgrounds are made in this way. Knowledge about vertical transmission of HIV amongst focus groups of asylum seekers has been shown to be highly variable (Collard and Rigge, 2001). A woman may be the first family member to be diagnosed. And in consequence responsibility for initiating the discussion about HIV within a family often lies with the woman. The associated burden of disclosure to partners can lead to blame and breakdown of relationships.

The introduction in 1997 of combinations of potent anti retroviral drugs to treat people with HIV infection (Highly Active Antiretroviral Therapy – HAART) has resulted in a dramatic improvement in both morbidity and mortality (Palella, 1998). Such an approach is now standard in parts of the world with adequate money and medical infrastructure. It remains largely unavailable to the resource poor areas of the world. Despite the steep rise in new infections in the Britain the numbers of people developing or dying of AIDS has fallen sharply since 1997. This decline is however significantly less prominent among the UK black African population, although there is no suggestion of a difference in disease progression. Once started on HAART immunological and virological responses are equivalent in African and UK white patients (Frater et al., 2001) and are at least as good in women as in men (Moore et al., 2000). Despite medical and technological advance none of the available drugs provide a cure. The aim of therapy is to secure long-term suppression of viral activity and to preserve or attempt to restore the function of the immune system.HIV has a rapid and error prone replication rate. In the presence of sub-optimal drug levels, resistant mutations are selectively produced with consequent treatment failure. For patients this means a major commitment to long-term medication to maintain viral suppression, the best responses to therapy being associated with adherence levels of at least 95 per cent. The currently available compounds have substantial limitations. For some, drug absorption from the gut is influenced by the presence or absence of food, making it important to be able to control the content and the timing of meals. Numerous bulky tablets may be required to provide an adequate dose. The timing of doses is often critically important to maintain adequate blood levels. Despite this inhospitable pharmacological milieu the levels of adherence to HAART are overall considerably better than in other populations with chronic illness. The optimal time to start therapy remains uncertain. There is clear evidence that people with symptoms and signs associated with HIV infection have much to gain from taking medication, both in terms of improved well-being and for their longer term prognosis. For those who are asymptomatic therapeutic decision-making is based on laboratory markers of viral activity and immune system function. Use of antiretroviral drugs in pregnancy has been shown to reduce the rates of vertical transmission from mother to baby and HIV positive women who are pregnant must consider the needs of two individuals, themselves and their unborn child.

A variety of cultural and social factors may impinge on the medical management of HIV infection in African and other migrant groups. In the African community in which HIV is highly stigmatised, being observed taking specific HIV medication or its visible side effects may risk disclosure of HIV status to others. Poverty may prevent individuals following the necessary dietary advice associated with appropriate adherence. Care of others, especially children, may mean that the needs of others take priority over those of the patient. Africans with HIV infection participating in both the Padare project and in Project Nasah report that religious belief is important in taking antiretroviral medication as prescribed (Chinouya and Davidson, 2003; Weatherburn, 2003).

It has been suggested in one focus group study that African patients have specific difficulties with HIV services and health care professionals (Erwin and Peters, 1999). In contrast only 3 per cent of the respondents in Project Nasah reported problems with access to anti HIV treatments and most expressed satisfaction with the ways in which clinical decision making took place. In addition talking with clinic staff was reported as the most helpful way to access appropriate information concerning anti HIV treatments (Weatherburn et al., 2003). The beliefs held concerning the causes of ill health and thus the rationale for treatment decisions are critically important in this area if the extremely high levels of adherence to antiretroviral agents required both for optimal efficacy and to minimise the emergence of resistant viral mutants are to be met. Cultural differences of understanding on the origins of ill health and misfortune between doctor and patient must be recognised and addressed.

The Perspective of African Women Living in London

To better understand the experience of African women living with HIV in London a qualitative study was carried out in the summer of 2001 (Anderson and Doyal, 2003; Doyal and Anderson, forthcoming). Sixty-two women with HIV infection who were born in 11 different African countries participated. Using a narrative approach, women were asked to talk about their HIV status in the broader context of their life history. Recruitment took place in 5 hospital based specialist HIV clinics. With a median age of 33 years (range 20–58 years), most women were educated to at least secondary school level although only a quarter were either working or studying. Despite a variety of differences between the participants (in particular nationality, reasons for leaving Africa, income, education level and legal status in the UK) there were a number of marked similarities.

Almost all had received their HIV diagnosis in Britain. About 20 per cent had been diagnosed in pregnancy and for a further 70 per cent the diagnosis was consequent upon ill health – either their own or that of a close family member. A majority reported serious stresses in their lives, which were exacerbated by their HIV status. For many, such difficulties were layered onto previous life trauma. Almost half had direct experience of HIV related illness or death in close family members and some had experienced the death of a child from HIV.

Approximately 50 per cent the women were in the UK as a result of political pressures, particularly those coming from East and Central African countries. Rape, murder of family members and a variety of other forms of persecution had been experienced by at least a quarter of participants. One third were asylum seekers at the time of the study and a further one third had variable periods of leave to remain in the UK. The uncertainty of their position in the UK coupled with the paralysing impact of the UK immigration system emerged as an important theme, which exerted a major influence on the ability to make autonomous choices, both in the present and the future. This contributed to high levels of uncertainty, financial problems and restrictions of movement.

Most of the women had children, although for some they were still in Africa. Women with dependant children in the UK were usually the primary carers, frequently alone and without the levels of family and social support that would be normal in African communities. Some women regretted the inability of UK society to provide an appropriate cultural upbringing for their children. Anxiety about the welfare of children in the event of death was common and staying alive for the sake of children was cited frequently as the major motivating factor in life. For those with children in Africa women were attempting to sustain family connections and relationships across at least two continents, often at considerable emotional and financial cost.

The reality of life in the UK was not as many women had expected and most had experienced very poor housing and financial conditions at some stage. Women subsisting on the limited resources available to asylum seekers had described serious difficulties in ensuring an adequate diet, warm clothes and the bare school essentials for their children. Women described forgoing their own needs for food and clothing to ensure that their children were adequately fed.

Almost all (95 per cent) of the women talked about the stigmatising nature of HIV especially within the African community. About a third reported direct experience of HIV related stigmatisation such as rejection by husband or partners, eviction from their home, marking or special washing of kitchen utensils and refusal to allow contact with children. Others described witnessing discrimination or unsympathetic responses towards HIV related topics or known HIV positive people. Another third expressed considerable anxiety that they would be subject to discrimination if their HIV status were known. The consequent need to control information about their HIV infection had profound effects on how women related to other people, health services and voluntary sector agencies.

The limiting effects of physical ill health consequent upon HIV were described by about half the women. Commonest complaints were of weakness, tiredness, and side effects of medications and unpredictable periods of poor health. Five were visually impaired and two were in wheel chairs. HIV associated ill health in others, either sick partners, sick children or in some cases both, imposed further limitations. The unpredictability of health was one of the most difficult aspects, making forward planning difficult. Feelings anxiety and uncertainty were common. Of particular concern was the possibility that that their diagnosis might be revealed. The greatest fear for many was that their situation might become public knowledge in African communities in London. In consequence they frequently felt the need to lie and many described the problems involved in leading a secret life.

One of the main topics explored in this study was the management of daily life. How do women look after themselves when faced with such a variety of obstacles? A powerful sense of resilience existed amongst study participants with three emerging themes: the management of information, the use of medical services and importance of religious faith.

Disclosure of information about HIV serostatus emerged as a major theme. Many shared their diagnosis only with the clinical team or with a limited group of people. Reasons cited were fear of rejection by family, partners and friends, fear of stigmatisation and shielding others from anxiety. Anxiety that family in Africa might acquire the information via a third party made women disinclined either to discuss their diagnosis with others from their home country or to attend support groups for fear of meeting people that they knew. Controlling information lead to secrecy and lies, which were difficult to sustain and caused some women to curtail their activities. A number of women said that the issue of disclosure of HIV status was a barrier to the establishment of emotional and sexual relationships. Revealing details to infected and affected children was identified as particularly difficult. For those who did discuss HIV with others the easiest relationships were those with other HIV [positive people. And the support given by various voluntary sector organisations was highly praised by those who used them.

For this particular group of women who were attending specialist hospital clinics health workers and clinical services were a central source of both physical and psychological support. The hospital and clinic were regarded as safe environments and for many these were their major source of information and support. The importance of continuity of care was emphasised. Many women travelled considerable distances to outpatient appointments, either to stick with familiar clinical teams or to preserve confidentiality by being seen away from their local area. Two thirds of the women interviewed had experience of antiretroviral drug therapy. Most women were fearful of side effects prior to initiating treatment and many had experienced adverse events on starting therapy. In most cases, these had either resolved or treatments had been changed to provide a manageable regimen. Most women on antiretroviral treatment were strongly committed. Many had given up a great deal to maintain their access to the drugs and they tried very hard to make sure the regimen worked. However a minority described their unwillingness to start treatment despite clinical advice to do so. Fear of side effects, anxieties about long term harm from drugs, apprehension about confidentiality and the impact of religious beliefs were important determinants of their decisions.

The vast majority of the women (92 per cent) described their religious faith as extremely important in their lives and a major source of support in coping with their difficulties. In addition the direct and indirect healing potential of prayer was a common theme. All but one of the women were of various Christian, denominations. Most (but not all) were regular churchgoers and church was described as a place where an HIV identity could be forgotten for a while. Despite the importance of religious faith only a minority had discussed their HIV infection with their priest or other spiritual adviser.

In response to the question of what would most improve their lives the commonest response was a desire to find something to do and to regain a sense of purpose in life. The importance of adequate accommodation and money was highlighted, as was the need for help with childcare in particular during times of ill health.

Conclusions

African women dealing with HIV in London have to manage a multiplicity of challenges stemming from their position as migrants, as women and as people with HIV infection Each factors alone has its particular problems with but when combined together the difficulties rise exponentially. The voices of the women themselves highlight, in particular, the profoundly stigmatising nature of HIV in the African community and this must be understood by all those involved in the planning and delivery of services. Working on strategies to overcome HIV associated stigma must be one if the most important health priorities. Stigma inhibits all forms of communication and progress both at an individual and community level as the women described in this chapter have so eloquently shown. For any grouping within a wider society both the factors that unite and those that divide need to be understood and taken seriously if they are to receive sensitive and appropriate services. The diagnosis and management of HIV infection has its own challenges and complexities and these need to be understood within the context of the life experiences of individuals and the other stresses in their lives. But at the same time it is essential that autonomy is respected and the mechanisms that are employed to deal with adversity are acknowledged. Women have demonstrated amazing resilience in the face of what are often extremely difficult circumstances. Recognition of this reality needs to be the starting point both for future research and for the planning of services to meet the needs of HIV positive women from Africa and others.

The African experience in the UK is a current worked example of the impact of global structures and processes in people's lives. Worldwide, people have been set on the move by war, economic factors and other pressures, all of which are likely to produce successive waves of migrants. Although each population will have its particular needs, generic lessons can be learnt and applied from those who have gone on ahead. Recognising the dignity, integrity and rights of others has never been of greater importance.

Acknowledgements

Particular thanks go to the African women who participated in the project and who gave so much information about their often painful experiences. Professor Lesley Doyal, School of Policy studies, University of Bristol was pivotal to the execution and analysis of the qualitative study on African women living with HIV in London and Private Patients Plan Health Care Trust provided financial support.

References

African Communities Involvement Association (ACIA) (1999), *An Evaluation of HIV/AIDS work with African Communities in South West London*. London: ACIA.

African HIV Policy Network (on behalf of the Department of Health) (2002), *Health and social care services for Africans affected by HIV and AIDS: A framework for action.* Draft report. London: Department of Health.

All Party Parliamentary Group on AIDS (2001), *The UK, HIV and Human Rights: recommendations for the next five years.*

Anderson, J. and Doyal L. (2003), Women from Africa living with HIV in London: A descriptive study, *AIDS Care* (In press).

Ankrah, M., Schwartz, M., Miller, J., (1996), Care and Support Systems, in L. Long and M. Ankrah (eds), *Women's Experiences with HIV: an international perspective.* New York: Columbia University Press.

Barnett, T. and Whiteside, A. (2002), *AIDS in the twenty first century – disease and globalisation.* Basingstoke: Macmillan.

Barry, S.M., Lloyd-Owen, S.J., Madge, S.J., Cozzi-Lepri, A, Evans, A.J., Phillips, A.N., Johnson, M.A. (2002), The changing demographics of new HIV diagnoses at a London Centre from 1994 to 2000, *HIV Medicine*, 2002, 3, pp.129-134.

Baylies, C. and Bujra, J. (1999), Rebels at risk: young women and the shadow of AIDS in Africa, in C. Becker, J–P. Dozon, C. Obbo and M. Toure (eds) *Vivre et Penser le SIDA en Afrique/Experiencing and Understanding AIDS in Africa.* Paris: Karthala.

Baylies, C. and Bujra, J. (2000), *AIDS Sexuality and Gender in Africa. Collective strategies and struggles in Tanzania and Zambia.* London: Routledge.

Berer, M. and Ray, S. (1993), *Women and HIV/AIDS: an international resource book.* London: Pandora.

Burgi, D. and Fleury, F. (1996), A National AIDS prevention programme for migrants in M. Haour-Knipe and R. Rector (eds). *Crossing borders: Migration ethnicity and AIDS.* London: Taylor and Francis.

Burnett, A. (2002), *Guide to Health Workers providing Care for Refugees and Asylum Seekers.* London: Medical Foundation for Care of Victims of Torture.

Buve, A., Bishikwabo-Nsarhaza, K., Mutangadura, G. (2002), The spread and effect of HIV-1 infection in sub-Saharan Africa, *Lancet*, 359, pp. 2011-17.

Chinouya, M., Davidson, O., Fenton, K. (2000), *The Mayisha Study – sexual attitudes and lifestyles of migrant Africans in inner London.* London: AVERT.

Chinouya, M. and Davidson, O. (2003), *The Padare Project: Assessing health related knowledge, attitudes and behaviours of HIV positive Africans accessing services in north central London.* London: African HIV Policy Network and Camden primary Care Trust.

Collard, S. and Rigge, M. (2001), *Mother to child transmission of HIV – talking about it.* London: College of Health.

Dallison, J. and Lobstein, T. (1995), *Poor Expectations: Poverty and undernourishment in pregnancy.* London: Maternity Alliance.

Del Amo, J., Goh, B.T., Forster, G.E. (1996), AIDS defining conditions in Africans resident in the United Kingdom, *International Journal of AIDS*, 1996, 7, pp. 44-47.

Del Amo, J., Petruckevitch, A., Philips, A.N. (1996), Spectrum of disease in Africans with AIDS in London, *AIDS*, 1996, 10, pp. 1563-9.

Del Amo, J., Petruckevitch, A., Philips, A. (1998), Disease progression and survival in HIV infected Africans in London, *AIDS*, 1998, 12, pp. 1203-9.

Department of Health (2001), *The National Strategy for Sexual Health and HIV.* London: Department of Health.

Doyal, L. and Anderson, J. (2003), 'My fear is to fall in love again..' How HIV-positive African women survive in London, forthcoming.

Doyal, L., Naidoo, J. and Wilton, T. (eds) (1994), *AIDS: Setting a Feminist Agenda.* London: Taylor and Francis.

Elam, G. and Chinouya, M. (2000), *Feasibility Study for Health Surveys among Black African Populations living in the UK: Stage 2 diversity among Black African Communities.* London: Department of Health.

Elam, G., Fenton, K., Johnson, A., Nazroo, J., Ritchie, J. (1999), *Exploring ethnicity and sexual health.* London: Social and Community Planning Research.

Erwin, J. and Peters, B. (1999), Treatment issues for HIV+ Africans in London, *Social Science and Medicine,* 49, pp. 1519-1528

Frater, A.J. et al. (2002), Comparative response of African HIV-1-infected individuals to highly active antiretroviral therapy, *AIDS,* 2002, 16, pp. 1139-1146.

Glynn, J.R. et al. (2001), Study Group on the Heterogeneity of HIV Epidemics in African Cities. Why do young women have a much higher prevalence of HIV than young Men? A study in Kisumu, Kenya and Ndola, Zambia, *AIDS,* 2001, 15, pp. 51-60.

Greater London Authority Policy Support Unit (2001), *Refugees and asylum seekers in London: a GLA perspective,* draft report for consultation. London: GLA.

Green, G. and Sobo, E. J. (2000), *The Endangered Self: Managing the Social Risk of HIV.* London: Routledge.

Haour-Knipe, M. and Rector, R. (eds) (1996), *Crossing borders: Migration ethnicity and AIDS.* London: Taylor and Francis.

MacPhail, C., Williams, B.G. and Campbell, C. (2002), Relative risk of HIV infection among young men and women in a South African township, *International Journal of AIDS,* 13, 5, pp. 331-42.

McLeish, J. (2002), *Mothers in Exile. Maternity experiences of asylum seekers in England.* London: The Maternity Alliance.

McMunn, A.M., Mwanje, R., Paine, K., Pozniak, A.L. (1998), Health service utilisation in London's African migrant communities: implications for HIV prevention, *AIDS Care,* 1998, 10, pp. 453-62.

Oxfam, Refugee Council, the Asylum Rights Campaign and Body Shop (2000), *Token Gestures. The effects of the voucher scheme on Asylum seekers and organisations in the UK,* Submission to the Home Office. London: Home Office.

Schoepf, B. (1998), Inscribing the body politic: women and AIDS in Africa, in M. Lock and P. Kaufert (eds), *Women and Biopower: what constitutes resistance?* Cambridge: Cambridge University Press.

Schoepf, B. (2001), International AIDS research in Anthropology: Taking a critical perspective on the crisis, *Annual Review of Anthropology,* 30, pp. 335-361.

Chapter 10

The Politics of Identity and Community: Migrant Women from Turkey in Germany

Umut Erel

Research on post-war migration to Western Europe has long constructed the male migrant as the prototype. If women migrants were acknowledged, it was as dependants. Migrant women have been portrayed as victimised on the one hand by the global structures of inequality forcing them to migrate, and on the other hand as women within the particularly oppressive gender relations of their families and wider ethnic communities. These notions of the passive, oppressed migrant woman dominated much of the research. In the literature on migrant women in Germany, both in quantitative and qualitative terms images of women of Turkish background came to represent migrant women: 'From the 1970s onwards, a clear tendency towards the orientalization of migrant women can be identified: the debate on "foreign women" (*Ausländerinnen*) became a debate on Turkish women' (Inowlocki and Lutz, 2000: 307). The key themes along which research on migrant women from Turkey has been structured for the last three decades have been that of 'the (uncivilized) stranger, the victim of patriarchal honour and being "twice rootless"' (Inowlocki and Lutz, 2000: 307). The modernity-difference hypothesis (Apitzsch, 1996) constructed migrants as backward and in need of catching up with modernity in Europe. In particular migrant women, due to their important role in the family were seen as representing tradition and the more originary type of the culture of origin. Migrant women's commitment to the family was therefore seen as 'a particular obstacle in the process of modernisation' (Apitzsch, 1996). This analytically locates migrant women firmly within the domestic sphere, which is often seen as a privileged site for passing on the 'essence' of an ethnocised or nationalised culture (Yuval-Davis, 1996). Portraying migrant women as particularly linked to the family was thus seen as a confirmation of their underachievement of modernity.

　　　Other factors contributing to migrant women's particular positioning such as the gendered institutional regulation of migration have rarely been taken into account in the explanatory frameworks of migration research. Thus, immigration legislation, recruitment contracts and intermediaries play a crucial enabling and constraining role. For women who enter under family reunification legislation, this severely constrains their possibilities to take up work in the first years. Those who enter as tourists, students, au pairs, undocumented or asylum seekers, also face restricted (or illegalised) access to the labour market, and social rights. Often these immigration statuses increase their gendered vulnerability. Factors such as the lack of rights to work as legally dependent spouses, formal and informal discrimination in the labour market, as well as in civil society (Akashe-Böhme, 2000; Erdem, 2000) are rarely included into an analysis of migrant women's lives. However, 'being deprived of rights of entry and settlement as well as broader rights of citizenship, are central reasons for the forms of domination faced by migrant men and women' (Anthias, 2000; 26).

Assumptions about migrant women's culturally reified passivity and reduction to family life are problematic explanatory frameworks, fostering tautological arguments as well as the reproduction of oppressive truths and social realities through the social policy approaches they inform: they fix migrant women as passive and within the private sphere, while ignoring their interventions into community building and both participating in established public spheres, as well as creating their own public spheres. Therefore, a shift in the approaches, methods and theoretical underpinnings of research on migrant women is necessary. Such an approach should not view migrant women just as passively enduring migration (Lutz, 1998). This article hopes to contribute to a growing feminist literature that views migrant women as social actors in their own right and examines their agency and subjectivity.

> The role of agency is particularly vital for a gendered account of migration because it is so often assumed that women simply follow men and that their role in migration is reactive rather than proactive. (Kofman et al., 2000: 23)

This chapter[1] explores how notions of gendered and ethnocised identity and 'identity politcs' are articulated in social and political activism of migrant women. This is based on a study on the life stories of skilled and highly educated migrant women in Britain and in Germany.[2] Here, I will only look at two life-stories of migrant women living in Germany this enables me to explore in detail the ways in which they view their activism as contributing to their subjectivity. The use of biographical interviews and their in-depth analysis is particularly suited to exploring the subjectivity and agency of migrant women, that is, the ways in which the interviewees make sense of their lives and act upon their personal and

---

[1] This paper is based on my PhD 'Subjectivity and Agency in the Life Stories of Migrant Women of Turkish Background in Germany and Britain' at the Faculty of Humanities, Nottingham Trent University, UK 2002. It was written under the supervision of Prof. Richard Johnson, Prof. Eleonore Kofman and Dr. Tracey Skelton, whom I wish to thank for their intellectual guidance, encouragement and support.

[2] The sample consisted of 10 first and second generation interviewees. The interviewees' were all skilled and highly educated, with diverse occupations and routes of migration. Their involvement in social and political activism also varied. A common issue that all the interviewees adressed was how their position as migrant women related to their social, and political activities. Here it is important to point out that most of them saw their professional activities as constituting a form of social intervention, also.

collective circumstances (Lutz, 1998). My sample of highly educated and skilled women is due to their neglect in research on migrant women. This absence is not just problematic empirically, but theoretically it also does not take account of their role as 'mediators' between ethnic minority people and the ethnic majority society (Lutz, 1991) and as 'organic intellectuals' articulating specific knowledges of gendered and ethnocised marginalization and organizing anti-racist and anti-sexist resistance (Rodriguez, 1999). Thus, my findings indicate that skilled and highly educated migrant women, despite their activism and their contributions to shifting the discursive terrain of citizenship are marginalized as social actors on the basis of their gender and ethnic identities in theories and policies of citizenship.[3] This is an exploratory study and does not claim statistical representativity, indeed skilled and highly educated migrant women from Turkey form a very small minority among the population. Instead, I am interested in an in-depth exploration of the processes of giving meaning to gendered and ethnic identities as articulating a personal and a collective subjective of politics. As such, the following narratives are at once highly personal and at the same time inform wider discourses and practices of migrant women's activism. The biographical approach aptly characterises the conjunction of these in elaborating a politics of the self and its relation to a wider 'identity politics'.

In the following I am interested in the interviewees' fields of activism. This refers to two levels: on the one hand what issues they choose to politicise, and on the other hand how they articulate them. Moreover, I analyse the organisational forms they choose, including elements of both identity politics and other forms of politics. This relates to notions of belonging and the question of community building. The interviewees cited here construct community both within and across ascriptions of gendered and ethnicised identity. However, at the same time they challenge simplistic identity ascriptions which fix them to a single ethnic and gendered subject position.

The notion of identity politics is problematic, as will be discussed in more detail below. However as a working definition I use the notion of identity politics as elaborated by the Combahee River Collective:

> We realize that the only people who care enough about us to work consistently for our liberation is us. Our politics evolve from our healthy love for ourselves, our sisters and our community, which allows us to continue our struggle and work. This focusing upon our own oppression is embodied in the concept of identity politics. We believe that the most profound and potentially the most radical politics come directly out of our own identity, as opposed to working to the end of somebody else's oppression. (Combahee River Collective, 1998: 522)

In this paper, I am most interested in aspects of identity politics where forms of political activism and organisation reify essentialist identity positions as the privileged subject of knowing and doing politics. In this sense, I view political

---

[3] While my study focuses on highly educated and skilled migrant women, it should not be read as indicating that women with less formal education are therefore less agentic.

activism as a site of negotiating identity and thus elaborating specific politics of identity. The privileging of (sets of) essentialised identities can take place in an overt or hidden form, I argue. However, the politics of identity as elaborated by the interviewees also importantly entails a willingness to deconstruct and cross boundaries and construct new political subjects, across multiple identities. This entails highlighting different dynamics of inclusion and exclusion on the basis of gender, ethnicity, sexuality and class. Moreover, I examine how notions of belonging are expressed and how this relates to the stories of activism. These are central elements for understanding the interviewees' constructions of identity and community an issue at the heart of the citizenship debate.

Following Yuval-Davis (1997) I view citizenship as a multi-layered and multi-dimensional concept. In this paper I look at the ways in which the interviewees locate themselves vis-à-vis local, national and transnational communities. This includes their activism in the countries of residence as well as Turkey. Baubök's (1994) concept of transnational citizenship emphasises the viability of residence and social rights of migrants in their country of residence. While the interviewees all had a secure residence status at the time of interview, and residence rights did not form a problem for them, their activism shows how they articulate their membership in the society of residence. Soysal's concept of post-national citizenship (Soysal, 1994) emphasises the importance of the country of residence for the legal and social aspects of identity and agency, however underemphasises the salience of political rights in the substantiation of citizenship. The interviewees' stories on their activism testify on the one hand to their social and political contributions to the countries of residence through their professional, social, cultural and political activism. Another important aspect is how the interviewees conceptualise the political. The notion of the private/public divide posits women's activities of childbearing, and caring as merely reproductive and ignores its social and political aspects. The interviewees' stories contradict this. Thus, mothering is an important aspect of articulating, transmitting and negotiating belonging, also vis-à-vis institutions of the society of residence. Women's continuing responsibility for caring can however limit their access to the labour market and to the exercise of political rights (Lister, quoted in Sales, 2000). While citizenship entails passive aspects of access to rights, here I focus on the active and participatory aspects.

Migrant women's contributions to the societies they live in are rarely recognised, and most often their 'citizenship practices' (Sassen, 2000; Turner, 1993) are presented as merely being passive recipients of social rights. However, as Kofman et al. (2000: 190) state: 'Far from being passive victims of patriarchal social systems and racist imigration policy, migrant women have challenged the constraints on their political activities and engaged in and reworked the definition of the political.'

Pinar

Pinar is a 36 year old social worker, she has a daughter, aged 9 and is a single mother. Her professional work and social activism has focused for a long time on improving the living conditions of migrant women in Germany. I have chosen to present Pinar's story on her activism on the one hand because she articulates a complex and dynamic view of identity and activism. Moreover, through her activities she has participated in creating communities and concepts of identity and activism, thus acting in some ways as an 'organic intellectual' (Gutierrez, 1999).

Becoming an Activist

As a young woman, through friends of Turkish and Kurdish background, Pinar got involved in left-wing activitism: she attended meetings and participated in activities of different left-wing groups. She emphasises that even at the time, she viewed some aspects of these organisations critically.

> These were all left wing organisations and they had the aim of building communism in Turkey, so to speak. To make a revolution. (...) [I got to know different organisations], I found all of them (...) too dogmatic. Many things bothered me, I have to say, because I found it too much directed towards Turkey.

For Pinar the experience of being a migrant was a central political issue, already at the time, although there was little collective articulation of a migrants' political position. This led to conflicts with the members of the left-wing organisations, both about determining the privileged field of politics and about authority. They denied the second generation any political competence 'You haven't got a clue, you're the second generation, you are mostly socialised here and you aren't even refugees, your parents are not even politicised', 'You look at these issues too much like a European'. These were the arguments put forward to disqualify Pinar's interventions.

This is a typical conflict where the generation of migration is used to construct a privileged, authentic knowledge position to claim superior authority. Such a strategy constructs an ethnic authenticity as a necessary basis for gaining knowledge and political authority. The field of politics – 'revolution in Turkey' – is pre-given, as well as its conceptualisation. The argument of a necessary experiential basis for doing politics or for participating in strategic decision-making is highly problematic (cf. Anthias and Yuval-Davis, 1992). It constructs politics as statically expressing a pre-given subjectivity, where any re-conceptualisation of the process or political aims amounts to deviation. Moreover, it assumes a set of fixed characteristics and opinions as a pre-condition for participation at the level of decision-making. It does not allow for differentially positioned people to articulate any political or strategic differences. Such differences are seen as a deviation, threatening the aim or unity of an organisation. The gender- and age-based hierarchies within this type of political organisation also contributed to Pinar's standpoints and opinions as a young woman being marginalised.

Despite this de-valuation of her standpoints, Pinar views her contributions to these organisations as important. These organisations needed the second generation people for 'translating leaflets, or fly-posting them etc. And I do think that we allowed ourselves to be instrumentalised.' Pinar was not a member in one organisation, but sympathised with different organisations and participated in those activities she supported. When in the late 1980s, there was a meeting for left-wing women activists across party political divides, she helped to organise it and sees it as an important achievement (cf. Avrupa Kadin Bülteni, 1991). This was the first time that migrant women got together to discuss the role and position of women in left-wing organisations critically and to develop women-centred or feminist left-wing political projects. However in this forum also, Pinar recalls conflicts on issues of authority between the generations. Thus, while Pinar values the overcoming of party political divisions on the basis of a common gender identity, she also recognises that other differences and hierarchies on the basis of generation of migration remained intact in this forum, too.

Through her marriage, Pinar unselfconsciously became part of the organisation her husband was a member of. Although she was never formally a member of the organisation, she stopped attending other organisations' meetings and was perceived to belong to this one organisation. Retrospectively, Pinar is self-critical about this. This is a common mechanism, whereby women get subsumed under their male partner's political attitude and status. One of Pinar's criticisms of her husband during their marriage was that he used his political ideals to postpone his actual social responsibilities, to which Pinar responded: 'The revolution starts here at home, not outside in the big world.' Thus, she debated also with her husband about the status of politics in everyday life. While she presents her husband as expecting social change from outside to solve the problems in Turkey, Pinar characterises her own approach as taking small steps to achieve concrete change from where she lives. A turning point in her political work was the experience of political violence, in her husband's organization that resulted in the accidental death of a close friend. While Pinar had opposed political violence all along, this experience prompted her decision to quit this type of political organisation: 'After this it was clear that I would quit. This finally convinced me.'

Politics of Experience and Place

The personal and the political were closely intertwined in Pinar's involvement with a woman's NGO. As she had recently separated from her husband and had to redefine her role as a single mother, in this group, she started doing 'grassroots work (...) with women in situations of separation, counselling, everything on a voluntary basis.' This constituted a change in her field and conception of politics, compared to her earlier involvement with her husband's organisation. Pinar was soon elected into the management committee of the NGO and became involved in its international projects. She participated in planning, evaluating and setting up women's projects, such as refuges, health projects, etc. in Third World countries.

At first she found that the new responsibilities put a great strain on her. Gradually, as she trained and familiarised herself with the work, she enjoyed it a lot since she 'saw the direct benefits' of her work. She worked in this NGO for four years, until it was dissolved. At the same time she began paid part-time employment at a migrant women's centre. This job gradually developed into a full time job and recently Pinar has entered a managerial position in this women's centre. After her involvement with the NGO, she continued to work politically on women's issues:

> P: My interest to work on women's issues developed very quickly. Through the personal but also through the political.

> U: Do you mean your experience of the pregnancy and your marriage?

> P: But also through the experiences at home with my parents, you know. And it was very important to reflect on all this. We founded a group for migrant girls and women and we had an exchange about things we had experienced ourselves.

Pinar participated in the foundation of a women's group for migrant and Black women, where they had 'a lot of space to work through' their own experiences, including traumatic experiences of gendered or racialized violence. The consciousness raising methods employed in this group enabled Pinar and others to give meaning to her personal experiences in a collective process. These could then be articulated as collective political concerns. The shame that is often attached to experiences of victimisation and violence gave way to a political articulation of an identity defined by actively and collectively 'struggling' rather than being victimised. The group offered seminars and workshops for migrant women and girls in various cities on issues of racism and violence against women. The group thus formed part of an emergent vocal and visible movement of migrant and black women and articulated their specific political position.

> There were the first books where migrant women started to- we really *fought* for this, against the white structures here, to say that we do not want to be researched about (...) by white Germans. Instead we want migrants to research about us, you know. And we do not want to be seen as objects, (...) on whose back (...) others make a name for themselves, but we want to be involved creatively and actively and we want to participate more, also in political events. And legally and everything.

They organised a series of workshops and conferences, inviting international speakers, also to develop strategies in the areas of political, cultural, legal and social representation. This was a phase in the early 1990s, in which a political subject of migrant women was formed in opposition and delineation to white German feminism which was the 'direct milieu'. In this story of her political work Pinar articulates two related issues. She had previously articulated a subject position of an independent fighter for herself which was resistant to her parents' projects of femininity for her, as well as in contrast to the passive and merely supportive role that she rejected in her marriage. In the leftwing organisations directed towards Turkey, she had contested the relegation of her standpoints to a secondary position as inauthentic. Pinar's participation in the creation of a migrant and black women's movement articulates her personal strategies for creating a subject position as a collective political subject. The strategy of fighting for a space to be recognised as agentic pervades her life story and informs her conception of the political collective and its strategies, as she elaborates in the above quote.

Pinar presents this period as very significant on a personal level as a 're-socialisation into the culture of origin.' This process she feels had already started in her relationship with her husband. I think this raises an important and interesting issue of how Pinar conceptualises 'the culture of origin'. The reference to her 're-socialisation' into a culture of origin through her husband can be read as her increased interest in learning and speaking Turkish and engaging with the political situation in Turkey and its leftwing Diaspora politics. However, it should be noted that Pinar's ex-husband, a political refugee, is Kurdish, so that the process of learning about and engaging with 'Turkishness' or 'being from Turkey' in dialogue with her ex-husband already constitutes a construction of a cross-ethnic or differentiated 'culture of origin'. In this narrative, the 'culture of origin' with which Pinar engages is ethnically differentiated and open. The meaning of 'culture of origin' in the context of her engagement with migrant and black women on the other hand is consciously cross-ethnic and relates to different trajectories of migration and processes of racialisation. The engagement with differentially racialised women and the construction of shared political projects contains a process of cross-ethnic community building. When she presents this community building as a 're-socialisation into the culture of origin', she uses the metaphor of a shared origin. This metaphor subverts the myth of common origin that is commonly employed to naturalise and legitimise national and ethnic cohesion (Anthias and Yuval-Davis, 1992, Bhabha, 1990). Pinar's strategy of projecting a commonalty of migrant and black women in Germany into the past contains elements of fantasy in the sense of myth-making. That Pinar's presentation of 'origins' appears more constructed than naturalised national historiographies, I think is due to the marginality of such a cross-ethnic project of doing and representing history, rather than its lacking coherence. Thus, Ohliger (2000) argues for a de-nationalisation of historiography, to engage more adequately with the present and future concerns of globalisation instead of reifying national paradigms and narratives.

> In such a view, marginal populations such as immigrants and minorities could become central. They would offer the possibility of researching history from the periphery, narrating it from the margins, partly against the *telos* of the centre and thus opening up historical imagination for much larger, more open but also more conflictual interpretations. (Ohliger, 2000:2)

Pinar's representation of history is part of her project of constructing a cross-ethnic political subject of migrant and black women, and thus part of a construction of community based on shared political projects of a gendered and racialized subject position.

In Pinar's story of her political work, not only the subject and field of politics, but also its location have changed. During her involvement in Turkish left-wing organisations, their efforts were directed at the long-term goal of building communism in Turkey. Retrospectively, she criticises this approach for neglecting practical political work that takes one's own life and living environment as a starting point. When she worked in the women's NGO, she worked internationally co-operating with local partners. At this international level the starting point of politics was not her own life, however the women's projects she helped set up worked for tangible changes locally. In this context Pinar refers to a shared experiential basis of the identification as woman that constitutes a link to her own life, which she presents as more concrete than the Diaspora politics. The meta-discourse of a shared gender position and its underlying experiential basis allows her to construct her international field of political activism as related to her own living environment. In this context, an essentialised notion of womanhood serves to de-essentialise a national identity basis for politics in order to delineate this type of activism from her previous Diaspora politics.[4] Currently Pinar's focus of political work are migrant and black women in Germany for whom she tries to achieve practical changes in their living conditions. She emphasises the importance of this shift for her own identity construction, since to her it signifies that the centre of her life is in Germany, not Turkey. She finds it difficult to follow political and social developments in Turkey, since 'everything moves so fast there'. She does not follow the Turkish press on a daily basis, but keeps informed of broader developments there through monthly journals. She concedes that her visions have changed, also, and are now based on her life in Germany. She sees her political connection to Turkey as one of supporting individual projects such as a woman's refuge or a woman's journal she helped to set up as part of a German NGO with funding from Germany. She contrasts this with her in-depth knowledge of the German political process that enables her to intervene effectively on different political levels.

Germanness?

Pinar presents her decision to take on German citizenship as a contradictory and ambivalent processes. For a long time she had thought of taking on German citizenship as a form of 'treason'. She explains this through having had partly internalised the logic of either belonging to Germany or to Turkey. However she now thinks that the second generation of migrants have a 'bi-cultural' identity by virtue of growing up in Germany. Thus, she resolved the conflict of formal

---

[4] Räthzel gives an example of a group whose 'essentialist notion [of womanhood] is a basic motor for their commitment to make boundaries between nationalities and *ethnic* groups more permeable' and at the same time aimed to change masculinities and femininities (Räthzel, N: Hybridität ist die Antwort, aber was war nochmal die Frage? in Brigitte Kossek (ed.) Gegen-Rassismen. Konstruktionen Interaktionen Interventionen. Hamburg p. 209).

loyalties through positively evaluating her subject position as dual. Her decision to take on German citizenship was triggered by the increasing racist violence at the beginning of the 1990s as a reaction to German unification. At the time, Pinar felt frightened and feared 'that with underlying economic developments it would not improve but get more difficult.' She argues that taking on German citizenship enabled her to get more actively involved in the political process in Germany. The fact that she could later-on take on Turkish citizenship, too, eased the decision and allowed her to formally express her dual allegiance. However, she evaluates the taking on of German citizenship as a:

> detour (...). Why should people who have decided they want to stay here, why should they not be able to be elected or to participate in elections. For me (...) this totally contradicts the universality of human rights.

Pinar delineates her strategy of taking up German citizenship from assimilation or one-sided integration. Instead, she views it as enhancing her possibilities of articulating political dissent and furthering the impact of her advocacy of migrant and black women's rights.

Throughout the narrative Pinar emphasised the political salience of her paid employment. Working in a migrant women's centre to Pinar is one way of intervening politically. Her professional and political activities are not clearly bounded. Thus, through her job she is part of a number of local and regional governmental committees in which she enjoys participating and making her presence felt. She is often criticised for 'complicating everything' when she intervenes against the normalisations of dominant identities. 'It is always in situations like this that one is uncomfortable for people. (...) But of course this has psychological effects.' Pinar views her job as a field of political activism, where she offers services to migrant women but at the same time is able to 'give voice' to their concerns, including the initiation of legal changes. In this sense, the professional field is a central area in which Pinar articulates her citizenship as social participation. This includes the levels of community building, giving services but also initiating and sustaining campaigns. This political activism also initiates legal changes, Pinar gives the example of a campaign to end the dependent residence status of married migrant women to the marriage. In this instance, her political activism aims at broadening the basis for citizenship, of which residence rights are a crucial component.

Pinar's story of her political activism can be seen as part of a community construction shared by other interviewees, mainly second generation migrants. Identity politics as coming to consciousness and gaining a voice both in terms of gender and as (second generation) migrants are the key themes. The issue of locating oneself vis-à-vis claims or denial of belonging to national communities is a further commonality in the narratives of the second generation interviewees. While not all of them share Pinar's internationalist outlook, none of them identified primarily in national terms. Instead, the idea that the position of in-betweenness gives privileged access to questioning social relations and their power basis was commonly shared. Other second generation interviewees shared Pinar's view, that their professional work or paid employment, relating to migrants or migrant women, formed part of their social or political activism. While these themes are not limited to the second generation, they are elaborated differentially in the first generation migrants' stories. Among the first generation migrants, identity politics and the relation to place plays a different role. The first generation interviewees do not present the process of ethnic identification as an articulation of political subjectivity. However they share with the second generation interviewees a claim to a 'double consciousness' (Gilroy, 1993) of being both from Turkey and from Germany. In contrast to the second generation interviewees, they present their experiences of power relations and inequalities and their own responses to these in Turkey as a constitutive part of their political positioning. This is most articulate in the life stories of those who were politically active in Turkey.

Birgül

Birgül is a 40 year old medical doctor. She is a single mother, and her daughter is six years old. She fled to Germany in 1980, after the coup d'etat in Turkey, where she had been a political activist.

While Birgül's political activism in Turkey is clearly decisive in her life story, in the interview, she only referred to it as a trigger for her migration experience, while she elaborates on her activism in Germany. This indicates a biographical strategy of locating herself firmly within the German context in which she lives, rather than in a retrospective or future 'homeland'.

Identity Politics: 'As if there's a different politics for the Germans and the Turks'

Birgül underlines her interest and involvement in the political and social life in Germany. When she started her professional specialisation she experienced severe difficulties in terms of professional and foreigners' law in obtaining the necessary permits. Birgül sought advice from and became involved in 'antiracist resistance'. She contributed to setting up different antiracist groups. In this way, she used her own experiences of institutional discrimination and her personal struggle against them as a motivation for organising antiracist groups. While Birgül had been active in leftwing politics in Turkey, the area of antiracist politics was new to her. As she points out throughout the interview, the experiential dimension of racism has been formative for her self-representation and how she views her part in German society.

In this sense, Birgül's activism involved some central elements of identity politics. She recognised and analysed her personal experiences of institutional racism as a valid starting point to organise collectively. In the early 1980s antiracist politics were not seen as a central field of leftwing politics in Germany, and leftwing groups of Turkish origin focused their analysis and activism on homeland politics. Thus, Birgül's formulation of an antiracist politics that politicised experiences of racialization rather than adapting the prevalent paradigm of enmity to foreigners and submitting to the role of client of 'foreigner-friendly' German activists and mediators (cf. Radtke, 1994) constituted an agentic subject position for migrants. This challenged not just the hegemonic analyses of racism as 'enmity to foreigners', furthermore it challenged the reified relation between migrants as victims of racism or inversely as recipients of support and protection of 'foreigner-friendly' Germans. The pitfalls of identity politics as essentialising and homogenising personal and collective identities are well-known. Still, they carved out a space for gaining political agency for migrants disenfranchised and excluded from party politics and marginalised in other forms of political organisation.

Apart from her antiracist activism, Birgül was also active in traditional leftwing organisations, dominated by Germans. She describes her experiences there as follows:

> Birgül: I was involved in political activities here. However in the political groups I also experienced that they treated us as if we didn't know Marxism: 'Have you ever read anything of Lenin?' they asked me. 'Have you read this book of Karl Marx?' 'Of course' we said, 'we have read it.'
>
> U: (Laughs) As if they had written it themselves.
>
> B: No, there wasn't a bit of difference to those experiences in the hospital, there was no difference to that in the political groups, either.
>
> U: Yes.
>
> B: There, as well, as I said earlier as if there is a different type of medicine, you know, for the Turks and the Germans. As if there's a different politics for the Germans and the Turks, as if there were different books that we read and different books that they read. If you have read the classics, we have read them, too. That was the approach, you know. And then we made anti-racist politics, but we are the only ones responsible for this. We were not included in the general politics, the decision making and discussion and so on. Only when the issue of racism came to the agenda they asked us for our ideas.
>
> U: Yes.
>
> B: Well, there as well we experienced racism.

In this extract, Birgül points out the similarity of her experiences of racist discrimination and the denigration of her abilities and knowledges at the workplace with those in the political group. She critiques the German members' claim to authentically own what was considered generalisable knowledges of Marxism and its classic foundational texts. Her claim to this knowledge, as a migrant woman from Turkey, was questioned and de-legitimised. On this basis, her claim to participation in decision making was reduced. She points out that her analytical skills and her capacity of decision-making were only recognised in relation to the issue of racism, where she was identified as competent due to personal experience. I think it important to recognise the specific knowledges that experience gives access to. However, by ascribing the topic of racism to the sole responsibility of their migrant comrades, the marginalisation of the topic of racism is reified, once again. This group was not based on identity politics, but instead on universalist leftwing ideological and organisational premises. However, I would argue that some of the epistemological and organisational elements that Birgül recounts contain a logic of invisible identity politics. By 'invisible identity' politics, I mean an identity politics that is taken for granted, both constituted by and constitutive of the normalisation of dominant identities, their legitimated standpoints, epistemologies and decision making processes.

The term identity politics is usually ascribed to the organisational and epistemological forms developed by marginalised groups to articulate their interests and organise around these (Alice Echols quoted in Rowbotham 1992: 274). Thus, women, migrants, disabled people, gays and lesbians' organisations are seen as doing identity politics. When men, members of the ethnically dominant group, heterosexuals or able bodied people organise, they claim to do so on the basis of their political interest which they present as based on generalisable knowledges, rather than on specific experiences or interests (Harding, 1991).

As Anthias and Yuval-Davis (1992) point out, members of dominant identity groups have privileged access to the state, media, economic and other resources to present their view of the world as valid and neutral. This is also true for oppositional groups and the resources of their oppositional institutions and networks, albeit that the resources and the reach of their knowledges may be more restricted. These representational resources can strengthen their claim to define what counts as generalisable knowledge in the interest of all and what counts as specific knowledge based on specific identities. This representation is so generalised that the normalisation of dominant identities appears as neutral.

Birgül emphasises that in her political activism, her gendered and ethnocised identity has been fixed as different. This reflects a 'compulsory difference',[5] where the content and boundary of difference is ascribed and defined by Germans in order to uphold group boundaries and as a means of upholding the subject-object relation between Germans and 'Ausländer'. Thus, Birgül had previously delineated her interest in and involvement with political groups and issues in Germany from the lack of involvement of many other migrants from Turkey. However, she feels that the German members of the leftwing group, and

---

[5] By compulsory difference I mean a practice of constructing the racialized Other as culturally different that involves a fixing of boundaries, whose content has been defined by the ethnically dominant side. Difference and its content are ascribed often in contradiction to the racialized Other's self perception. An example is the irritation of multiculturalists or liberals towards those Others who do not perform the cultural, social or political norms they ascribe this group.

later on of feminist groups did not allow for such an internal differentiation of the category of migrant:

> The workers here, or the Turkish families here, Turkish or Kurdish, they live here in a rather isolated way, they are ghettoised, because they are not at all *recognised*. If you try to do the opposite then you get put into a different position, too. You are discriminated against, although you are not that way. As I said, you are constantly struggling.

Birgül's activism belies her equation with people who 'live here in a rather isolated way' and are 'ghettoised'. However, the German activists' refusal to recognise her activism reinforces the ascription of sameness with a 'ghettoised' Turkish community. This refusal of recognition denies any agentic subject position to migrants, whether they withdraw or not. Thus, the compulsory difference ascribed to her as passive or isolated structures her relationship with German activists, so that she is 'constantly struggling' for a recognition of her activism, as a legitimate participant in social and political processes.

Politics of Belonging

Birgül makes sense of this experience of margnialisation through explanations of cultural differences in socialisation.

> B: Well, the people from Turkey, me as a person, too, we come from a different socialisation, we have a mania for social life. Well, our political struggles before 1980, there was no individual, everything was collective. When I came to Germany I realised that the individual had more importance. That was very exhausting and difficult for many people, for me, too. Because all of a sudden you can see how important the individual is. Still however the collective or community is very relevant for the people from Turkey and I see this as very positive, too. In the German groups, be they political or personal or other, everybody lives very much for themselves, they are very individualised. That disturbs me, it still disturbs me.

Thus, Birgül expresses what she perceives as a crucial difference in the forms of sociality. While she finds it valuable to recognise the importance of the individual, she does not want to give up her value of collectivity or community. To her these are 'Turkish' values, however she specifies that they are values relating to her own political socialisation and historically specific. This can be seen as an instance where nationally specific forms of sociality articulate other, political identities (Johnson, 1993).

Her critical evaluation of belonging is reflected in her view on national belonging, too. Birgül values the position of 'foreigner':

because to be able to get to know two different ways of life, cultures, can enable you to see many things more from outside and observe them. (...) But on the other hand, the negative side of being a foreigner is that after a while you loose the roots anyway. You don't feel *at home* anywhere.

She juxtaposes this to her daughter's claim for belonging to both Germany and Turkey. Instead of claims to Germanness, she finds that other migrants are the people with whom she can most easily generate a community on the basis of their common experiences of racism. The experience of non-recognition and marginalisation is central to Birgül's experiences of social and political participation in Germany. She gives examples of this experience in other areas of life, such as her participation in creative writing groups, where German participants question her status as a writer on the basis of her ethnicity and the fact that she is writing in German, her second language. This is an example of how her linguistic and cultural competence is de-legitimated because she is seen as not belonging. However, it is important to point out that there is no automatic relation between feelings or recognition of belonging and participation. Thus, while Birgül has become active in social and political groups relating to Germany soon after she arrived in Germany, for a long time this did not correspond to her feeling settled in Germany. Until very recently she emotionally evaluated her stay as 'temporary'. At the time of interview, Birgül still felt that she was not recognised as a legitimate part of the society she lived in. Nonetheless, she had projects relating to this society, such as doing research, as well as a creative writing project. Birgül's story of her political and cultural activism calls into question any a priori assumptions about the relation between identity, belonging and social participation. She points out that her feeling of 'belonging is reduced', both towards Turkey and Germany. However, she follows political events and developments in both countries. After her migration she has participated in social and political campaigns in both countries. However, she critically evaluates the groups that she has participated in, in terms of their hidden identity politics. This means that Birgül does not construct belonging as a given, but rather as negotiated and struggled over. Despite her experiences of marginalisation and de-legitimisation both in her political and cultural activities she values what she perceives as her 'Turkish' value of constructing community. She acknowledges that there is a tension between collective and individual priorities. However she tries to negotiate this tension so as not to reify one over the other.

I examined two interrelated forms of politics that Birgul was engaged in: on the one hand her antiracist activism in the early 1980s, was a challenge to pre-existing forms of foreigner's politics because it formulated a critique of German institutions' racist practices on the basis of her own experience as a 'foreigner'. This constituted an agentic subject position for herself as a participant in antiracist struggles, rather than being merely the object of these struggles as formulated by Germans. In this form of politics, Birgül articulated a link between identity, experience and resistance, which I view as an integral element of identity politics. She was however also part of other political groups, such as a German dominated socialist group, whose organisational form and field of politics was not explicitly built on identity. I analyse the marginalisation and the ascription of compulsory difference she experienced there as a hidden identity politics of dominance. These tensions between identity political organisational forms and universalist organisational forms appear in the narratives of all interviewees who were politically active, although, of course, they deal with them in different ways.

For many interviewees, the fantasy of a new migration elsewhere or the longing for Turkey co-exists with a strong commitment to participating in and being part of the society of residence. This underlines the importance of differentiating between a fantastic form of longing for 'elsewhere' (Rodriguez, 1999) as opposed to a concrete 'integration work' (Lutz, 1998) into the society of residence. By 'integration work' Lutz means those efforts, often overlooked both by researchers and migrants alike, to 'maintain an everyday order, restructure or reorganise it under changed everyday conditions' (Lutz, 1998: 286) this includes a self reflexive negotiation of the biographical scheme of agency in a lifeworld which may be experienced as contravening it. This notion emphasises the agentic aspects and the competences of migrants, rather than viewing them as passively suffering the changes of the migration situation.

Conclusion

In this chapter I have examined the social and political activism of some migrant women. The neglect of the active dimension of migrant women's citizenship in the literature suggests that, as they are often marginalized from political and other representation in the nation-states they live in, they do not participate in the society, either. The interviewees' stories contradict this. Instead, I argue for a more differentiated examination of political activism, including women's work in community groups, voluntary work, as well as informal activism (Kofman et al., 2000). The fields of politics the women chose are diverse, ranging from 'homeland politics', internationalist or transnational feminist or socialist activism, to voluntary work in community organizations, and local feminist politics. One commonality in the women's activism is that they view their gendered and ethnocized experiences one important element of their political identities. However, they also use other principles of knowledge and organizational forms. Thus, Pinar's work with and for migrant women importantly constructs common epistemologies, strategies and interests across ethnic differences. She self-consciously articulates a common history of experiences of subjection but also of struggles and resistance with migrant and Black women in Germany.[6] Birgül's experiences of marginalization

---

[6] The notion of political Blackness as articulated in the late 1970s in Britain has been adapted for the context of migrants in Germany in the late 1980s. Although some of the literature claims that this concept has been overcome during the 1990s, others (e.g. Brah, 1996; Sudbury, 2001) argue that it should not be simply discarded. They argue that political Blackness has never been unequivocally accepted to start with, however that it continues to be an important notion to highlight the commonalties of experience, outlook and activism.

within a German dominated socialist group highlight that the exclusionary aspects of identity politics are also at work in groups that explicitly organise around universalist principles. I analysed this as a form of hidden identity politics of dominance. While I think it is important to highlight the diverse fields of migrant women's political activism, I would also like to call attention to the field of formal politics and formal citizenship rights. As argued above, the term identity politics is most often used to refer to organizational forms of marginalized and oppressed groups. However, in the German context one of the most powerful institutions relying on principles of identity politics remains that of formal citizenship.[7] While formal citizenship in itself is not sufficient to end gendered and ethnocised power relations, it remains of continuing importance to give migrant women access to all levels of political participation. Indeed formal citizenship can be an enabling tool towards achieving substantial citizenship rights.

I have further examined the notions of belonging the interviewee's put forward. Avtar Brah's concept of diaspora space argues that it is necessary to distinguish between 'homing desire' and the desire for a 'homeland' (1996: 180).

> When does a location *become* home? What is the difference between 'feeling at home' and staking a claim to a place as one's own? It is quite possible to feel at home in a place and, yet, the experience of social exclusions may inhibit public proclamations of the place as home (Brah, 1996: 193).

These contradictions are borne out in the interviewees' narratives of belonging. Thus, Pinar who locates herself firmly in the space of German society and on different levels struggles for changes in this society, claims a bi-cultural identity in which she wants to protect an allegiance to what she views as 'Turkishness'. Her claim to both Germanness and Turkishness contests exclusionary discourses of nationalism. Birgül, while having participated actively in the professional, social, political and cultural life of German society claims a position of outsider, and non-belonging, both vis-à-vis Germany and Turkey. Her refusal to proclaim national belonging does not prevent her from her activism, however. This reveals that 'home' can be sought on the basis of different commonalties, not only nationality. However, even in such non-national constructions of 'home' or community, conflicts, hierarchies and differences are at work. 'Home' need not be, indeed never is, a place of pure harmony (cf. Räthzel, 1994). For some interviewees, their homing desire is maybe best expressed in the fantasy of a new migration, which articulates 'home' as 'somewhere else'.

Some interviewees construct community and commonality across ethnic differences. They either feel they most easily relate to other migrants, like Birgül, consciously construct a political and emotional community of migrants and Black people in Germany, like Pinar, or overcome linguistic difficulties to reach out and

---

For a discussion of multiracial Blackness in British Black feminist groups and its articulation of difference and commonalty cf. Sudbury, 2001.

[7] While recent changes have provided easier access of migrants to citizenship, it is still conditional on the migrants' criminal records, economic self-sufficiency and other factors.

learn new things about themselves and others in cross-ethnic friendships with both members of the dominant and other minority ethnicities. There are, of course, also interviewees, who do not give such centrality to cross-ethnic social and political relations, however these interviewees also incorporate cross-ethnic relations in their life stories. I stress this finding because often the experiences of migrants are examined only within a binary frame of reference of 'Turkishness' versus the ethnically majoritarian society of residence. This does not take account of the multilayered, complex process of locating and positioning themselves in a multi-ethnic, 'differentially racialised' (Brah, 1996) social space.

References

Akashe-Böhme, F. (2000), *In Geteilten Welten: Fremdheitserfahrungen zwischen Migration und Partizipation,* Frankfurt: Brandes und Apsel.

Anthias, F. (2000), Metaphors of Home: Gendering New Migrations to Southern Europe, in F. Anthias and G. Lazaridis (eds), *Gender and Migration in Southern Europe.* Oxford: Berg.

Anthias, F. and Yuval-Davis, N. (1992), *Racialized Boundaries.* London: Routledge.

Apitzsch, U. (1996), Frauen in der Migration, *Frauen in der Einen Welt,* 1.

Arbeitsgruppe Frauenkongress (ed) (1985), *Sind wir uns denn so fremd? Ausländische und deutsche Frauen im Gepsräch.* Frankfurt: Sub-Rosa-Frauenverlag.

Bauböck, R. (1994), *Transnational Citizenship: Membership and Rights in International Migration.* Aldershot: Edward Elgar.

Bhabha, H. K. (1990), The Third Space, in J. Rutherford (ed), *Identity, Community, Culture, Difference.* London: Lawrence and Wishart.

Brah, A. (1996), *Cartographies of Diaspora.* London: Routledge.

Combahee River Collective (1998), A Black Feminist Statement, in P. Nardi and B. Schneider (eds), *Social Perspectives in Lesbian and Gay Studies.* London: Routledge.

Erdem, E. (2000), Mapping Women's Migration: A case study of the economic dimensions of female migration from Turkey to Germany, Paper presented at Humboldt University Berlin, October 2000.

Gilroy, P. (1993), *The Black Atlantic: Double Consciousness and Modernity.* Cambridge, MA: Harvard University Press.

Harding, S. (1991), *Whose Science, Whose Knowledge?* Ithaca: Cornell University Press.

Inowlocki, H. and Lutz, H. (2000), The 'Biographical Work' of a Turkish Migrant Woman in Germany, *European Journal of Women's Studies,* 7, 3, pp. 301–320.

Johnson, R. (1993), Towards a Cultural Theory of the Nation: A British Dutch Dialogue, in A. Galema et al. (eds), *Images of the Nation.* Amsterdam: Rodopi.

Kofman, E., Phizacklea, A., Raghuram, P. and Sales, R. (2000), *Gender and International Migration in Europe.* London: Routledge.

Lutz, H. (1991), *Welten verbinden. Turkische Sozialarbeiterinnen in den Niederlands und in der Bundesrepulik Deutschland.* Frankfurt: Verlag fur interkulturelle Kommunikation.

Lutz, H. (1998), Migration als soziales Erbe, in H. Lutz (ed), *Wissenschaftliche Veröffentlichungen.* Munster.

Ohliger, R. (2000), Making European Immigrants Visible, Paper presented at conference on Historical Perspectives on Immigrants and Host Societies in Postwar Europe, Humboldt University, Berlin, October 2000.

Radtke, F. (1994), The Formation of Ethnic Minorities and the Transformation of Social into Ethnic Conflicts in a So-Called Multicultural Society: The Case of Germany, in J. Rex and B. Drury (eds), *Ethnic Mobilisation in a Multi-Cultural Europe*. Aldershot: Avebury.

Räthzel, N. (1994), Harmonious 'Heimat' and Disturbing 'Auslander', *Feminism and Psychology*, 4, 1. pp. 81–98.

Räthzel, N. (1999), Hybridität ist die Antwort, aber was war nochmal die Frage?, in B. Kossek (ed), *Gegen-Rassimen. Konstruktionen Interaktionen Interventionen.* Hamburg: Argument Verlag.

Rodriguez, E. (1999), *Intellektuelle Migrantinnen – Subjektivitäten in Zeitalter von Globalisierung*. Opladen: Leske und Budrich.

Rowbotham, S. (1992), *Women in Movement. Feminism and Social Action*. London: Routledge.

Sassen, S. (2000), Gender and Market in Global Spaces, Lecture at the International Women's University, Hannover, 9 August 2000.

Soysal, Y. (1994), *Limits of Citizenship. Migrants and Postnational Membership in Europe.* Chicago: University of Chicago Press.

Sudbury, J. (2001), (Re)constructing multiracial blackness: women's activism, difference and collective identity, *Ethnic and Racial Studies*, 24, 1, pp. 29-49.

Toksöz, G. (1991), *'Ja, si kämpfen – und sogar mehr als di Männer.' Immigrantinnen-Fabrikarbeit und gewerkschaftliche Interessenvertretung*. Berlin: Verlag für Wissenschaft und Bildung.

Turner, B. (1993), Contemporary Problems in the Theory of Citizenship, in B. Turner (ed), *Citizenship and Social Theory*. London: Sage.

Yuval-Davis, N. (1996), *Gender and Nation*. London: Sage.

Yuval-Davis, N. (1997), Women, Citizenship and Difference, *Feminist Review*, 57, pp. 4-27.

Yuval-Davis, N. (2001), Contemporary Agenda for the Study of Ethnicity, *Identities*, 1, 1, pp. 13-24.

Chapter 11

From Maids to Entrepreneurs: Immigrant Women in Greece

Gabriella Lazaridis

Introduction

This chapter explores the phenomenon of ethnic entrepreneurship in Greece
through the eyes of three African women. It uses these brief biographical accounts
as a heuristic device to open up a series of debates about ways in which one can
understand the migration and working experiences of these self-employed migrants
in the Greek context. By picking out key extracts from their life stories, among the
questions I will try to provide answers for are the following: why did they become
entrepreneurs (was it their individual characteristics that laid them towards this
direction or availability of ethnic resources, or racialised labour market structures
in the host country)? what kind of business did they opt for and why? where did
they find the start-up capital (personal savings, loans from family and co-ethnics,
banks)? what factors have affected business success or failure? what was the
impact of the business on their personal life; how are we to interpret this
phenomenon vis-à-vis their experiences of discrimination, exclusion and
racialisation? Migrant entrepreneurs will be viewed as social actors, whose careers
are not merely circumscribed by the existing structures of opportunity in the host
country, but also by the meaning they themselves attach to their work choices. This
chapter attempts to answer these questions in the context of recent migration into
Greece and the multiple forms and degrees of racist and sexist discrimination and
abuse suffered by the black women. It draws on research carried out by the author
on the self-employment of ethnic minority groups in Athens.[1] The study is
contextualised within existing theoretical approaches to self-employment, and the

---

[1] This chapter is based on the research carried out under a three-year project (1997-2000)
funded by the EU's TSER (Targeted Socio-Economic Research) initiative. The project was
on 'Self-employment practices in relation to women and minorities: their success and failure
in relation to social citizenship policies'. Gabriella Lazaridis was director on the Greek part
of the project. The author would like to acknowledge the financial contribution of the
European Commission on this project (grant no. CEC: SOE2-CT97-3042). Special thanks to
Maria Koumandraki who worked as research assistant on the project.

empirical work presented here aims to provide a critical reflection on the relative adequacy of the various theoretical approaches to explain the situation in Greece.

Theoretical Context

The literature on entrepreneurship is vast. Narrow definitions arguing that only medium and large firms comprise entrepreneurship or only innovators are entrepreneurs, have been challenged by those who argue that non-traditional types of entrepreneurs such as marginalised self-employed workers (domestic workers, street vendors, flea market sellers etc.), should be included in the definition. 'The market activities of marginalised self-employed workers are often labelled as informal and underground, or have been dismissed as a pseudo-economy comprised of the poorest, most unqualified and desperate pool of recently-arrived illegal immigrants' (Valenzuela, 2001: 337).

Ethnic entrepreneurship has attracted considerable interest in the US, Canada and Western Europe (see for example, Rath and Kloosterman, 2000; Uneke, 1996; Waldinger et al., 1990a and 1990b; Wilson, 1983). In Greece however, research so far has focused on the socio-economic position and employment experiences of migrant waged workers in the construction industry, in agriculture, in the domestic sphere and in the sex industry (see for example, Lazaridis and Romaniszyn, 1998; Lazaridis and Wickens, 1999; Lazaridis, 2000 and 2001; Lazaridis and Psimmenos, 2000), but not on ethnic entrepreneurship. This is an attempt to fill this vacuum.

A variety of approaches have been used in explaining ethnic entrepreneurship. Some stress the importance of psychological/individualistic factors, such as the need for autonomy, creativity, self-fulfilment and making money; others put emphasis on the effect of ethno-cultural factors, such as cultural predisposition to self-employment (Uneke, 1996: 530; Valenzuela, 2001: 338), ethnic solidarity and access to ethnic social networks and possession of social capital or social embeddedness (see Portes and Sensembrenner, 1993; Granovetter, 1985); yet others stress the impact of structural elements, such as discrimination in and exclusion from the formal labour market. Migrants become entrepreneurs because they are disadvantaged in the labour market (Aurand, 1983); disadvantage emanates from unemployment, underemployment, illegal status, lack of proficiency in the host country's main language, unrecognised or low educational qualifications (Valenzuela, 2001: 349). In many cases, entrepreneurship is the outcome of a combination of all three factors mentioned so far. Rafiq (1992: 44) for example, argues that 'the most important determinants of entrepreneurial activity of any group and between groups are a combination of culture, socio-economic status and the economic opportunity structures open to them'. Uneke (1996: 530) shares this view too; ethnic business is the result of interaction between 'individual and group attributes and dimensions of opportunity structures provided by the social environment'. Although this approach is shared by many scholars (Kloostermann et al.,1998; Rath and Kloosterman, 2000), it has been criticised for not taking into account the subjective point of the entrepreneur. Kupfeberg (1999) distinguished between subjective-interpretive and objective approaches to entrepreneurship, depending on whether one takes into account the view of the entrepreneur or not. The interpretative or social constructionist approach puts emphasis on the meaning of business entrepreneurship to the owner and thus sheds light onto the complex issue of motivation; it considers the owner as an actor who is able to interpret the social world and take action.

The gender dimension is still an area very much neglected in research on ethnic business. This chapter shows that an understanding of the processes and practices of gender relations is crucial in understanding how far these contribute in facilitating or constraining the development of business activities by migrant women, and in determining the prospects of success or failure of these activities.

Methods

The empirical material is based on qualitative research grounded in individuals' accounts from selected ethnic minority groups, namely Africans. There are no available data on self-employed migrants in Greece. The data available from the ESYE (Greek National Statistical Service) on employment activities of migrants are rather crude: information is available only on the type of employment activities, such as work in manufacturing, construction industry. No differentiation is made between employee and self-employment status. In addition, some business activities are neither registered as these operate within the informal economy, nor can these be identified through local organisations, directories held in the local chamber of commerce etc. Hence interviewees were identified through the snowballing technique and via established contacts with migrants and their associations.

The non-directive biographical approach was chosen, because it gives voice to marginalised and socially excluded subjects and gives them the chance to reconstruct and narrate their life experiences and life-styles or parts of they wish to share (Lazaridis and Koumandraki, 2001: 284). Information has been collected from a cross-section of individuals, trying to understand the respondent's viewpoint during the telling of his/her story, at the same time being aware that this was mediated by the individual's social positioning and the time and the social context of the interview itself (see Lazaridis and Koumandraki, 2001: 286).

The life-story approach used is based on narratives about one's life or relevant parts of thereof (Bertaux and Kohli, 1994). Two features of this approach distinguish it from other qualitative approaches. First, its 'holistic' character and breadth of coverage – it covers the totality of a person's life. As Rosenthal (1993: 62) put it, this 'must rather be interpreted in a gestalt sense of biography as a comprehensive, general pattern of orientation that is selective in separating the relevant from the irrelevant'. Second, the 'process'; to quote Rosenthal (1993: 63) again, ' the individual has their own history of personal development and change and they "process" along their life course ... [In addition], historical events and social change at the societal level impinge upon the individual's own unique life history'.

Interviews were conducted at the interviewees' workplace during working hours. The women were busy serving customers, answering the phone giving short instructions to their helpers and therefore there were breaks of shorter (2-3 minutes) or longer duration (10-15 minutes), which may have influenced the interview situation. Despite these unavoidable interruptions however, the interviewees managed to produce a narrative account of their life. In the interviews/life-stories selected for this paper, the emphasis is on the individual as 'a unique entity located in a complex network of social relationships that change and evolve over historical time' (Miller, 2000: 10). From the total of 18 narrative interviews conducted with a heterogeneous group of migrants living and working in Athens since the early 1990s, 4 life-stories of migrant women engaged in self-employment activities have been selected for this paper. The material on experiences of self-employment presented below represents a general construct of biographical experiences derived from 'past interactional episodes and future expectations' (Rosenthal, 1993: 65). As mentioned elsewhere, 'from this coagulate of past and future, a creation of the lived present was obtained in the form of a narration, based on the narrator's choice of stories and/or memories to be narrated and the way in which s/he perceived them at the time of the interview' (Lazaridis and Koumandraki, 2001: 285).

The Greek Context

Immigration

Although the immigration flows into Greece have their roots in the late 1960s and early 1970s (Lazaridis, 1996), since the early 1990s an increasing number of third-country migrants arrived in the country, a substantial proportion of which are illegal (Lazaridis and Poyago-Theotoky, 1999). The number of potentially active illegal migrants who entered the country in the 1990s is 'guestimated' to be around one million.

As stated elsewhere (Lazaridis and Wickens, 1999; Lazaridis and Koumandraki, 2001), immigration has evoked a variety of negative reactions among the Greeks, including stereotyped and stigmatic labelling; for example the word 'Filipina' has become synonymous with domestic worker, the word 'Albanian' denotes a criminal or a hard working man (Lazaridis, 1996), the word '*kafros*' is used to identify those with dark skin, especially Africans. Anti immigration agitation, often shaped by negative representations of migrants in the Greek media (Lazaridis and Wickens, 1999), is often legitimised in public discourse as a reaction against 'the problem', the 'threat presented to the fabric of society' by the influx of these 'dangerous others'. Such sentiments are often used to: (a) legitimise racialisation and discrimination of 'the other', who 'is fixed in public imagination as the irredeemably "different"' (Lazaridis and Koumandraki,

2001: 288); and (b) justify the introduction of stringent anti-immigration laws[2] and the government's 'sweeping operations' known as *skoupa*, as the massive forced deportations of undocumented migrants have become known. At the same time, there is a 'silent' policy of tolerance towards the entry of cheap labour due to pressures from employers of small labour-intensive units, trying to remain competitive in the global economy. For this same reason, the 1998 regularisation of migrants commanded little support from employers of cheap labour.

Economy and Society

In 1991, the year when an increasing number of migrants started arriving in Greece, the country's primary sector was producing about 18 per cent of the GDP at current prices, employing 23 per cent of the labour force, while the corresponding figures for the secondary sector were 25 per cent and 27 per cent respectively and for the tertiary sector 57 per cent and 50 per cent. A very distinctive characteristic of Greece's labour force is the high percentage of second job-holding, which is impossible to measure and the high percentage of the self-employed and non-paid family members that work in small family enterprises.[3] According to the Greek Labour Survey of 1997, 45 per cent of the labour force was self-employed or worked as 'family aides'. Another key feature of Greek society and economy interrelated with sectoral employment changes just mentioned is expansion of activities in the informal sector, which represents around 30 per cent to 45 per cent of the GDP (Canellopoulos, 1995; Petmesidou, 1996). Self-employment and small enterprise have long been characterised by operation in the informal economy. Their income activities lie outside the protection or regulation of the state or other bodies entrusted with enforcing established rules concerning property relationships, labour contracts, social security, etc.

Reinforced by informalisation is labour market flexibility and segmentation. The tertiarisation of the economy, the existence of labour-intensive employment in small family based businesses, created a structural demand for the recruitment of a flexible, mobile labour force which will be willing to undertake casual, seasonal insecure jobs at low payment rates and no insurance coverage. An increasing competition amongst Greeks for getting higher-status jobs, meant that such work not attractive to indigenous labour force, was now left to migrants and other underpriviledged groups. Hence the rise of flexible forms of production has created a plethora of niches for inexpensive forms of flexible labour, such as migrant cheap, easy-to-manage easy-to-sack workers. As argued elsewhere, migrants do not form a single niche but rather cluster in particular niches, undertaking a variety of low-skilled, low-paid jobs (Lazaridis and Romaniszyn,

---

[2] For a critical account of Greek immigration laws and policies see Lazaridis 1996 and Lazaridis and Poyago-Theotoky 1999.

[3] The percentage of self-employed in 1991 was around 36 per cent, while the percentage of non-paid workers in family business was estimated to be 11.66 per cent (Petmesidou and Tsouloubis 1994).

1998). At the same time, traditional family ties and reciprocal support structures are weakening (Katrougalos and Lazaridis, 2003). In a country like Greece, where collective forms of solidarity, the tradition of contractual relations and an active civil society are weak and the role of the family in welfare delivery has been important, the process of corrosion of the social fabric[4] means that today women who have to get a job to contribute to the family budget or want to pursue a career and cannot find much support in the relatives or the state for child and other forms of care, have to turn to migrant labour for support. It is now not only permissible for women to pay for care to be brought in, provided that the setting within which the provision of care may take place is provided for, but also employing a domestic worker is also regarded as a status symbol by families with relatively large disposable incomes (Lazaridis, 2000: 59). Moreover, in Greece, as in Italy (Andall, 1998), migrant domestic workers are not perceived as competitors in the employment market as they are occupying a sector which bares a considerable degree of social stigma and which has been increasingly shunned by local women.

The feminisation of entire sectors of the labour market is of particular importance to this study as the women under study, prior to becoming self-employed worked in the domestic sector and/or nursing. As stated elsewhere, for a closer examination of the sectors employing women migrant workers, one must consider the connection between gender and race, and racism and sexism, if one is to understand the position of migrant women and the kind of racialisation they face (Lazaridis and Koumandraki, 2001: 287; Lazaridis, 2000; Lazaridis, 2001). In the section on migrant women's profiles, I will look at ways in which racism which is interwoven into the fabric of everyday living in Greece has affected the work and life trajectories of these women.

Moreover, statism and particularistic-clientelistic forms of social organisation are prevalent. 'Access to clientelistic networks and the state by individuals and social groups constitutes the primary means for appropriation of resources and benefits, a condition which converts social conflicts into individualistic power feuds and thus hardly favours collective solidarity' (Petmesidou, 1996: 102). The widely legitimised practice of using political means to appropriate resources is not an option available to the migrants, unless tied to a Greek spouse. Migrants have to rely on their own strategies and networks for compensating for the lack of social citizenship rights.

This schematic outline of some important aspects of the Greek socio-economic formation gives an idea of the environment within which labour migration and self-employment activities of migrants occur.

---

[4] Urbanisation and emigration in the 1960s and 1970s have weakened the traditional family relationships and related inter-generational reciprocal arrangements (Lazaridis 2000:57). This has had implications for care of dependants which now falls under the responsibility of women (mothers and daughters).

Self-Employment

Similar to Western Europe and the Unites States (Waldinger et al., 1990a and 1990b), ethnic entreperneurship[5] in Greece is limited to labour-intensive light industries, like for example, service industries (restaurants, petty trading, taxis, hairdressing saloons, small food stores etc.) run by the entrepreneur him/herself and family members or co-ethnics. In the Greek setting however, ethnic business activities comprise of a mosaic of formal and informal activities of migrants who are active agents in creating an economic niche by making use of their ethnic and socio-economic networks to facilitate their business operations (however modest) and promote their profits. Whether a migrant will engage in a formal or informal activity depends largely on one's legal status, economic resources and access to ethnic and non-ethnic networks. A few migrants who have legal documents run registered businesses, such as retail businesses (food stores, electronics shops), restaurants, wholesale trading, hairdressing and beauty saloons. But the majority are undocumented and these tend to embark on business ventures which survive in the twilight of the Greek economy, such as decorating, petty trading (mainly street-hawking), domestic work, hairdressing and prostitution, that is sectors which require little skill and small capital. Indeed the local environment plays a decisive influence on the creation and performance and survival of such 'enterprises'. Some businesses cater for an ethnic and others for a non-ethnic clientele. Therefore, migrant entrepreneurship in the informal sector can be seen as the 'poor person's survival strategy' to secure inclusion in the host country's economy. Opportunities for participation of migrants in informal economic activities occur because of the high demand for informal provision of services and goods at competitive prices. In addition, in the case of informal activities, the entrance barriers are even lower, since one usually does not have to rent premises and meet costs related to the running of the business such as rent, taxes, electricity, heating and other bills.

The rest of this chapter shows that an understanding of ethnic entrepreneurship in the Greek context must take into account the dynamic interaction between ethno-cultural resources, labour market, economic and institutional structures of opportunity as well as subjective/interpretive meanings attached to business ownership by the entrepreneurs themselves. Thus, entrepreneurship is not viewed as an economic behaviour per se, structured by the existing economic and socio-political environment, but as also having an important subjective meaning for the self-employed women interviewed for this study.

---

[5] Waldinger et al (1990a and 1990b) equate ethnic enterprise and immigrant business. Although there are some problematics with applying the term in the Greek context due to lack of such terminology in the Greek language to describe the business of persons who are third-country migrants and to distinguish it from either foreign business, foreign investors with substantial capital, for practical purposes these terms will be used here.

Migrant Women's Stories

This section starts with three case-stories of migrant women as these were narrated by them, and use these as a heuristic device to open up a series of discussion about the phenomenon of ethnic-entrepreneurship/ethnic business in Greece. In all three cases, migration is 'both an escape ... from the original homeland and a search for a better life and some kind of a new home if not a new homeland' (Anthias, 2000: 15). To guarantee anonymity, some changes have been made to the personal details. The interviews were conducted in English at the interviewees' preference, and the interviewees imperfect English is left as it was spoken.

The case of Adama:[6] *owner of a beauty shop, a cosmetics shop and a hairdressing saloon*

Adama is a 27 year old, single mother of two, from Sierra Leone. Although there was war and unrest in Sierra Leone at the period when she migrated, she did not present lack of peace in her home country as the reason for leaving. Her decision was rather a voluntary one, triggered by her wish to live independently of her parents and build a better future for herself which would enable her to support her family back home via remittances. Her migration was also chain migration, facilitated by a series of contacts in Greece; her sister, already in Greece together with a close Greek friend played an important role and made all the necessary arrangements for her to come to Greece.

She migrated to Greece after obtaining a student visa in 1991, but dropped out of the university because of difficulties with the language. She worked for some years cleaning houses and later as an employee in a hairdressing salon. Her decision to become self-employed was her own, a planned action in order to make a better living for herself. She gathered a modest capital and in 1997 she set up her own business – a hairdressing salon. The choice of this enterprise obviously reflected her previous work experience and acquired skills but was also her former Greek husband's objection to her working outside the home. From her narration, it become apparent that a set of additional to the above mentioned factors have acted cumulatively in her decision to become self-employed in the host country. These were the following: (a) she realised that there is a high demand for African hair style hairdressing services amongst the ethnic community; (b) she had the relevant skills, working experience and knowledge of existing competition in the area; (c) her eagerness to have control over her work; and (d) her ability to develop a clientele and develop a good reputation for her skills while working part-time for another hairdressing saloon.

She attributed her success to the good services she provides to customers in competitive prices, to self-exploitation (working hard for long hours to the detriment of her health) and to personal qualities, such as ambition, emotional

[6] The case of Adama has also been used in and borrowed from Lazaridis and Koumandraki (2001:293-294).

strength, determination in pursuing and achieving one's dream. She narrated in detail her work experiences with various Greek employers and how she decided to provide Afro-Caribbean hairdressing services at home:

> Wherever I was working – the men, the women [she refers to her employers] they didn't treat me nice. I worked in houses in Filothei, Kolonaki [areas of Athens], and elsewhere. And I worked for one employer – in Palaio Faliro, who didn't pay me. Because of this I got very angry [with emphasis]. I will never forget the way he treated me [vividly]. He employed me to look after his father-in -law. I was staying with the old man. I was cleaning. There was a lot of work to be done. I worked for them and at the end of the month. I asked him "where is my payment?". He answered to me: "I don't have any money to give you". I asked him "why?". He replied "I don't have money to pay you, what do you want me to do?" [vividly]...And he wanted to fuck me. I said "no, I don't want" [with emphasis]. I said "I'm not doing this kind of job". I am doing house cleaning. I am not a whore [vividly]. And I quit this job ... But I was afraid to do such thing because I didn't have any legal documents at the time. Thus, I didn't complain to anyone [vividly].

> Then I worked in Filothei. The people were nice there. They didn't cause me any trouble. But my sister had a problem. She was held in the Foreign Office. She was held there for 3 days. I got crazy and I wanted to help her. I asked my employer for three days leave to help my sister. But she replied to me "no you can't. If you decide to leave now you should go and find a job elsewhere". I said "OK" because I had to help my sister.

> Then I got another job. I was looking after the grandfather and grandmother. The grandmother was very ill; she couldn't walk. I cleaned and everything and the grandmother was very satisfied with my work. But then one day, they told her husband "Giannis your house looks like a salad. A black woman is coming to your house. There are various colours. You should get a white woman to work for you". I was working for them for 6 months and I asked the grandmother "why?" [she asked why you want to sack me?]. She said "nothing in particular. I don't want you to work for me anymore". I realised that they didn't want to keep me. I got depressed. I cried, cried, because I had a lot of problems [she implies she was in financial difficulty].

Migrant women, desperate at securing employment in the host country, meet the demand of employers who seek reliable, hard-working women readily available at below-market rates. Entrepreneurship is a way out of a 'no-option' job of the type described by above. Entrepreneurship serves as a viable alternative to wage employment (e.g. in a patriarchcal Greek household) that pays at best poorly, and exposes these women to risks associated with sexual harassment and possibly physical violence – 'others' are desired for their exotic beauty or supposed submissive nurturing natures. If this is brought to the notice of the state, deportation is likely to be the result for the worker as an illegal migrant, while the employer is likely to go free. The burden of the proof is shifted to the 'undesirable alien'. Therefore, for many, entrepreneurship is a 'survivalist strategy'.

> My sister suggested "why don't you stay at home with me to provide Afro-Caribbean hairdressing services? (.) But I didn't like this idea because we would have work one day but not the next day. And I wanted to work continuously, do you understand? And I started working again [she means she started working as a domestic]. But I encountered problems again [vividly] Her husband one morning took off his bathroom towel in front of me [sound surprised] Ooh I got out my mind, I said what is going on? [vividly]. His wife was a very good woman and nice to me. But he wasn't nice. I asked him "what are you doing?" And he said "would you like to (..)". I replied to him "no, I don't want. This isn't my job. I am working but I am not a whore". I said to his wife that I had to leave and that I can't stay in this job. I didn't want to tell her what really happened. And I left that job and from then on I started to provide hairdressing services with my sister at home. And we worked ... slowly we obtained a clientele and saved some money.

The initial capital to set up a business came not from a bank, but from Adama's and her cousin's savings. She did not have any skills and know-how on running the business.

Business ownership should not be seen only as the outcome of racial discrimination, sexual harassment and economic exploitation. Unlike Adama, some women had the 'dream' to become entrepreneurs. For them, the need for independence, autonomy, creativity and self-fulfillment were the primary motives for becoming self-employed. This is the case of Sofia (see below), a 44 year old Ghanaian woman who initially worked as a midwife-nurse and now runs a hairdressing salon and an ethnic food store; the idea of having a 'second career' by setting up a business came to her by chance. As she said:

> I worked in a hospital for the past seventeen years...It wasn't my idea to open a shop but then my sister lived in London ... most of the items we needed I had to ask her to bring them over. My sister was bringing everything, posting and all (.) she said "what are you doing? You can do something. I mean you can open a shop and...be able to supply other people too".

The case of Adamse: owner of a hairdressing saloon

Adamse is a 30 year old mother of two, who migrated to Greece from Nigeria in 1994 because the father of her children is Greek. Her integration into the Greek labour market and society was not easy. Like Adama, she initially worked as a domestic worker. She decided to become self-employed in order to escape from the exploitation and sexual harassment she became subjected to at the workplace. She described the exploitative conditions under which she worked when she came to Greece (no insurance coverage, very low wages for long working hours, no bonus, no break, racist abusive remarks and sexual harassment) and how she had to come to terms with this because of lack of any alternatives, as follows:

> My first job was in Kolonaki ... He had a bar and my sister was working in a hairdressing saloon in Kolonaki at that time. And I started working there and one

day … I was cleaning the bar … it was time to leave … he said "come back here". I said, "what's going on? Have I done anything wrong? Haven't I cleaned well that spot?" He locked the door- I said "what's going on?". I couldn't speak Greek at the time. I've been working there only for three weeks. I couldn't understand what was going on. He was talking to me, but I couldn't understand what he was saying. And he went and locked the door. He said "would you like to come close to me?" And I started running. He was chasing me around the tables. He kept saying "would you like to come closer?" and I continued running around because I couldn't understand. I kept saying "what's going on? What's happening?" And he was chasing me around and he took off his clothes and his trousers. I ran towards the telephone and I called my sister, because my sister was working close by … My sister came along with her boss, with Daniel. He is a Greek. They came and knocked at the door. They shouted "open the door" and he (...) he opened the door. Daniel who is Greek asked me "what happened? What happened here?" I explain to him in English and he said to my boss "I am going to call the police". But my boss begged him "please don't do that, don't do that". Daniel said "give her salary". He gave me my money and I quit that job.

The second employer I worked for in Kolonaki was a policeman, he had a high post [with emphasis]-. He employed me to look after his father-in-law. I was staying with the old man. I was cleaning. There was a lot of work to be done. But he wouldn't pay me.

And I left and I got a job in Paleo Faliro. There was a lot of work to be done there. She got twins and the apartment was on the top floor, on the fifth floor. There wasn't an elevator to go up to the fifth floor. The elevator goes up till the four floor. And I had to walk up the stairs to the fifth floor. And they were giving me to carry all the heavy things (..) And I got very tired /and one day I collapsed in a bus, in Akadimias. Because I was working hard and my head was [vividly] (..) Some people took me to the hospital. I phoned my employer and told her "I am not feeling well. I am at the hospital". I said to her "I want my salary to buy some medicine". But she said she won't give it to me because I had to work two more days. I was getting paid every 15 days. I needed to work two [more] days to get my payment. Thus, she told me that she couldn't give me my salary. What could I do?

It is clear that Adamse, like Adama, encountered many problems while working as a domestic, mainly sexual harassment, she worked for long hours and was getting paid little money. But she didn't have any other alternative but to do this type of job. The exploitative conditions under which she was working under are clear. Adamse's decision to become self-employed was driven by the need to escape from bad working conditions and sexual and racial harassment she was subjected to while working as a domestic. So, similar to Adama, she used her savings to set up the business. Her business mainly relies in her labour input. She works long hours and has little free time. Unlike Adama, Adamse did not have any prior skills and know-how on running the business, apart from some tacit hairdressing skills which every African woman acquires when young, as part of her regular hair combing routine. She gradually developed a clientele working from home, saved some money and decided to set up her business.

Adamse's self-employment was 'a response to hardship, uncertainly and discrimination' she was faced with. Like Adama, she was not fully aware of the risks involved in her lack of knowledge on how to work her way around the Greek bureaucracy, lack of experience to run a business. As shown below, her case reflects the difficulties and problems faced by migrant entrepreneurs when setting up a business in a foreign country which they know little about and where there is lack of state policies to address their needs.

The initial capital came not from a bank but from her savings. Family members (husband and brother) helped. Like the previous case study, she too tapped on the demand created by 'cultural needs' among co-ethnics, and was able to turn her African hairdressing saloon into a profitable business.

The case of Sofia: owner of an Afroansian food shop, a beauty cosmetics shop and a hairdressing salon

Sofia originates from Ghana; coming from a middle-class family; she had 'a good life in Ghana', as she said. Sofia wanted to be a midwife and initially went to London to study. Her family met the cost of her education abroad. After meeting her Greek husband, she came to live in Greece. So, although her initial migration to UK was 'a wish for independence' and 'get away', as she said, her migration to Greece is an example of a dependent move determined by her relationship with the man she eventually married. Greece became her home – hers is a settling down migration. The fact that she held a degree from a British university and the high demand for qualified nurses gave her a comparative advantage in getting a first job in Greece.

Unlike *Adama and Adamse*, Sofia's self-employment was 'a pleasant surprise', it was not 'an action she was driven to by economic necessity or bad treatment'. As she explained, the initial idea to set up her own business was her sister's. When she arrived in Greece, she had to order ethnic products she needed for personal use from her sister in London. The un-fulfillment of Sofia's consumer needs due to lack of availability of specific ethnic products in the Greek market was one reason that contributed to her becoming self-employed. Another was her sister's emotional and financial support and encouragement.

Her initial plan was to set up a business and hire someone to work for her, thus retaining her full-time permanent and secure job as nurse in an Athens hospital. This reflects her seeing the business as a way of meeting her needs and making an easy profit, and not necessarily as a future employment prospect. 'I loved being a midwife', she said. She had no previous relevant experience and skills and was not fully aware of the implications her decision to set up a business would have on her life. To quote her, 'I decided to get personally involved in the day-to-day running of the business in order to ensure that I would not loose the money I borrowed to invest in the business'.

The initial modest capital came initially from Sofia's and her husband's savings and shortly after her sister chipped in. So family members played a very important role. Her association and marriage with a Greek man, his established contacts and know-how in pulling the strings within the Greek highly bureaucratic patronage riddled state system played an important role in her getting smoothly integrated into the host society and in dealing with the Greek state agencies. She started with a cosmetics business and three years later she expanded into the food store and a hairdressing saloon.

Gradually, Sofia's personal involvement in the business and being herself a member of the African community, made her realize that there was a large number of foreigners in Athens who had needs similar to hers. Her being a member of the African community in Athens provided a pool of clientele with similar needs to hers. Tapping on the demand created by the 'cultural needs' of the African ethnic communities, she expanded in other areas too so as to meet a variety of ethnic needs, hairdressing being an important aspect of their identity which they try to preserve in the host country. This supports Light and Gold's (1999) argument that the entrepreneurial performance of migrants depends upon the fit between what the market in the host country requires and what the migrants have to offer. She stressed the constant need for further training in order to keep up with changes in fashion; possession of necessary skills and up-to-date knowledge on new products and styles is according to her essential for running a successful business. The need for further training derives, as she explained, also from her need to control the business, be able to give instructions to her employees, and 'be in charge'. She has 'to observe, guide and suggest' to her employees and 'devote time for things that the employees wouldn't care to pay attention to'. 'I am the heart of the business', 'I am hooked in entrepreneurship', she added.

She attributes the success of her business to her role and the personal, individualized services that she is offering to customers. Her success depends on the personal relationship with the clients and the time, as she emphatically said, she takes to answer their questions. It is on the personal, friendly and close relationship with the customers that such businesses capitalize on in contrast with big businesses like super-markets which operate on a self-service basis.

The above narrations reveal the complexity of issues surrounding entrepreneurial motivation in the case of female ethnic business owners in Greece. Structural factors interact with ethno-cultural features and individual aspirations and lead to the emergence of self-employment careers. In some cases, like Sofia's for instance, motivation for setting up a business lies on individualist motives relating to self-fulfilment and ambition. It is a career largely discovered 'by chance' and could be seen as the outcome of a 'turning point' in one's life. The cases of Adamse and Adama on the other hand, exemplify the so called 'disadvantage theory' following which self-employment is seen as a 'way out' from exploitative working conditions in the domestic and care work (see Lazaridis, 2000). They decided to become self-employed in order to escape from restricted employment opportunities and segregation in the labour market and entrapment in positions of inferiority in the Greek informal economy – the economic opportunity structure described above may be determining which migrants come to Greece, encouraging a gravitation of these migrants towards the informal sector. The establishment of formal ethnic businesses is seen as a 'survivalist strategy' which promises higher economic gains and a relatively flexible work schedule and an escape from racial and sexual harassment by the employer.

Restricted employment opportunities also resulted in the development of certain niches in hairdressing and petty-trading. Migration itself has lead to this niche creation. These women capitalise on ethnic resources such as hair combing, in order to make a living. Tapping on the demand created by 'cultural needs' turned out to be a profitable business. Niches are likely to collapse if the demand for a skill (hairdressing) or specific products (African food) is reduced. If migration stops, because demand will fall, the niche may disappear, unless demand for the product is sustained amongst the host population.

Problems Encountered: Institutional and Everyday Racisms

The procedures a migrant woman needs to follow in order to become self-employed in Greece are rather complicated. A number of prerequisites, such as the requirement to produce certain certificates necessary for the recognition of qualifications, obtain a 'white card', become a member of an insurance scheme, makes the setting up of a registered business almost an unattainable dream. None of the above mentioned women received any relevant information or help from the Greek state agencies, as there were no programmes developed for the inclusion and integration of these migrants into the host setting. Undocumented migrants like Adamse are in general not eligible to take part in programmes promoting self-employment. They do not receive any information about potential sources of help (for example programmes encouraging self-employment of minorities like INTEGRA) and are themselves reluctant to approach those agencies because of their illegal status and fear of deportation. This gets further complicated by the fact that migrants do not have the necessary knowledge to manipulate the existing patronage system and thus create pathways to success. Therefore, access to informal networks (family and acquaintances) is important in helping with the setting up of the business. Some, Sofia for instance, used another person's – a Greek person's, usually a Greek spouse – name to register the business under.

In addition, lack of fluency in the Greek language is another factor that renders it difficult to understand and complete the necessary documents. Adamse's experiences, for example, with the Greek state agencies show that she is confused and frustrated by the 'way things work' or the 'Greek way' as she called it. She complained about the long queues and the delays in the issuing of relevant documents and the high cost and unfairness of having to hire a Greek lawyer to help her renew her permit. Being acquainted with a Greek man played an important role in solving part of her problems. She narrated her experiences of becoming regularised (a main prerequisite for setting up a legal business) and renewal of her residence permit as follows:

Another problem that I have here is getting a work permit. When you go to the Foreign Affairs office for renewing the permit they say [you have to wait] two months. One has to go to a lawyer who will ask 1,500 [Euros] for his services. Where can one find this amount of money? They should have renewed my permit for a year, but they renewed it instead for seven months. And they delayed for five months to give it to me ... I went to renew it again and two months have passed now and I haven't got it ...I have to pay around 200 Euros in order to issue the residence and work permits ... But this doesn't bother me ... what irritates me a lot is that I have to pay the lawyer...

They also encountered many problems with obtaining a licence to become self-employed and set up the business. She explained:

When we wanted to set up the business it was very difficult ... From one problem we run to another ... The tax office wouldn't give us a licence. There is a huge bureaucracy. That's in all state agencies. A lot of bureaucracy and wherever we went there was trouble [vividly]. We are coming from third world [countries], you know [vividly]. Later, she added: Wherever we went we had to go twice, three times till the job was done ... It took us two, three, four months to get the licence [vividly].

She added:

I didn't know about racism, you understand?... When I came to this place I started realising that people treated us differently, you understand? They, some people, they don't even want to touch you, some people when they see you they will do the sign of the cross, as if they seen a bad thing, you understand? Sometimes they will insult you. School children will laugh at you. Look, look black people ... they will laugh ha, ha ... They will mock you ... .

Adama had to put up with racist in-laws. She said:

His mum, his sisters, they don't like me ... They were always abusing me that I am black, I am foreigner. Even the mum told me once that she will pay my ticket to go back to my country, make me run away ... the woman was [interfering] with my life until I say to my husband I can't stand it anymore. I have to find my own house ...

She left the house and went to stay with some relatives of hers.

The experiences of these women suggest that there is a markedly differential provision of services towards black people, depending on whether one has access to a 'Greek protector', be it a husband or a friend. Black people are racialised because they are 'different', and this is accompanied by practices of inferiorisation, subordination and exploitation (see Lazaridis and Koumandraki, 2001: 291). The 'other' is inferior; s/he may have a place in the Greek society, but it is an inferior one. This falls under what Wieviorka (1994: 182) calls 'classical inegalitarian racism'. As a result of this behaviour these women feel intimidated. This is exacerbated by media discourse on immigration which fuels feelings of opposition towards the 'other', based on assumptions concerning the natural boundaries between Greeks and the 'other', on the basis of 'race'.

Their racialisation is often intensified and interwoven with sexism. Two sets of gender relations, those of the minority and those of the dominant majority produce a particular class structuration for different groups of migrant women in conjunction with labour market processes and racialisation (see Anthias, 1998). Moreover, as indicated with the interviews above, racialised sexual violence was common, 'often justified in terms of the lure of the exotic sexuality of the black woman or the control of the "superior" Greek over the "backward" ...[African]... whose sexuality can be "owned" by the Greek male' (Lazaridis and Koumandraki, 2001: 294).

Other problems they encountered included lack of 'inderetminancy', that is a body of formal rational knowledge, which has a tendency towards built-in codification that renders it more accessible to the educated public. It is difficult to see how this type of knowledge could be acquired by these women. They therefore need to hire a professional to deal with the legal and administrative systems in the host country, maintain the accounts, and perform many other activities that are conducive to the working of the business. They also lack knowledge of the patronage system and the related reciprocities, which require considerable exercise of judgement in their practice, but the exercise of judgement is on the basis of knowledge that these women do not see as being sufficiently esoteric to justify the cost. It appears to them as being 'everyday' rather than professional knowledge. And it may be 'everyday' and mundane in many respects for members of the Greek culture. But in the case of the migrant women, the judgement must be exercised by the professional who has acquired mastery of the habitus; help in this occasion is often based on a superior, patronising position, and on qualities that were never rally taught, qualities that the Greeks have from their families. Hence, migrant women are often unable to conduct their own affairs, to gain access to the offices of senior officials and to make suggestions of offering secret gifts and money bribes without embarrassment in exchange of a favour, such as get public servants to relax certain regulations whose implementation lie in their own hands.

Factors Affecting Business Success or Failure

Embeddedness in social networks and personal contact

As Velanzuela (2002: 337-338) argues, 'ethnic entrepreneurs possess unique advantages (and disadvantages) due to their ethnicity'. Ethnic resources, are important. As the cases of Adama and Adamse show, ethnic entrepreneurs benefit from their ethnicity in terms of co-ethnic loyalty (clients and employees), ethnic traditions attitudes and values; also, ethnicity serves some type of inclusionary mechanism for other migrants seeking to be employed in this type of work.

Adama presents herself to be a good professional. She is not after making easy profit, but rather tries to offer good services at reasonable, affordable prices. She narrates:

> I am a boss and how can I say, worker and boss together. – Mostly I do have problems. You know people if they know you for doing their hair, they don't want another person to touch their head. So like customers because these ones are not... are no regular customers ... I try to do my best for them, to do what they want. I don't look too much for the money (...). What is not right, I don't do it... the more you do good work- the more they come. I've never done advertisement [with emphasis].

Adamse added:

> When we started to provide hairdressing services in Greece it was difficult in the beginning to get clients. ... First, we [Adamse and her sister] combed our own hair in the Afro-Caribbean hair style for people to see. And people started asking us where did we come from and what's our telephone number. Thus, we started to develop our clientele and we had many clients , we had lots (...).

Sofia on the other hand stressed the provision of personal services and the personal contact with the customer as being essential for the success of the business. She explained:

> [It is important] to show more interest in the customer. It could be that eh ... they have their own problems too [with emphasis] ... Maybe I could help ...when they are passing by they see me here they come in. Because they know they will get the full services they are looking for [with emphasis] –. And the full service is me ... with the ethnic food... they wanted to know every use of every other thing.... Maybe they are not ready to buy but out of curiosity they want to know. You have to have the time to explain. Because that's the reason why you are here. Otherwise if it's not different thing the supermarket will be selling the same items. So I have to be there... Not only the food. On the cosmetics side... You have to be with the client. Make sure that what you are doing will suit her... See the face ...

Therefore, small enterprises base their success on the personal relationship with the customer and the importance of this personal contact for the business's success. Unlike big businesses like supermarkets, which operate on a self-service basis, it is on this personal, friendly and close relationship with the customers that the small business capitalises on.

Sofia explained that the investment of money in the business and the problems the business encountered in the beginning made her decide to get personally involved. As she explained, she realised that she couldn't watch from a distance but had to take action. Sofia thus demonstrates a strong sense of responsibility towards the business and the money invested. Furthermore, she presented herself as a 'fighter', an active and not a passive person who wants to be successful in what she is doing.

Sofia closes this topic by stating the importance of being close to her employees, 'she is with them' and for this reason 'they are with her too'. She presents herself as a 'good' boss. A boss who is friendly, understanding, caring for his/her employees, who is always willing to hear their opinion and take it into consideration the suggestions they put forward to her. Showing a 'human' attitude and concern towards her employees, contributes to the smooth and successful running of the business.

Impact on Women's Lives

Lack of Free Time

Although for some entrepreneurship is a 'solo project', Adama, Adamse and Sofia employ a small number of employees (ethnic and non-ethnic) on a permanent, part-time or temporary basis, depending on the business needs and finances. Nevertheless, they do try to save on labour costs by over-exploiting themselves and relying on family members for support. When asked about the time she devotes to the business, Adama said:

> We don't go nowhere, we don't do nothing. All of our time is just spend for this. Eight o' clock morning we start working ...I am not sleeping well, eating well because when you are doing this ones you don't have time to eat. I don't sleep early at night because we always work at night. I couldn't, I couldn't stop the work, I had to continue working- because we don't say no to the customers... I don't go nowhere my love. I spend most of my time with my work ... I belong to my work.

Adamse said:

> I open the shop around ten o'clock. In the morning I take my daughter to school. I will come to the shop, I open it, if I have somewhere to go I will go there and I will come in here and then around three o'clock in the afternoon I will go to and pick my daughter from school. Take her to the house. I will eat and I will come back to the shop. I stay the rest of the day in the shop.

Being a businesswoman and being able to work flexitime gives Adamse the chance to combine more successfully the work and family responsibilities. She explained that in the afternoons her mother looks after her children. Thus, the role of familial resources in helping proves to be crucial for a newly established business.

Sofia on the other hand explained that when she got involved in the business she was working on Sundays as well. Then, a year ago, she realised that she had to devote some time to her children. They have a summer house and she decided that the whole of the family will spend the weekends there. In this way, as Sofia says, the family has the opportunity to spend sometime together. Sofia compares the working hours while she was working in the hospital with her working in her business; she was working eight hours, five days a week whereas now she leaves the house at eight o clock in the morning and returns home at twelve o' clock in the evening. Sofia referred to the lack of free time to be spending with friends as she used to do in the past, while working in the hospital. Now she admits that she doesn't have the time and although they do keep in touch, they don't see one another as often as they used to.

Sofia narrates that people including her husband couldn't understand why a woman with a stable working career suddenly in her late 30s decided to become self-employed. She said:

> The beginning was difficult for people to understand even my husband. he hated me so much for what I'm doing [with emphasis] . He hated me so much for it because I was giving more time here than I was giving to them …in the end he realised there is no way out "put water in his wine".

What becomes clear is that the most significant investment these women make is their labour input; hence, copying with family responsibilities is a matter of constant effort and poses restrictions in their economic activities. Despite being a successful businesswoman, Sofia still operates under the existing patriarchal regime in Greece where a woman albeit economically active, is still expected to fulfil her responsibilities in the domestic domain and is still seen as being the primary carer. 'Women are subjected to ideologies about their 'place' and their obligations to the household and the family and these affect perceptions of their economic activity' (Allen and Truman, 1993: 2).

Job Satisfaction

Adama is being asked whether she feels satisfied with what she is doing. She starts explaining that when there isn't work to do she goes home to rest. She contrasts her current position with the one in the past when she was working as a cleaner and a hairdresser at the same time. She doesn't express her argument clearly and she provides a confusing account. What she wants to say is that it is better to run her own business, rather than being an employee. She prefers running her own business and she sounds satisfied with her choice. Being self-employed gives her a sense of value and worth. Becoming self-employed was seen as a way of working independent and being able to have control over the work process and timing. Thus, Adama doesn't mind self-exploiting herself because this gives her the opportunity to be independent and make a better living.

Conclusions

In the last decade immigration into Greece has grown rapidly, becoming one of the main features on the political agenda of a country whose institutions were largely unprepared to cope with the newcomers; even twelve years later, and despite being a Schengen Agreement signatory, Greece remains without any coherent policy and without success in controlling the inflow. In spite of the social alarm in public opinion, migrants proved to be functional in the maintenance of some crucial components of the Greek economy. Greece is a country of small businesses. In the ethnic-business sector, migrants have been marginally involved in self-employment and entrepreneurial activities. New forms of migrant businesses have begun developing and some new kinds of trading activities have begun spreading. Migrant entrepreneurship, although increasingly diverse, is still strongly oriented towards specific segments of the opportunity structure. Migrant women entrepreneurs usually sell exotic goods mainly acquired by migrants themselves or provide specific services.

Taking as a yardstick the stories of three migrant women, I tried to understand and explain ethnic entrepreneurial strategies and in doing so took into account ethnic and socio-cultural factors; however, explanations cannot only be directly linked to ethno-cultural traditions, ethnic behaviour patterns, ethnic loyalties and markets. To do this would be to reduce migrant entrepreneurship to an ethno-cultural phenomenon existing in a politico-economic vacuum. Immigrant entrepreneurs do not operate in a vacuum; they operate within a politico-economic space where there are specific opportunities for businesses, especially small-size ones. As shown in section four, the shape of this space is contingent multifarious factors including the presence of a large informal economy, which have to be taken into account in order to put the opportunity structures actors operate within into a proper perspective.

In the Greek setting, migrant women gravitated towards self-employment because there are so few alternatives; blocked mobility, an inability to find a job that fits their skills, interests and ambitions due to racist practices, pushed these women towards self-employment. On the other hand, the increase in immigration from developing countries to advanced economies has created a demand for small firms catering for ethnic needs; such firms are intimately associated with processes of flexibilisation and informalisation and their expansion serves as a magnet for new migrants in 'global cities' (Sassen, 2001) where the high end of the service sector creates a demand for low-end activities by outsourcing directly (producer services) or indirectly (consumer services), thus pulling these women towards self-employment. Flexible specialisation seemed to be the answer.

In the Greek case, the match between potential entrepreneurs and opportunities for small firms seems to be straightforward. This is not to say that one should take much of the broad context for granted or that the role of agency is underestimated. On the contrary here I tried to combine agency and structure perspectives, following Klooserman and Rath's (2001) concept of mixed embeddedness, where they took into account the shape of the opportunity structure, the institutions mediating between aspiring entrepreneurs and concrete openings to start a business and the characteristics of the immigrant entrepreneurs to be. Within this framework, I discussed the realities of the everyday circumstances and experiences of three self-employed migrant women in Greece and showed that the independent small ethnic business, using flexible labour, self-help and private capital, was the answer to many of the problems these women were faced with in the Greek economic and social setting. However, entrepreneurship has done little to facilitate socio-economic advancement and incorporation. Discrimination remains the rule. In other words, entrepreneurship appears no more likely than domestic work to offer a ladder of success. Restricted access to capital and collateral is a key barrier to them achieving financial security.

References

Allen, S. and Truman, C. (1993), Women and Men Entrepreneurs: Life Strategies, Business Strategies, in S. Allen and C. Truman (eds), *Women in Business: Perspectives on Women Entrepreneurs*. London: Routledge.

Andall, J. (1998), Catholic and State Constructions of Domestic Workers: the Case of Cape Verdean Women in Rome in the 1970s, in K. Koser and H. Lutz (eds) *The New Migration in Europe: Social Constructions and Social Realities*. Basingstoke: Macmillan.

Anthias, F. (1998), Rethinking Social Divisions: some Notes towards a Theoretical Framework, *The Sociological Review*, 46, 3, pp. 505-535.

Anthias, F. (2000), Metaphores of Home: Gendering New Migrations to Southern Europe, in F. Anthias and G. Lazaridis (eds) *Gender and Migration in Southern Europe: Women on the Move*. Oxford: Berg.

Aurand, H. W. (1983), Self-employment, and last resort of the unemployed, *International Social Science Review*, 58, 1, pp. 785-809.

Bertaux, D. and Kohli, M. (1984), The Life Story Approach: a Continental View, *Annual Review of Sociology*, 10, pp. 215-237.

Canellopoulos, K. (1995), *Parallel Economy and tax Evasion*. Athens: Centre of Planning and Economic Research.

Granovetter, M. (1985), Economic action and social structure: the problem of embeddedness, *American Journal of Sociology*, 91, 3, pp. 485-510.

Kloosterman, R., van der Leun, J. and Rath, J. (1998), Across the border: immigrants' economic opportunities, social capital and informal business activities, *Journal of Ethnic and Migration Studies*, 24, 2, pp. 249-268.

Kloosterman, R. and Rath, J. (2001), Immigrant entrepreneurs in advanced economies: mixed embeddedness, *Journal of Ethnic and Migration Studies*, 27, 2, pp. 189-201.

Kupferberg, F. (1999), *What entrepreneurs do, how and why? An Interpretative theory of entrepreneurpship*, Paper presented at the Aalborg TSER Workshop, 2-4 October, Denmark.

Lazaridis, G. (1996), Immigration to Greece: a critical evaluation of Greek policy, *New Community*, 22, 2, pp. 336-348.

Lazaridis, G. (2000), Filipino and Albanian women migrant workers in Greece: Multiple layers of oppression, in F. Anthias and G. Lazaridis (eds), *Gender and Migration in Southern Europe: women on the move*. Oxford: Berg.

Lazaridis, G. (2001), Trafficking and prostitution: the growing exploitation of migrant women in Greece, *European Journal of Women's Studies*, 8, 1, pp. 67-102.

Lazaridis, G. and Katrougalos, G. (2003), *Southern European Welfare States: Problems, Challenges and Prospects*. Basingstoke: Palgrave Macmillan.

Lazaridis, G. and Koumandraki M. (2001), Deconstructing naturalism: the racialisation of ethnic minorities in Greece, in R. King (ed), *The Mediterranean passage: migration and new cultural encounters in Southern Europe.* London: Longman.

Lazaridis, G. and Poyago-Theotoky, J., (1999), Undocumented migrants in Greece: Issues of regularisation, *International Migration*, 37, 4, pp. 715-738.

Lazaridis, G. and Psimmenos, I. (2000), Migrant flows from Albania to Greece: economic, social and spatial exclusion, in R. King, G. Lazaridis and C. Tsardanidis (eds), *Eldorado or Fortress? Migration in Southern Europe.* London: Macmillan.

Lazaridis, G. and Romaniszyn, K. (1998), Albanian and Polish undocumented workers in Greece: a comparative analysis, Journal of European Social Policy, 8, 1, pp. 5-22.

Lazaridis, G. and Wickens. E. (1999), "Us" and the "Others": ethnic minorities in Greece, Annals of Tourism Research, 26, 3, pp. 632-655.

Light, I. and Gold, S. (1999), *Ethnic Economies.* San Diego: Academic Press.

Miller, R.L. (2000), *Researching Life Stories and Family Histories.* London: Sage.

Petmesidou, M. (1996), Social Protection in Southern Europe: Trends and Prospects', in G. Lazaridis (ed) *Southern Europe in Transition*, special issue of the *Journal of Area Studies*, 9, pp. 95-125.

Petmesidou, M. and Tsoulouvis, L. (1994), Labour market Restructuring and Pressures for Modernising Social Policy in Greece. Paper presented at the conference on Greece: Prospects for Modernisation, LSE, London.

Portes, A. and Sensenbrenner, J. (1993), Embeddedness and Immigration: notes on the social determinants of economic action, *American journal of Sociology*, 68, 6, pp. 1320-50.

Rafiq, M. (1992), Ethnicity and enterprise: a comparison of Muslim and non-Muslim owned Asian businesses in Britain, *New Community*, 19, 1, pp. 43-60.

Rath, J. and Kloosterman, R. (2000), Outsiders' business: a critical review of research on immigrant entrepreneurship, *International Migration Review*, 34, 4, pp. 657-681.

Rosenthal, G. (1993), Reconstructing life stories: principles of selection in generating stories for narrative biographical interview, in R. Josselson and A. Lieblich (eds) *The Narrative Study of Lives.* London: Sage.

Sassen, S. (2001), *The Global City: New York, London, Tokyo.* London: Princeton University Press (2nd Edition).

Uneke, O. (1996), Ethnicity and small business ownership: contracts between Blacks and Chinese in Toronto, *Work, Employment and Society*, 10 , 3, pp. 529-548.

Valenzuela, A. (2001), Day labourers as entrepreneurs?, *Journal of Ethnic and Migration Studies*, 27, 2, pp. 335-352.

Waldinger, R., Aldrich, H. and Ward, R. (1990a) (eds) *Ethnic entrepreneurs: immigrant businesses in industrial countries.* London: Sage Publications.

Waldinger, R., Aldrich, H., and Ward, R. (1990b), Opportunities, Group characteristics and Strategies, in R. Waldinger, H. Aldrich and R. Ward (eds), *Ethnic entrepreneurs: immigrant businesses in industrial countries.* London: Sage Publications.

Wieviorka, M. (1994), Racism in Europe: Unity and Diversity, in A. Rattansi and S. Westwood (eds) *Modernity and Identity on the Western Front.* New York: John Wiley and Sons.

Wilson, P. (1983), Ethnic minority business and bank finance, *New Community,* xi, ½, pp. 63-73.

Index

sans-papiers, meaning 35
Schengen Agreement (1985)
   and Amsterdam Treaty (1997) 5
   asylum and refugee policy 6
   and external borders 5
   and third-country nationals 5
second job-holding, Greece 177
Secure Border, Safe Havens... White
   Paper (UK) 28
security, and immigration 4
self-employment, Greece 178-9
September 11 (2001) attacks, and
   immigration 4
sex industries
   Germany, Thai women 129
   globalisation 127-30
   Greece 130
   Spain 55, 59, 100-1
      personal histories 60-3
   women migrants 8, 82, 123-4
   see also prostitution; trafficking
sexual orientation, asylum system,
   France 48-9
slavery, France 50
Social Action Fund (FAS), France 109
Spain
   employment statistics, inadequacy 91-
   2
   migration to, strategies 57-64, 74
   trafficking, organised crime 71-2
   women migrants
      Colombian 56
      compatriot networks 96-7
      country of origin connections 93-4
      discrimination against 103-5
      domestic work 92, 98
      economy
         formal 98-9
         informal 99-101
         monetary 97-101
      Ecuadorian 56
      family networks 94-5
      finance sources 64-71
      labour market, integration 91-105
      payments home 103
      sex industries 55, 59, 100-1
      social security benefits 102
      taxes paid 102
      types of work 92-3
Straw, Jack 23
Structural Adjustment Programmes

(SAPs), gender issues 128
sub-contracting, cleaning work 79-81
Sweden, prostitution 133-4

terrorism, and immigration 4
Thai women, Germany, sex industry 129
third-country nationals
   EU integration 4-5
   Schengen Agreement (1985) 5
trafficking
   Amsterdam Treaty (1997) 125
   Anti-Slavery International 127
   causes 122-4
   data, lack of 121-2
   definitions 120-1
   EU responses 124-5
   European Parliament, resolutions
      124-5
   France 50
   immigration
      distinction 55
      problems 119-20, 125
   Italy 126-7
   networks 125-6
   numbers 122
   and poverty 122-3
   Spain, organised crime 71-2
   UN protocol 121
   see also prostitution; sex industries
Turkey, women migrants
   in France 40
   in Germany 153-70

UK
   African women, HIV/AIDS 139-49
   Asylum and Immigration Act (1996)
      30
   asylum and refugee policy 20-31, 141
      European Convention on Human
         Rights 30
      Fairer, Faster, Firmer White
         Paper 22, 28
      'safe countries' 28-9
      Secure Border, Safe Havens...
         White Paper 28
   asylum seekers
      'bogus' vs 'genuine' 7, 20, 22
      financial support 22-4, 30
      numbers 20

For Product Safety Concerns and Information please contact our EU
representative GPSR@taylorandfrancis.com
Taylor & Francis Verlag GmbH, Kaufingerstraße 24, 80331 München, Germany

www.ingramcontent.com/pod-product-compliance
Lightning Source LLC
Chambersburg PA
CBHW050710280326
41926CB00088B/2907